SMALL BREWERY
FINANCE

Accounting Principles & Planning for the Craft Brewer

By Maria Pearman, CPA

BREWERS
PUBLICATIONS®

Brewers Publications®
A Division of the Brewers Association
PO Box 1679, Boulder, Colorado 80306-1679
BrewersAssociation.org
BrewersPublications.com

Printed in the United States of America.

Library of Congress Cataloging-in-Publication Data

Names: Pearman, Maria, 1979- author.
Title: Small brewery finance : accounting principles & planning for the craft brewer / by Maria Pearman, CPA.
Description: Boulder, Colorado : Brewers Publications, [2018] | Includes index. | Summary: "Your brewery is much more than just a small business-it's the fulfillment of your dream to share a love for quality craft beer and beverages. Build success from start-up to expansion with a solid foundation of finance principles geared specifically toward small beverage producers. Learn how to build and interpret financial reports and create basic pro-forma financial statements for launching a brewery, purchasing additional equipment, or determining a new location. Explore the various business models available to you as a craft brewery. Discover pricing models that maximize your profits. Learn how to build a budget and how to use it to hold staff accountable. This book is written to teach complex topics in simple terms. Written in an accessible style, it will help brewery owners and their staff understand the importance of a strong financial foundation. The insights and results-oriented content will help you run a more successful brewery"-- Provided by publisher.
Identifiers: LCCN 2019028683 (print) | LCCN 2019028684 (ebook) | ISBN 9781938469527 (paperback) | ISBN 9781938469534 (ebook)
Subjects: LCSH: Breweries--Accounting. | Breweries--Finance.
Classification: LCC HF5686.B5 P43 2018 (print) | LCC HF5686.B5 (ebook) | DDC 663/.420681--dc23
LC record available at https://lccn.loc.gov/2019028683
LC ebook record available at https://lccn.loc.gov/2019028684

Publisher: Kristi Switzer
Technical Editor: Larry Chase, Adam Robbings, Audra Gaizunas
Copyediting: Iain Cox
Indexing: Elizabeth Walker
Art Direction: Jason Smith, Danny Harms
Interior Design: Danny Harms
Production: Justin Petersen
Cover Photo: Luke Trautwein

TABLE OF CONTENTS

FOREWORD

Many times when I go into an Iron Hill establishment, I will sit at the bar and do a product evaluation with the brewer. It's a process of doing a sensory evaluation of a selection of beers currently on tap. Inevitably, a customer at the bar will see us and shout out, "Hey, how do I get that job?" As craft brewers, we are certainly living the dream. But rarely will someone outside of our circle recognize the difficult road we took to get here. Craft beer lover, passionate homebrewer, tired of working for The Man, willing to risk it all, friends and family crazy enough to part with some of their disposable income—even if many of us share similar stories getting into this industry, our journeys don't all take the same path. Some are wonderful success stories, while some end badly. In Philadelphia, I am part of a small group of brewers (there are eight of us) who all opened their breweries around the same time (1995–97) and are still in business today. We get together every year and brew a collaboration beer called Brotherly Suds. We all opened at exactly the wrong time in craft brewing, during the burst of the mythical first "craft beer bubble." The late 1990s saw the shuttering of so many small breweries, despite the fact that, as Paul Gatza will tell you, craft beer sales never declined during those years.

So how did the we all survive this long, while so many others from back then have long since been shuttered? It's easy to say great products, but that has almost become the price of admission for long-term viability in our business. The other key element is a disciplined approach to running our businesses profitably. This sounds like simple and obvious advice for running your business, but it has been the downfall of so many craft brewers.

Financial knowledge or discipline is rarely in our nature. Very few of us who jump into this business come from a strong financial background, and it's certainly not what we are passionate about. Just look at the seminar rooms at any craft brewers conference. The packed rooms are where the talks on barrel-aged beer, sour beer, brewing techniques, and equipment design happen. These are the subjects we are passionate about. A snoozer on building the profit and loss (P&L) statement is never going to fill a room.

My partners and I are two engineers and a restauranteur. We had to learn about P&L statements when building them by hand for our initial pro formas (this was pre-internet!). Everything was learned in bits and pieces and through trial and error as we were starting and growing our business. And there were no resources for the brewing industry. But we were also data geeks, and pulling and reporting the numbers helped clarify what we needed to do to run the business. Eventually, my partner went back and got his MBA to help move the business forward with better financial guidance. Through the last 23 years, Iron Hill has seen a lot of ups and downs, but developing strong financial knowledge and discipline has helped us weather so many storms over the years. Along with our products and people, those skills are what set us apart and have brought us success.

A key element of craft brewing that attracted so many of us to the industry is the willingness of everyone to share and collaborate, to help each other even as competing businesses. Yet, as the industry has grown over the last 30 years, the information available on the financial side of the industry has been disproportionately low compared to information on topics like technical brewing, marketing, distribution, and ingredients. *Small Brewery Finance* is the missing piece we have all been waiting for. Maria Pearman has done an outstanding job of taking a subject that is foreign to most brewers and presenting it in terms that are easy to understand for the non-financial business owner. She starts by giving an instructive narrative, telling the tale of Mike and Erica, a husband and wife team following their passion. This is a familiar story to many of us and one that you are probably hoping to make your reality or may even be currently living. This narrative is a wonderful way to take the reader through the ups and downs of starting and growing a business. Maria then does a deep dive into the fundamentals of accounting and finance, giving you the understanding you need for your small BREWERY business. This book puts so much brewery-facing financial information and guidance all in one place. I wish we had a resource like it when we founded Iron Hill in 1996.

The information and guidance that *Small Brewery Finance* provides is not just a valuable resource to start-ups, but to existing businesses as well. This industry has seen great momentum in recent years and a surge in public excitement over local breweries. And for many, that local excitement results in early success, but early financial success does not prepare a small business for the inevitable storm that lies ahead. When you open a small business, you wear all of the hats and deal with all of the issues. It becomes difficult to prioritize work and set up tighter financial controls, particularly if you appear to be doing well financially. But is your business really doing as well as you think? Executing the principles expounded in this book will allow you to discover what you previously didn't know about your business.

The second part of running your business financially is financial discipline. Once you have better clarity on what needs to be done, you have to actually take action. There is enormous pressure in this business, particularly as it is driven by passion and craft, that it is not all about the numbers and profits. But it really needs to be a lot about it. Every beer can't have an insane amount of hops in it and be priced to keep your friends happy. Tough financial decisions have to be made constantly. And if they are not being made, then you either don't have the right information or you are ignoring it. Financial discipline cannot be taught by this book, but it is the key to using its guidance successfully.

So why do you need to read this book and be more disciplined? Because the bad times are coming for your business, you just don't know it yet. It comes in so many forms. Sure, there is the business cycle, but there are a hundred more reasons that are specific to your business or market. And you won't see it coming. You need to be ready and have the financial structures and data in place to help you react quickly and weather the storm. Think about everyone that is relying on the financial success of your business. It starts with you, your significant other, and your immediate family. But that circle starts to grow. As your business grows, think about everyone that has bought into your dream and passion. It's not just your business anymore. So many of your managers, brewers, and staff all put in the extra hours and effort because they believe in what you are doing. You begin to owe it to them as well. We started our first Iron Hill with 65 employees. We now employ over 1700 people that share in our dream and rely on us for their livelihood. Use the resources in this book to their fullest extent and make your business great for years to come.

Mark D. Edelson
Founder/Director of Brewery Operations
Iron Hill Brewery & Restaurant

ACKNOWLEDGMENTS

One of my favorite things about the craft beer industry is its sense of collaboration. This book is a perfect example of that spirit, as it would not be possible without the generous input of many friends and colleagues. Thank you to Mark Boelman and the craft beer accounting group for allowing me to be a fly on the wall to soak up wisdom and inspiration. Feedback and opinion was offered by so many of you, including Fred Bowman, Mike Corneille, Ben Crowl, Oceania Eagan, Jamie Floyd, Audra Gaizunas, Gay Gilmore, Quinton Jay, Jeff Jones, Mike Musson, Marty Ochs, Evann Rodgers, Amie Ruggles, Kris Spaulding, Ray Veillet, and Emily Wenner.

If accounting is one cornerstone of small business success, legal counsel is certainly its mate. Thanks to Marcus Reed for his professional expertise, eye for grammar, and suggesting a better turn-of-phrase than I could produce. Marc Sorini, Jesse Lyon, and Laura Warf each went to great lengths to provide rich content. Thanks for making all of us readers a little smarter.

I would like to specially thank my personal proofreader, Mo Wark, who enthusiastically took on terribly tedious tasks to ensure coherent continuity of this material. Mo was truly a pleasure to work with in the final stages of this project. This project wouldn't be possible without the patience, guidance and support of my publisher, Kristi Switzer. Kristi has a deep dedication to the craft beer community, and she shares it in each publication that she shepherds through to completion.

The growth of this industry has, for years, been the result of newer brewers learning from more experienced brewers. It's true in this book as well. Many industry professionals shared a window into their process so that we can all learn from their experience. Thank you Arlan Arnsten, Aaron Brodniak, Larry Chase, Patrick Corcorran, Rocky Fiore, Adam Firestone, Matt Greenberg, John Harris, Patrick McCarthy, Heather McCollum, Adam Robbings, Mel Smith, Nicole Smith, Richard Strauss, and Rick Wehner.

INTRODUCTION

What is craft beer? Aside from the liquid, it's an artistic expression, a catalyst that creates community. If you're passionate about craft beer and choose to make it your profession, it's a physical manifestation of a brewer's hopes and dreams, a personal sandbox to explore building a brand, a livelihood, a business.

If you are starting a brewery, you're probably quite capable at making beer, but haven't had a lot of business experience. This book is intended to be a resource for those who are striking out on their own in the world of beer.

Regardless of industry, every business needs at least a basic understanding of finances because it is the foundation that allows an organization to function. Financial reports are an objective assessment of a business's performance. An ability to understand accounting allows you to see a company's risks and opportunities, and its strengths and weaknesses. A solid financial core will allow a company to grow faster with more stability, while having enough flexibility to weather trends and growing pains. The principles you'll learn in this book translate to many industries, but this book is presented through the lens of a small brewery.

This industry-specific focus on a brewery's financial function will, I hope, allow you to make the most of your company's accounting results. I will teach you the basics, and will get specific on the points most relevant for breweries.

We all learn differently, so I have presented the lessons two ways. Chapter 1 is a narrative that tells the story of a brewery from start-up through exit. Within the story you'll be exposed to many accounting concepts and can learn through example. The remaining chapters are the technical material, which is presented in a more traditional textbook manner. This will be a good option for those of you who want to go right to the heart of the material. We will progress into cost accounting concepts as they apply throughout the production process and conclude with an overview of a brewery's life cycle.

Throughout the book I have added "Expert Advice" sidebars, which are relevant to the material and based on years of brewery finance experience. Additionally, I include some helpful advice from industry professionals based on their reflections on lessons learned. I hope that their words of wisdom will be beneficial.

Readers will walk away with the necessary financial knowledge and templates to improve existing operations, consider expansion, or to create a business plan for a new craft beverage entity. My goal is to help brewery owners understand the importance of a strong financial foundation and to help unlock the power of financial knowledge to run a more successful brewery.

Your craft is a force of good in the world. Throughout the ages people have gathered around a pint to appreciate, debate, collaborate, connect, dream, and solve. A strong business core allows you to bring more good to the masses. Let's get there.

1

FROM DREAM TO REALITY

A CRAFT BEER BUSINESS JOURNEY

Mike was a very talented brewer. In college he'd gone the safe route and earned an engineering degree. He started homebrewing as a creative outlet that perfectly intersected with his left-brain job. After eight years in a corporate job he was bored and burned out. Mike's creative side tugged hard enough at his shirt sleeve that he finally listened; he ditched the corporate gig, went to work at a brewery, and began brewing full time. When Mike took the position, he knew it was a departure from the well-paved path of job security and certainty, but he'd always been headstrong. A firm believer that you only live once, Mike decided to give the brewing world a whirl.

Mike had been in the brewing industry for about four years when he started to daydream about opening his own brewery. He believed that he had what it took. Many of his peers, who had much less experience in the industry than him, were going for it. Why shouldn't he?

After serious consideration, Mike decided to take the first step and started drafting a business plan. Four months later, his first draft plan was complete and he shared it with his wife, Erica. As she read the business plan she found herself warming to the idea. With more revisions, Mike thought he had a good vision and a plan that would work.

Mike had a number of contacts in the brewing industry and entrepreneurs from other businesses who agreed to sit down over a beer to vet his business plan. The information he received was invaluable. He was able to get a realistic idea of costs and processes. They shared basic tools like recipe sheets and production planning charts. The best input came from Mike's own boss, who realized that if he was going to lose a good employee because he wanted to start his own shop then it was a win for the industry.

Mike and Erica started to think about the logistics of the idea. The first consideration was financial— how much money would they need to get started? How long before the brewery became profitable? Based on his business plan, Mike made a list of required equipment to get through the first two years of operations. Then he considered space, how much he would need and the average rent per square foot. Next, he planned for personnel. In his business model, Mike had sketched out what positions he would need and when to hire for them over the next two years. The result of all these deliberations was a very basic idea of how much money Mike and Erica would need to get started and fund expenses for two years. From there, Mike made a crude assumption of expected revenue and subtracted that from the total expenses. The result was an estimate of how much capital the couple would need to fund the project for the next two years.

> See appendix A for what to include in your business plan.

While they didn't yet know exactly how much the whole project would cost, Mike and Erica agreed to spend up to $50,000 of their own money. Based on Mike and Erica's estimates, their start-up cost would total about $250,000[1] and they would have to finance $200,000 of that to make the project happen.

The second major consideration was **entity** type. Since neither of them had experience with legal matters, Mike and Erica asked for advice from an attorney who had helped several other breweries. After the attorney walked them through various options, the couple decided to organize as a limited liability company (LLC) taxed as a partnership. This structure gave them personal protection from the activity of the brewery and provided flexibility to add partners and investors for future capital needs.

> See chapter 9 and appendix F for more information on organizational structure and financing your brewery.

Mike and Erica really wanted to start their brewery project on their own without investors, which meant getting big loans from a bank. They called a few bankers recommended by friends in the brewery business. They learned that, because their company was a start-up, lenders would consider Mike and Erica's personal credit and assets when deciding whether or not to loan them money. The bank was also going to need financial projections for three years, and a bank loan would not be extended to them for several more months. These early conversations helped them understand what would be needed for the bank to make a decision. It was also a good opportunity to get to know a few different bankers. One of Mike's colleagues told him that their relationship with a banker would be one of the most important business partnerships of the brewery, so they wanted to choose wisely.

Next on the list was an Alcohol and Tobacco Tax and Trade Bureau (TTB) license. This part of the process was more time-consuming than they would have liked. Before Mike and Erica could get licensed they had to have a location, and in their town real estate was at a premium. Finding a helpful real estate broker was easy, but they had to be patient for the right property to come along.

After looking for five months, Mike and Erica secured a retail location on the main street of downtown that fit their plan for a brewery and taproom. Plus, the city was encouraging small businesses to contribute to downtown revitalization. Specifically, the city wanted to attract a brewery as a catalyst for more investment, believing that a brewery could be a hub for economic activity and help revitalize the area. Mike and Erica even got a grant from the local community development fund. Further, the landlord agreed to cover the cost for a significant amount of the improvements needed for the production space. It is common for landlords to pay for leasehold improvements because they can control the process and quality of improvements. Often it also allows the landlord to charge more in rent over the long-term.

During an interview with a potential landlord, Mike and Erica had been asked the name of their brewery, to which Mike replied that they were planning on calling it Core Brewing. The landlord replied that it sounded familiar and that he had heard of a Core Cidery on the other side of the state. He asked if the two were related entities—at that moment it dawned on Erica that they had not even considered completing due diligence of naming trademarks.

Over the next two weeks the couple spent a lot of time researching brewery names and brand identity concepts. They enlisted the help of a trademark attorney, who helped them weed out possibilities and counseled them to use a name different than Core. After much deliberation, Erica and Mike chose Happy Hour Brewing Company as their brewery name.

---

[1]   All costs in the text are USD, use US customary units, and are based on 2018 prices.

They had the beginning of a budget based on the preliminary financial sketches that had been prepared by Mike. One of the banks had given them a worksheet to format their financial plans. This was Mike and Erica's first encounter with financial statements. They did their best to complete the worksheets and, even though they didn't fully understand the results, the banker coached them through the process. The banker explained that, based on their projections, they would be cash flow positive by the second year. Based on the projected numbers, and their personal assets and credit score, Mike and Erica were able to secure a $200,000 Small Business Administration (SBA) 7(a) loan.

As the application for the TTB license was working its way through the system, Mike and Erica began searching for equipment. Thanks to Mike's connections in the industry, they were able to secure a used system with three fermentors. It was enough to get started. In their budget, they had planned to buy new equipment. Saving money so early in the process felt like a real win for them.

Using the money saved on brewing equipment, the couple enlisted a designer to bring their logo and color palette to life. This investment gave them a solid beginning structure for basic marketing needs.

In their initial assumptions, Mike and Erica had not planned on spending money on brand design. It was clear that their rudimentary budget was quickly becoming obsolete. Prices and needs were changing frequently, and before long they couldn't keep a running tally of actual cost versus budgeted cost in their head. Up to this point, expenses had been paid out-of-pocket and receipts were kept in a shoe box. As the receipts started piling up, keeping track of expenditures became overwhelming. They went to the local branch of the Small Business Development Center (SBDC), where they were paired with a woman named Shannon who guided them through a few key steps:

- opening a checking account for the business;
- buying accounting software for the business;
- using the software daily to keep up to date on all expenses.

At first, the use of dedicated software did not seem necessary to Mike and Erica due to the limited number of transactions involved. It had seemed easy to keep track of every transaction in their head. Further, if they needed to know the bank balance, they could simply look online. But as things progressed, they had reached the point where the pace of activity was too much to keep in their heads. Mike and Erica found themselves in the position of having to schedule vendor payments based on when cash was available, and not making payments when the bill arrived. The situation was requiring them to be much more organized.

Erica agreed that getting software was a natural next step. Shannon, the SBDC advisor, helped her find a product that suited their needs. Erica was able to purchase it online and start the basic set-up that day. The software walked her through the process of establishing some basic accounts. Shannon then helped her refine the accounts to meet the company's needs. Shannon also advised Mike and Erica to use the accounting software on a frequent basis to ensure financial records could be produced in a timely manner.

In the accounting software, the couple created accounts for each credit card being used for expenses and they set up two partner capital accounts: "Members Equity – Mike" and "Members Equity – Erica," Based on their business plan, Erica knew that they would need to secure additional financing from either a bank or investment partners. They also had plans to buy a vehicle, and she was certain that purchase would be financed. Erica was unsure how the **chart of accounts** should be set up for items she knew would happen in the future. Shannon assured her that accounts could be added later when the need arose.

> See chapter 2 for a full explanation of the chart of accounts and financial statements.

Erica adjusted the fixed asset section of the balance sheet to include more categories:
Brewery Equipment
Computers
Vehicles
Leasehold Improvements
Accumulated Depreciation

Even though the brewery did not yet own a vehicle, it was part of future plans. The "Vehicles" account was

TABLE 1.1 SAMPLE BALANCE SHEET
JUNE 30, 20XX | CURRENT MONTH VS. PRIOR MONTH

	Jun 30, 20XX	May 31, 20XX	$ Change
ASSETS			
Current Assets			
Checking/Savings			
Checking	9,902.03	1,706.32	8,195.71
Total Checking/Savings	9,902.03	1,706.32	8,195.71
Total Current Assets	9,902.03	1,706.32	8,195.71
Inventory	17,291.85	18,662.20	(1,370.35)
Net Fixed Assets			
Brewery Equipment and Machinery	159,179.17	153,679.17	5,500.00
Leasehold Improvements	54,329.36	54,329.36	0.00
Start-Up Costs	6,804.00	6,804.00	0.00
Total Fixed Assets	220,312.53	214,812.53	5,500.00
TOTAL ASSETS	**247,506.41**	**235,181.05**	**12,325.36**
LIABILITIES & EQUITY			
Liabilities			
Current Liabilities			
Accounts Payable			
Accounts Payable	19,801.32	19,801.32	0.00
Total Accounts Payable	19,801.32	19,801.32	0.00
Credit Cards			
Credit Card	9,734.23	3,167.82	6,566.41
Total Credit Cards	9,734.23	3,167.82	6,566.41
Other Current Liabilities			
Payroll Liabilities	7,000.00	0.00	7,000.00
Total Other Current Liabilities	7,000.00	0.00	7,000.00
Total Current Liabilities	36,535.55	22,969.14	13,566.41
Long Term Liabilities			
Loans Payable			
SBA Loan	163,740.00	133,740.00	30,000.00
Total Loans Payable	163,740.00	133,740.00	30,000.00
Total Long Term Liabilities	163,740.00	133,740.00	30,000.00
Total Liabilities	200,275.55	156,709.14	43,566.41
Equity			
Members Equity	125,000.00	125,000.00	0.00
Retained Earnings	(2,069.99)	(2,069.99)	0.00
Net Income	(75,699.15)	(44,458.10)	(31,241.05)
Total Equity	47,230.86	78,471.91	(31,241.05)
TOTAL LIABILITIES & EQUITY	**247,506.41**	**235,181.05**	**12,325.36**

Notes: This is representative of a brewery that has been operational for some time to give readers insight into the structure of a balance sheet once a company is operational. It is not representative of Happy Hour Brewing Company's balance sheet during start-up

Negative values in this balance sheet, and all tables throughout this book, are presented in parentheses.

created so that it would be available when needed. During the start-up phase, most of Mike and Erica's large purchases were for brewing equipment and the build-out of the space, which were categorized as "Leasehold Improvements." Erica learned that the breakout of fixed assets into different categories, like equipment, vehicles, and leasehold improvements, would allow lenders to see assets owned by the company that could be **collateralized**. She also learned that, as the amount of collateral a business owns increases, the business's eligibility for a loan also increases. She didn't expect to need another loan in the near future, but this knowledge helped her understand how bankers or other lenders looked at her financial reports.

> To **collateralize** means to pledge property for a loan. In the event that a debtor defaults on payments of a loan, the lender will then have rights to the property that secures the loan. Often, this property includes the business and/or personal assets of the debtor.

> See chapters 2 and 3 for an introduction to accounting basics and an overview of the balance sheet and income statement.

EXPERT ADVICE

Let's pause the story here and consider the journey of Happy Hour Brewing Co. so far. Mike and Erica are experiencing issues common for start-up brewery owners, but that doesn't imply it's the best way to run a business. Some common behaviors I have encountered when working with smaller or early stage breweries include:

- gauging the availability of cash as a key measurement of financial health;
- recording transactions long after they have occurred;
- using bank and credit card statements for inputs rather than using the transaction source documents; and
- failing to recognize the importance of financial reports.

While it's true that a business cannot operate for long without cash, it's important to recognize that cash does not equal profitability. Cash is only one data point relating to financial health but it's far from the whole picture. To rely only on the cash position to determine a business's health is like determining someone's physical health solely by their diet. We know that many things factor into physical health: diet, exercise, sleep, stress, and a variety of other influences. Diet is a considerable factor, but certainly not the only factor.

The bank balance tells you how much cash is available at a certain moment in time. Cash does not provide information on revenue versus expenses, nor the value of invoices outstanding or owed to your business. Cash does not tell you the amount in checks outstanding, that is, checks written that have not yet cleared the bank. Imagine that you had $75,000 outstanding in **accounts receivable** (AR) and you were unaware because you are not tracking the money owed to you in accounting software. It may sound silly to imagine a scenario where a business owner would forget such a large amount was owed to the business, but when that balance is comprised of a series of small amounts it can happen. When the pace of business activity starts moving faster and faster, keeping track of all the small pieces of information can be impossible without a central store of information.

Business owners may put off bookkeeping because they are too busy. They think they will get around to it every couple of months by entering transactions from the bank statement. While this is better than nothing, it means that you are relying on the bank statement to be correct. With this method you are recording only transactions that have cleared the bank. What happens if you write a $5,000 check and the payee doesn't cash it right away? Your records won't reflect the transaction. Your income and available cash will be overstated, potentially causing cash flow problems in the future and leading you to believe that your business is more profitable than it actually is.

The best practice is to record transactions from source documents. Source documents are receipts, contracts, invoices, and other similar documents that help determine the classification and period of a transaction. Classification means the account type of a transaction: asset, liability, equity, revenue, or expense. Period is the time—month, day, year—that a transaction should be recorded. By using source documents to enter transactions into your accounting file you are able to **trace** all transactions to their origination. Bank statements are then used to reconcile your file at the end of the month.

Reconciliations allow you to **vouch** all transactions. Tracing and vouching are critical to ensuring a set of complete and accurate financial records.

Most accounting software programs have a specific reconciliation feature. Typically, this involves entering information from your bank statement, such as beginning balance, ending balance, and statement end date, followed by checking off all the transactions in your accounting software in that account for the specified date range. Ideally, after you mark off all deposits, checks, and electronic payments, your ending balance matches the statement. This gives you confidence that what is in the financial records actually happened (tracing) and what happened is in the records (vouching). In reality, you end up with errors in the "books" (the accounting records) that need to be cleaned up. Examples of common errors include transactions entered twice, transactions not entered, and amounts entered incorrectly. The reconciliation process helps you identify these errors; once they are cleaned up you can be confident in the report's results. I recommend reconciling monthly as soon as possible after receiving your bank or credit card statement. Loans should also be reconciled to the statement as frequently as possible.

Do you now see how Mike and Erica are at a disadvantage by not having complete financial records? As new business owners, they are not recognizing the importance of financial reports. By letting that part of the process move to the back burner they are hamstringing their future success. Complete records should yield accurate reports, and accurate reports allow a business owner to stay attuned to the rhythm of the company's finances and operations. The income statement will reveal seasonal trends, the strength of the overall business model, and expense categories that need to be better managed. The balance sheet (table 1.1) demonstrates a company's strength through the relationship of assets to liabilities and equity, in other words, the relationship between what you own (your assets) and how you financed the assets you own (through debt versus equity).

Shannon, the SBDC advisor, also recommended that Mike and Erica retain a certified public accountant (CPA) as an important part of the advisory team. A CPA can do much more than just prepare taxes. A CPA can also serve as a resource to advise on business decisions. Such advice can range from helping clients understand their financial reports, to providing recommendations for financial and operational systems, to sharing experience on expansion plans.

The next day, Mike and Erica asked friends who were business owners for recommendations for CPAs. The couple called multiple CPAs and had brief conversations with each—just enough to hear about the firm's area of expertise and to see if the personality might be a fit. They asked each CPA the same set of questions:

- How long has the firm had been in business?
- What are their areas of expertise?
- Do they have brewery clients and what size breweries do they work with?
- What services do they provide to clients aside from tax preparation?
- What's the fee schedule?
- Who would be the primary point of contact?
- Are they familiar with the software Mike and Erica are using?

Following recommendations from other local business owners and interviews of potential firms, Mike and Erica decided to work with Charles as their CPA. Charles's firm was not the least expensive option, but he appeared to provide the most value. Most importantly, Mike and Erica felt that he listened and understood their challenges.

Charles spent the first meeting getting to know Mike and Erica's company. He asked who would be responsible for the accounting, and Erica replied that she would be entering the data. Charles agreed that it was a good idea for one of them to take that responsibility initially so that they could stay close to the numbers, but he advised that most companies quickly made the transition to hiring a bookkeeper within the first year of operations. Based on his clients' experience, Charles knew data entry would become too much to keep up with and an experienced bookkeeper could do the job more efficiently. He provided a few recommendations that Mike and Erica could call when they were ready.

Charles then moved to the accounting file. He began by asking them to open the chart of accounts. While each company's chart of accounts is different, using a template for breweries is a good place to begin.

See appendix B for a few sample charts of accounts.

The first thing Charles noticed was that there was only one inventory account, called "Inventory Asset." He recommended adding at least the following:

- Raw Materials
- Packaging Materials
- Work in Process (WIP)
- Finished Goods
- Food Inventory

That degree of detail is needed because some of the **key ratios** relate to how much inventory is on hand relative to revenue. If the ratio is off, the company will want to know what part of inventory should be adjusted.

Next Charles recommended creating a few income and **cost of goods sold** (COGS) accounts to give sufficient detail to sales. Mike and Erica planned to start selling beer in the taproom and kegs to a few accounts via self-distribution. The food in the taproom would be limited to snacks and easy-to-prepare items. Eventually they would add beer in bottles and cans, merchandise, and growlers. To the revenue accounts they added:

- Beer: Packaged
- Beer: Draft
- Merchandise
- Food

Then Charles scanned through the income statement to the COGS section and added:

- Beer COGS: Packaged
- Beer COGS: Draft
- Merchandise COGS
- Food COGS
- Excise Tax
- Production Labor

See chapter 2 for information on organizing your financial reports by activity and chapter 3 for a detailed discussion on COGS.

EXPERT ADVICE

Having accounts where the revenue and COGS mirror one another is important so that different types of COGS can be measured specifically against the corresponding type of revenue. More detailed accounts will allow business owners to mine rich data. Building a chart of accounts that can grow with your business is important even if some of the accounts remain unused for a period. Understand that the chart of accounts isn't set in stone, and you can alter it to meet your needs. Future changes should be made thoughtfully and carefully to avoid unnecessary clutter and complexity. Consider the comparability of reports from period to period. If detailed inventory accounts are added next year, and the prior year's inventory accounts are a simple summary, then a current to prior year comparison of accounts will not align. Using the same accounts year to year will allow an apples-to-apples comparison.

Charles also noticed that Mike and Erica had only one account for "Payroll" and one account for "Payroll Tax." Following the same logic as matching types of revenue and COGS, labor needs to be broken out as it relates to brewery, restaurant, sales, and admin. This departmental allocation adds more detail to the financials so that business owners have a better idea of the performance of different divisions (e.g., brewery vs taproom). He gave them advice on specifically how to book their payroll expense so that it's more clearly defined.

See chapter 6 for a detailed explanation on how to record payroll by department.

Charles recommended one more change to the chart of accounts. Within their operating expenses, Mike and Erica had an "Excise Tax" subaccount under "Taxes." Charles proposed that Excise Tax be moved up to the COGS section. Often, breweries leave excise tax in operating expenses, but the best practice is to have it in COGS because that expense is directly tied to the sale of goods.

Charles also asked the couple about the requirements of their loan and how much of the equipment and build-out they would be responsible for individually. He wanted them to think about when cash would be used, and to carefully consider the timing of purchases so that they wouldn't run out of cash. One of the tools that he provided to them was a simple cash flow forecast template.

> See chapter 4 for more information on cash flow.

After setting up their chart of accounts, Mike and Erica were excited to get to work on the building. They had received their Brewer's Notice from the TTB, so they could now start building the brewery. They decided that Mike would manage the construction side, while Erica managed the accounts side by entering receipts into the accounting software. She was still working her day job, so the data entry happened at night when she had time to devote to the brewery. Erica was committed to entering receipts every other day so that they didn't fall behind. Frequent and consistent attention to the books was a game changer. The couple were able to stay closely attuned to their expenses. And by frequently entering receipts, they actually caught a few billing errors by vendors. If Erica had waited a few weeks to enter the information, they wouldn't have accurately remembered what was purchased and those overcharges would have gone unnoticed. The couple started to be able to predict monthly rhythms of cash flow, as opposed to reacting to them. In sum, this close attention to the books allowed Erica and Mike to make smart business decisions, catch errors that saved them money, and positioned them to manage the business proactively.

At the end of each month Erica knew that the books had to be reconciled. She would get out the bank statement and credit card statement and ensure each was classified correctly. Along the way she caught a few items that had been entered twice, and a few transactions where the dollar amount was incorrect. At the end of the process she felt sure that she had a complete and accurate set of books.

With Erica's increasing proficiency with the accounting software, she could quickly pull up the "Reports" page and access last month's balance sheet. When reviewing the reports, Mike and Erica were able to see quickly that total assets equaled total liabilities and equity. They had cash in the bank and a large amount of accounts payable from debt that was financing the taproom construction.

However, when reviewing the reports, they realized there were still several accounts that seemed confusing. With the build-out continuing, they decided to set up another appointment with the SBDC to get a little help understanding the financials.

Later that week, their SBDC advisor, Shannon, sat down with them to review the reports. She too started with the balance sheet. Right off the bat Shannon identified a few things that seemed off: the hop contract that they had signed last month didn't show up on the balance sheet, and the Leasehold Improvement balance seemed low. Shannon knew Mike had contracted hops with a broker and had entered into an agreement for $10,000. The hops broker would hold the hops and ship to Mike as needed. Mike initially took a few 44 lb. boxes from the order, and the balance would be due as he took shipment of the remainder of the contract.

After digging, Shannon found the hops Mike brought back from the broker (for which he had paid $1,320) were not on the balance sheet but on the income statement as cost of goods sold; furthermore, the hops contract was not on the books at all, and some equipment purchases had been expensed as supplies. Shannon reminded Mike and Erica of their previous conversation concerning collateralized assets and the advantages of adding these to the balance sheet as opposed to expensing them. She also let them know that, since they had signed a contract with a hops broker, they were liable for the remaining balance of that contract and therefore it belonged on the balance sheet as a liability, much as a credit card or loan would be considered a liability. Shannon also let them know that a negative net income at this point was to be expected as they had not opened yet and therefore had no revenue.

Shannon could tell that Mike and Erica's financial education needed some fine tuning if they were going to be successful keeping the books and records themselves. She knew that they had a follow-up appointment with their CPA, so Shannon encouraged them to spend more time asking questions about the fundamentals of accounting.

> See chapter 3 for an explanation of what accounts are presented on the balance sheet versus the income statement.

During the last meeting with Charles, their CPA, Mike and Erica learned about their basic financial reports: Balance Sheet, Income Statement, and Statement of Cash Flows. When the couple looked at their own cash flow report for the build-out period, they found it sobering to see how much money they had spent. The construction phase had begun and, ready or not, the cash faucet was running. If all went according to plan, Mike and Erica would have an operating facility in six months.

Happy Hour Brewing Company's loan for equipment purchases required the brewery to purchase equipment and then turn in a receipt for reimbursement of 90% of the purchase price (Mike and Erica were responsible for paying the other 10%). In theory, there was plenty of cash to pay 10% of the cost of the equipment needed. However, the business would have to cover 100% of the cost for a few weeks due to the processing time for reimbursement requests. This left Mike and Erica in a position where cash was really tight for a few weeks at a time.

They were feeling the crunch. The build-out couldn't slow down because the brewery needed to open its doors so that they could generate revenue to contribute back to the company. There was a risk that the process might choke out all of Mike and Erica's cash before they could generate revenue. It was an anxious time for the couple. They even considered borrowing money from other people, or looking for an investor, but decided those were short-sighted solutions.

After their follow-up meeting with Charles, Mike and Erica appreciated the value of having someone on call who had counseled clients through this same process. In the meeting, Charles had advised them that planning for cash flow management was key.

Charles had explained that the key is to have a cash flow forecast. When looking at a cash flow *statement*, all the information is based on historical data. With a *forecast*, you determine what cash will be at some point in the future. The challenge with a forecast is that you don't have all of the data. Instead, you have to create assumptions about when you will incur

TABLE 1.2 CASH FLOW FORECAST

	Jan 7, 20XX	Jan 14, 20XX	Jan 21, 20XX	Jan 28, 20XX	Feb 20XX	Mar 20XX
Cash Flow from Operations						
Expense						
Business Licenses and Permits	100.00	–	–	–	–	–
Equipment Rental	–	–	320.00	–	–	–
Professional Fees	–	6,021.00	–	–	4,100.00	1,500.00
Sales Expense						
Supplies	200.00	200.00	200.00	200.00	800.00	800.00
Total Expense	300.00	6,221.00	520.00	200.00	4,900.00	2,300.00
Net Cash from Operations	**(300.00)**	**(6,221.00)**	**(520.00)**	**(200.00)**	**(4,900.00)**	**(2,300)**
Cash flow from Investing						
Equipment	(3,600.00)	–	–	–	(43,000.00)	(102,000.00)
Leasehold Improvements		(21,000.00)		(21,000.00)		
Net Cash from Investing	**(3,600.00)**	**(21,000.00)**	**–**	**(21,000.00)**	**(43,000.00)**	**(102,000.00)**
Cash flow from Financing						
SBA Loan					3,240.00	38,700.00
Owner Contributions						
Net Cash from Financing	**–**	**–**	**–**	**–**	**3,240.00**	**38,700.00**
Change in Cash	(3,900.00)	(27,221.00)	(520.00)	(21,200.00)	(44,660.00)	(65,600.00)
Beginning Cash	103,750.00	99,850.00	72,629.00	72,109.00	50,909.00	6,249.00
Ending Cash	**99,850.00**	**72,629.00**	**72,109.00**	**50,909.00**	**6,249.00**	**(59,351.00)**

expenses and generate revenue. It's good to look forward weekly for the coming month, then monthly for the next eleven months. With this in mind, Mike and Erica looked at their cash flow for the next couple of months (table 1.2).

EXPERT ADVICE

Note that in our story Mike and Erica's CPA helps them create a cash flow forecast, but this kind of guidance does not always have to come from a CPA. There may be other resources available that provide financial tools for start-up or early stage breweries. Agencies like the Small Business Development Center (SBDC) and even a banker can help clients create forecasting tools to help manage their business.

See chapter 4 for an in-depth discussion on cash flow.

Erica and Mike could clearly see from their cash flow forecast (table 1.2) that, on the current schedule, cash was going to run out in the next ninety days. They went back to Charles for advice. Charles first asked them to look at the options to change course, beginning with what was under the couple's control. Erica and Mike knew that the turnaround time for reimbursements of equipment purchases was causing them stress. What were the factors they could change to fix this?

Erica admitted that there was room for improvement in how records were organized. Usually, there was a three to four-day delay from when money was spent to when the reimbursement request form went to the SBA. And in this case time was critical. The loan was set up to reimburse the recipient after money had been spent on equipment. Receipts had to be turned in to the lender, who would then reimburse 90% of the cost back to the debtor. Because of the administrative effort to assemble the reimbursement package, Erica thought it was easier to submit fewer requests for larger dollar amounts. Unfortunately, the strain on cash flow demanded that the couple submit for smaller amounts of money as soon as possible. This would require more legwork on their end but would be the difference between staying afloat and choking on lack of cash. Up to this point, they had only received a portion of the

SBA funds, and the amount of the loan was sufficient to fund the project, but the timing of expenses was causing hiccups in cash flow.

Because the brewery and taproom were not yet open, there was zero cash inflow from operations. The only available cash was from the couple's own pocket or the bank. Should they consider taking a loan from friends and family? Should they look at selling a portion of ownership so that they could access more capital? Charles challenged them to dig a little deeper before taking those steps. First, he asked if they had evaluated the details of the project expenses. He knew the contractor had provided three budgets for the build-out: a low, a medium, and a high-priced option. The project was far from complete, so perhaps there was an opportunity to shave even more costs. Mike pulled up the detailed quote for the build-out to see if there were any adjustments that could be made.

The contractor was building in a fee for sourcing appliances and picking up building materials. Mike discussed this with the contractor and, after making the change to do that part himself, Mike was able to shave about $6,000 off the contract price. Furthermore, the finish of countertops in the prep area and bathrooms could be swapped out for a lower priced material without losing any functionality. This change had minimal effect on the aesthetics and brought down the price by another $4,000.

The quote also included a custom-built bar that was to be the centerpiece of the tasting room. If Mike and Erica went a different direction with the bar it could save them a lot of money, but there was more involved in the decision than just money. Mike's grandfather had owned a bar several years ago. He loved the place and it burned in a fire 20 years earlier. After searching high and low, Mike found a craftsman who was able to recreate the same style of bar from pictures. This centerpiece was to be an homage to Mike's grandfather, and Mike had thought of it as the soul of the space. The couple talked it over that night and, ever the voice of reason, Erica offered that the space was going to create a spirit of its own, and while the custom bar would be a really nice way to honor Mike's grandfather and family's history, they could always add it later. If they spent the time and money to do it now, they ran a risk of hurting themselves in the long run. Erica encouraged Mike to set a goal of putting in the custom bar if they met their revenue and income goals for the first year of business. Mike slept on it and woke up at peace with the decision to cut the bar from the initial build-out. That one change alone cut $23,000 from the budget.

With a little digging, compromise, and elbow grease, Mike and Erica were able to find $33,000 in savings. While this didn't solve all their cash flow problems, it certainly helped to close the gap. Erica then mentioned three more options for cash flow that they hadn't considered yet. Her first suggestion was to get a business credit card. She was sure they would get approved based on their personal credit scores, and the card would give them one more way to stretch out cash flow another 30 days. They would just have to stay committed to paying it off each month so that they would not rack up interest charges at a high rate.

The second idea to consider was taking out a home equity line of credit. They had purchased their home a few years ago and made extra payments toward the principal. However, while Erica and Mike thought that they could get at least $25,000 out if they needed to, this was not a viable option because the SBA loan had first position on their home as collateral.

Finally, Erica mentioned taking a loan from her 401(k). There were penalties associated with that, but it could be considered as an option of last resort. Mike resisted this idea, noting that he really hated the idea of building up debt. Erica agreed but encouraged him to be realistic about their situation. It was clear that they needed to cut expenses, shorten the timeline, have access to more cash, or some combination of all three. They decided to figure out exactly how short they were, and when they would need the money. At least that way they would know what their needs were and have that information to hand if they had to make some real decisions.

Erica and Mike went back to the cash flow forecast, and looked at it in more detail. It showed that money was going to run out within ninety days. They wanted to remedy the low points of cash and went after the easy cost-saving measures first. They decided to look further into the future in their forecast, extending it

from three months to six months. They quickly agreed that the cutbacks on the build project were the smartest way to improve their cash flow. Mike and Erica updated the forecast to account for the reduced costs, and the quicker turnaround time for reimbursement requests. Their results were much better, but still a little too lean for comfort (table 1.3).

Mike and Erica felt better about the cash situation. The forecast now showed no months of negative cash through the pre-opening phase, but the lack of wiggle room really made Erica uncomfortable. Looking at the ending cash balance, she noticed they'd have very little cash in the bank right around the grand opening at the beginning of July. Mike and Erica agreed that they would feel better if they could keep at least $5,000 in the bank, and so Erica returned to the idea of a business credit card. Mike hated the idea of being in debt. He had worked hard all his life to be debt free and, frankly, that was a large reason why they were able to get a bank loan for the business. But, again, Erica was the voice of reason. He knew that running a business was a whole different ballgame from running his personal affairs. The couple decided they would get a business credit card with a small approved credit balance, and they agreed to only use it when they really needed it. Mike's one stipulation was that they would get a business credit card with a great air miles program. He needed to reward his love of travel if they were going to go out on a limb and incur more debt!

> For more information on cash flow management see chapter 4, "Cash is King!"

In the haste of the build-out, Mike and Erica had fallen out of the habit of reviewing the financial reports thoroughly each month. They decided to get out the monthly financial review checklist that their CPA had given them during one of their first meetings. Erica was particularly interested in creating a regular rhythm of financial review. She knew there was tremendous value in reviewing the same data each month. It allowed her to reconnect with the data. As the financial manager, she started to understand the business at a deeper level by understanding the numbers.

TABLE 1.3 REVISED CASH FLOW FORECAST

	Jan 7, 20XX	Jan 14, 20XX	Jan 21, 20XX	Jan 28, 20XX	Feb 20XX	Mar 20XX	Apr 20XX	May 20XX	Jun 20XX
Cash Flow from Operations									
Expense									
Business Licenses and Permits	100.00	-	-	-	-	-	-	-	252.60
Charitable Contributions	-	-	-	-	-	-	-	-	-
Dues and Subscriptions	-	-	-	-	-	-	-	-	365.00
Equipment Rental	-	-	320.00	-	-	-	-	-	-
Guaranteed Payment	-	-	-	-	-	-	5,000.00	5,000.00	10,000.00
Insurance Expense	-	-	-	-	-	-	1,066.41	1,166.41	1,746.71
License & Permits	-	-	-	-	-	-	700.00	-	-
Marketing	-	-	-	-	-	-	-	2,000.00	-
Office Supplies	-	-	-	-	-	-	-	300.00	-
Payroll Expenses	-	-	-	-	-	-	-	-	7,000.00
Professional Fees	-	6,021.00	-	-	4,100.00	1,500.00	-	5,000.00	3,000.00
Rent Expense	-	-	-	-	-	-	9,533.33	7,572.16	7,374.47
Sales Expense	-	-	-	-	-	1,621.42	-	-	-
Supplies	200.00	200.00	200.00	200.00	800.00	800.00	800.00	800.00	3,000.00
Utilities	-	-	-	-	-	-	2,500.00	2,500.00	2,500.00
Total Expense	300.00	6,221.00	520.00	200.00	4,900.00	3,921.42	19,599.74	24,338.57	35,238.78
Net Cash from Operations	**(300.00)**	**(6,221.00)**	**(520.00)**	**(200.00)**	**(4,900.00)**	**(3,921.42)**	**(19,599.74)**	**(24,338.57)**	**(35,238.78)**
Cash Flow from Investing									
Equipment	(3,600.00)	-	-	-	(43,000.00)	(102,000.00)	-	-	-
Leasehold Improvements	-	(21,000.00)	-	(8,000.00)	-	-	(24,000.00)	-	-
Net Cash from Investing	**(3,600.00)**	**(21,000.00)**	**-**	**(8,000.00)**	**(43,000.00)**	**(102,000.00)**	**(24,000.00)**	**-**	**-**
Cash flow from Financing									
SBA Loan			3,240.00		38,700.00	68,850.00	22,950.00	30,000.00	30,000.00
Owner Contributions									
Net Cash from Financing	**-**	**-**	**3,240.00**	**-**	**38,700.00**	**68,850.00**	**22,950.00**	**30,000.00**	**30,000.00**
Change in Cash	(3,900.00)	(27,221.00)	2,720.00	(8,200.00)	(9,200.00)	(37,071.42)	(20,649.74)	5,661.43	(5,238.78)
Beginning Cash	103,750.00	99,850.00	72,629.00	75,349.00	67,149.00	57,949.00	20,877.58	227.84	5,889.27
Ending Cash	**99,850.00**	**72,629.00**	**75,349.00**	**67,149.00**	**57,949.00**	**20,877.58**	**227.84**	**5,889.27**	**650.49**

See chapter 5 for more detailed guidelines on a basic monthly financial review.

Monthly Financial Checklist
- Balance Sheet: comparative to prior period
- Income Statement: comparative to prior period
- Income Statement by class
- Statement of Cash Flows
- Income Statement: budget versus actual

Mike and Erica were getting close to opening day, and they decided they should review the books one more time before their grand opening. They began with the balance sheet showing the current period versus prior period, which had two columns, one for May and one for June (table 1.4).

EXPERT ADVICE

Adding data from another past period can be extremely helpful. Usually the comparative period will be either the month preceding the month in review, or the same month from the previous year. It's difficult to determine if performance is improving or not when you look at one period in isolation. Comparing the current month to the previous month adds context.

Cash and equipment had both increased, and Erica wanted to get excited because she thought of assets as good, positive things on the balance sheet. Mike reminded her that they needed to see the rest of the picture before judging the performance. Sure enough, when they moved to "Liabilities" they saw that most categories had increased. Erica noted that "Accounts Payable" (AP) had not changed at all. All of the bills they had as unpaid at the end of May were still unpaid at the end of June. Because cash was tight, bills did not get paid, and they had begun to use the new credit card for other expenses.

Charles, their CPA, had encouraged Mike and Erica to look at the changes period over period and make sure that they understood why the change happened. Then the couple could use that information to adjust behavior in the future.

One big issue jumped out to them during the review: there was no "Inventory" account on the initial balance sheet. This didn't make sense to Mike, because he had purchased a good amount of grain and hops to get ready to brew. Erica figured out that inventory items had all ended up on the income statement as COGS.

Erica felt a little embarrassed. Charles had explained how purchases of ingredients first go on the balance sheet and then get transferred to the income statement when the goods are sold. Shannon, their SBDC advisor, had also gone over this with Erica and forewarned her that it was a common error. Regardless of the education and warnings, Erica had made the same mistake. Erica recategorized the transactions so that they would show up correctly on the balance sheet (table 1.4, *see* Assets > Current Assets > Inventory). Admitting that she had made a mistake was hard for Erica, but being a business owner was quickly teaching her humility, and she was getting comfortable with figuring things out along the way.

Erica and Mike then moved on to the income statement (table 1.5), and the most obvious note was that they didn't have revenue in June. The couple were looking forward to adding numbers to the top of the report and, with the doors almost open, this was going to be the last month of zero revenue. They reviewed each line of the statement and felt comfortable with what they saw until they got to guaranteed payments, which was double the normal amount. Erica realized it was because they wrote one check for June in the early part of the month and another check for July on June 30th.

This was another topic that Shannon had brought up. Erica went back to her SBDC advisor meeting notes and found guidance relating to the **matching principle of accounting.**

> The **matching principle of accounting** states that you should record revenue and expenses in the period to which they relate. For example, if two checks are written in one month that relate to multiple months' expenses, then the second check should be recorded as a prepaid expense if you are paying for it in the month before. If you miss a month and need to pay later, then you would still record an expense entry for the month and credit a payable account.

TABLE 1.4 BALANCE SHEET
JUNE 30, 20XX | CURRENT MONTH VS. PRIOR MONTH

	Jun 30, 20XX	May 31, 20XX	$ Change
ASSETS			
Current Assets			
Checking/Savings			
Checking	9,902.03	1,706.32	8,195.71
Total Checking/Savings	9,902.03	1,706.32	8,195.71
Inventory			
Raw Materials	895.80	3,966.80	(3,071.00)
Work in Process	165.00	0.00	165.00
Finished Goods	2,906.00	0.00	2,906.00
Total Inventory	3,966.80	0.00	3,966.80
Total Current Assets	**13,868.83**	**5,673.12**	**8,195.71**
Fixed Assets			
Brewery Equipment and Machinery	134,179.17	128,679.17	5,500.00
Leasehold Improvements	4,329.36	4,329.36	0.00
Start-up costs	6,804.00	6,804.00	0.00
Total Fixed Assets	145,312.53	139,812.53	5,500.00
TOTAL ASSETS	**159,181.36**	**145,485.65**	**13,695.71**
LIABILITIES & EQUITY			
Liabilities			
Current Liabilities			
Accounts Payable			
Accounts Payable	21,801.32	19,801.32	2,000.00
Total Accounts Payable	21,801.32	19,801.32	2,000.00
Credit Cards			
Credit Card	11,701.03	7,134.62	4,566.41
Total Credit Cards	11,701.03	7,134.62	4,566.41
Other Current Liabilities			
Payroll Liabilities	7,000.00	0.00	7,000.00
Total Other Current Liabilities	7,000.00	0.00	7,000.00
Total Current Liabilities	40,502.35	26,935.94	13,566.41
Long Term Liabilities			
Loans Payable			
SBA Loan	163,740.00	133,740.00	30,000.00
Total Loans Payable	163,740.00	133,740.00	30,000.00
Total Long Term Liabilities	163,740.00	133,740.00	30,000.00
Total Liabilities	204,242.35	160,675.94	43,566.41
Equity			
Members Equity	50,000.00	50,000.00	0.00
Retained Earnings	(2,069.99)	(2,069.99)	0.00
Net Income	(92,991.00)	(63,120.30)	(29,870.70)
Total Equity	(45,060.99)	(15,190.29)	(29,870.70)
TOTAL LIABILITIES & EQUITY	**159,181.36**	**145,485.65**	**13,695.71**

TABLE 1.5 INCOME STATEMENT CURRENT MONTH VS. PRIOR MONTH
JUNE 20XX VS. MAY 20XX

	Jun 20XX	May 20XX	$ Change
Ordinary Income/Expense			
Income			
Merchandise Sales			
Shirt Sales	0.00	780.00	(780.00)
Total Merchandise Sales	0.00	780.00	(780.00)
Total Income	0.00	780.00	(780.00)
Cost of Goods Sold			
Merchandise Cost			
Shirt Cost	0.00	390.00	(390.00)
Total Merchandise Cost	0.00	390.00	(390.00)
Total Cost of Goods Sold	0.00	390.00	(390.00)
Gross Profit	0.00	390.00	(390.00)
Expense			
Business Licenses	252.60	0.00	252.60
Dues and Subscriptions	365.00	0.00	365.00
Guaranteed Payment	10,000.00	5,000.00	5,000.00
Insurance Expense	1,746.71	0.00	1,746.71
Payroll Expenses	7,000.00	0.00	7,000.00
Professional Fees			
Legal Fees	3,542.00	0.00	3,542.00
Marketing	0.00	2,000.00	(2,000.00)
Total Professional Fees	3,542.00	2,000.00	1,542.00
Rent Expense	6,200.00	6,200.00	0.00
Repairs and Maintenance	60.50	0.00	60.50
Utilities			
Natural Gas	10.99	0.00	10.99
Power	661.41	1,167.82	(506.41)
Water	31.49	0.00	31.49
Total Utilities	703.89	1,167.82	(463.93)
Total Expense	29,870.70	14,367.82	15,502.88
Net Ordinary Income	(29,870.70)	(13,977.82)	(15,892.88)
Net Income	**(29,870.70)**	**(13,977.82)**	**(15,892.88)**

Erica knew that they did not have a "Guaranteed Payments Payable" account in the chart of accounts. She and Mike considered the effects of adding such an account to the chart of accounts and judged that doing so would not jeopardize the comparability of the financial reports. Erica added the account and made an adjustment to the transaction. The effect was that guaranteed payments were correctly stated and they showed a new prepaid expense on the balance sheet.

In summary, the income statement showed they had spent over twice as much money as the previous month. While they didn't want to see losses, Mike and Erica knew to expect them because they had not yet opened the doors.

The next report was another version of the income statement, showing performance by class (table 1.6). Shannon had explained to Erica and Mike that turning on the Class function in their software helped them create departments in their financial reports. The brewery was a manufacturing operation and the taproom was a retail operation—using the Class function avoids having two different business models operating under one entity. Finances would look different for each operation, so it was important to have a mechanism to see that.

EXPERT ADVICE

An income statement by class gives the benefit of seeing brewery, taproom, and administrative activities separately. In our example (table 1.6), we only see taproom and admin class because this is pre-opening and the brewery is not active.

As Erica and Mike scrolled through each line in the income statement by class, they looked for expenses that were shared costs across classes. When they got to "Rent Expense," they noticed that 100% was in the Administrative class. Based on what he'd learned from colleagues, Mike recommended allocating the rent by square footage. They settled on splitting the rent with 10% to admin, 50% to the brewery, and 40% to the taproom. Each month going forward, even if the rent amount changed, the allocation percentages would stay the same. Erica made the adjustment to the expense entry (fig. 1.1).

> See chapter 2 for more information on using classes.

The "Repairs and Maintenance" and "Utilities" accounts were also both allocated 100% to admin. Mike decided that repairs should go to the class where the repair was needed, and utilities should be broken out to each department according to the department's use of the utilities. For example, when the brewhouse was installed, the burner on the kettle broke and needed replacing. By allocating that cost to the brewery, they could see the cost of brewing the beer. Categorizing the correct class for repairs seemed easy, but utilities were more difficult. After some discussion, the couple decided to leave utilities in admin because they were not yet open in June and most of the utility use was related to administrative tasks. Once open, they decided to use the same allocation as rent. Mike and Erica agreed to keep an eye on the distribution of utilities over time, and they agreed to fine-tune the allocation toward the end of the year.

Mike and Erica had made their way through the balance sheet and income statement. The final report they reviewed was the statement of cash flows, which illustrated cash inflows and outflows (table 1.7). The loss for the month of June was around $30,000, but about $13,000 of that total was either put on a credit card or booked as a liability that hadn't yet been paid.

Expenses	$6,200.00	Items	$0.00		
ACCOUNT		AMOUNT	MEMO	CLASS	
Rent Expense		620.00		Administrative	
Rent Expense		2,480.00		Taproom	
Rent Expense		3,100.00		Brewery	

Figure 1.1. Allocating shared expenses to different classes allows the business owner to see how each activity center affects the business's finances. In this case, the original $6,200 rent expense that was allocated 100% to admin is now split between the brewery, taproom, and administrative activities.

TABLE 1.6 INCOME STATEMENT BY CLASS
JUNE 20XX

	Administrative	Taproom	TOTAL
Ordinary Income/Expense			
Expense			
Business Licenses	252.60	0.00	252.60
Dues and Subscriptions	365.00	0.00	365.00
Guaranteed Payment	10,000.00	0.00	10,000.00
Insurance Expense	1,746.71	0.00	1,746.71
Payroll Expenses	0.00	7,000.00	7,000.00
Professional Fees			
Legal Fees	3,542.00	0.00	3,542.00
Total Professional Fees	3,542.00	0.00	3,542.00
Rent Expense	6,200.00	0.00	6,200.00
Repairs and Maintenance	60.50	0.00	60.50
Utilities			
Natural Gas	10.99	0.00	10.99
Power	661.41	0.00	661.41
Water	31.49	0.00	31.49
Total Utilities	703.89	0.00	703.89
Total Expense	22,870.70	7,000.00	29,870.70
Net Ordinary Income / (Loss)	(22,870.70)	(7,000.00)	(29,870.70)
Net Income / (Loss)	**(22,870.70)**	**(7,000.00)**	**(29,870.70)**

TABLE 1.7 STATEMENT OF CASH FLOWS
JUNE 20XX

	Jun 20XX
OPERATING ACTIVITIES	
Net Income / (Loss)	(29,870.70)
Adjustments to reconcile Net Income to Net Cash provided by operations:	
Increase in Credit Card Payable	6,566.41
Increase in Payroll Liabilities	7,000.00
Net cash provided by Operating Activities	(16,304.29)
INVESTING ACTIVITIES	
Increase in Brewery Equipment and Machinery	(5,500.00)
Net cash provided by Investing Activities	(5,500.00)
FINANCING ACTIVITIES	
Increase in Loans Payable: SBA Loan	30,000.00
Net cash provided by Financing Activities	30,000.00
Net cash increase for period	8,195.71
Cash at beginning of period	1,706.32
Cash at end of period	**9,902.03**

That meant that cash only actually decreased by about $16,000 from operations. They had also paid for $5,500 of equipment, so cash decreased to account for that. In terms of cash inflows, they had received $30,000 from the SBA loan. Between the cash outflows from operations and investing (roughly $22,000) and the cash inflow of $30,000 from loan proceeds, the net change resulted in a cash increase of about $8,000, leaving a balance of $9,900 in their checking account.

By the time they were done, Mike and Erica had spent about two hours reviewing the reports, but they felt that the knowledge they had acquired and their increased familiarity with the accounts would serve them time and again in the future. Now they could truly put this information to use when making decisions about their business.

The couple held their grand opening in July, and the neighborhood really supported them! Within the first 60 days of operation Happy Hour Brewing Co. had a steady group of regulars. The taproom was consistently busy from late afternoon until close. All signs were positive, except for how tired Mike and Erica were. Both of them were working in the business every day. On top of her day job, Erica continued to take the lead in managing the accounting. She spent nights and weekends entering data and paying bills.

The couple undertook a financial review after the first 60 days. When they dug into the brewery income statement, they noticed that COGS seemed high, being 3% higher than the previous month. Charles had shared some figures for industry norms with Erica and Mike that suggested they were already on the high end of costs, relative to income, for a brewery their size. Erica wanted to find out why.

Erica started by comparing the gross margin of "Food" and "Draft Beer." The ingredients cost for Food was in line with expectations, and taproom labor was under control too. It was clear that the issue was with their beer. Mike suspected that something might be off in their pricing. He loved to make big beers with multiple types of hops in each batch, plus dry hopping later in the process. All of that added up to an expensive beer. Plus, they were selling pints at a low price, $5.25, when the average in town was $6.

See chapter 7 for guidance on pricing.

Working with the theory that their pricing structure might be off, Mike came up with a list of questions that he wanted to answer:

- Did they need to find a new supplier of raw materials to bring down their costs?
- Were all the transactions correctly recorded in the books?
- Was the sales price too low?
- Did they need to cut out the big beers?
- Should they stop dry hopping? They knew that really affected the yields they got in the brewing process.
- Did they measure their production losses and brewhouse efficiency by style of beer?
- What if they changed to using fewer varieties of hops in their recipes? Could they buy in bulk and get a better price? How would this affect their hops contract?

The truth, Mike knew, was that he needed to understand all of the above, and the answer was a combination of several factors. The data in the accounting file wasn't detailed enough to help him understand how he could effect change. Mike decided to try to get more relevant data from the point of sale (POS) system, pulling a report for sales by item for the last month. He noticed that the amber ale they put on last month wasn't showing up. Surely they had sold pints of it?

When Mike asked his bartender that afternoon, she reminded him that a month earlier she had asked him to enter the new beer into the system so that they could log sales, but Mike had not done that. Everyone tending bar had been using a different beer style when the amber was sold because it wasn't in the system. Mike wanted to be mad, but he knew that this fell back on him. He had never given the bartender the POS system credentials to add items herself. The result was that, not only were data on sales of amber missing from the system, but also all of the brands' data were messed up for the prior month because everyone had been using random items in the POS system to record those sales. Mike decided that his only option was to correct the situation now and make changes so that, to the best of his ability, it wouldn't happen again. What had begun as an exercise in analyzing the pricing of beers had uncovered another operational issue that diverted Mike's attention and needed to be addressed before he could get back to the matter at hand.

Once the POS system settings were fixed, Mike turned his attention back to the analysis of revenue by brand. He wouldn't have good data on sales by brand for another month. But he did know how many pints they had sold last month. When he ran the numbers, he saw that if they charged the same as their neighboring bars—an extra 75 cents a pint—they would have made an additional $3,000. Their beers were being well received and they had a few styles available that the other neighborhood bars did not. Mike thought it might be a good idea to raise their prices to market level. After talking it over with Erica, they decided to make the change.

WORDS OF WISDOM

What do you wish you knew when you opened?
How word of mouth marketing works. When we opened we had a ton of great press, were making some great beers, but we weren't all that busy those first few months. What I didn't realize was that word of mouth marketing is an exponential growth curve, meaning that it starts incredibly slow, and then hits a tipping point. For us, the tipping point was around six months in, then we started getting really busy. If you're relying on word of mouth marketing for anything, expect those first six months to be slow as things work up steam.

Adam Robbings
Founder, Reuben's Brews

Next month Mike and Erica reviewed the numbers and, as expected, the change to price had a positive impact on gross margin. They had recaptured a few of the points that they lost in the prior month. Mike and Erica were happy, but Mike still wanted to get into the sales by item data now that they had a full month of accurate activity. He pulled up a new sales by item report for the last month (table 1.8). He saw that, as a percentage of sales, Happy Hour Brewing Co.'s IPA was the best seller; not surprising, as it was a popular

style, and Mike had to admit that he brewed a pretty good IPA. The Pilsner was the second highest seller, and the pale ale was third.

The IPA was expensive because it used a large quantity of hops; the Pilsner was expensive because it took longer to make than most other beers ; the pale ale was expensive because it used three kinds of hops. How could Mike make good profits if all of his beers were expensive?

After tracking the revenue of each brand, Mike pulled the cost per barrel from his recipe sheet. Just as he suspected, the most expensive beer, the IPA, was selling the most. One option was to still charge $6.00 per serving, but decrease the volume to a 12 fl. oz. pour. There were a couple of issues with this: first, Mike didn't know if it would be wise to make a change to pricing after they just went up to $6.00 per pint last month; second, he didn't have an adequate number of 12 fl. oz. glasses, so he'd have to purchase new glassware.

> See chapter 6 for guidance on proper costing, including calculating cost per batch.

Before making a final decision, Mike looked at the data another way. He pulled the ticket history of customers who had purchased the IPA and compared that to non-IPA purchases. He found that those who purchased an IPA purchased on average 0.6 pints more beer per ticket than patrons who purchased a beer other than IPA. The data suggested that the IPA drinkers were staying longer and ordering a second beer. Mike asked his bartenders if this pattern matched what they saw, and they confirmed the sales trends. Even though the margin for the IPA was lower, Mike knew the beer was still profitable and it was driving up overall sales. Mike felt this was a good tradeoff and he decided to make no change to the price per pint or quantity per serving for IPA sold over the counter.

Mike and Erica were planning to start selling kegs of the IPA next week, and Mike was glad that he'd done the above analysis before taking it to market. Based on the sales data, he felt confident that pricing the IPA kegs a little higher than their other brands was the right thing to do. He decided to sell IPA kegs for a price that was 7% above their other core beers.

TABLE 1.8 SALES BY ITEM
DEC 20XX

			Dec 20XX		
		Qty	**Amount**	**% of Sales**	**Avg Price**
Service					
Beers					
Pale Ale	Crowler	8.00	80.00	0.22%	10.00
Pale Ale	Pint	720.00	4,320.00	11.62%	6.00
Total Pale Ale			4,400.00	11.84%	
IPA	Crowler	16.00	160.00	0.43%	10.00
IPA	Pint	824.00	4,944.00	13.30%	6.00
Total IPA			5,104.00	13.73%	
Double IPA	Crowler	20.00	200.00	0.54%	10.00
Double IPA	Pint	852.00	5,112.00	13.75%	6.00
Total Double IPA			5,312.00	14.29%	
Pilsner	Crowler	18.00	180.00	0.48%	10.00
Pilsner	Pint	790.00	4,740.00	12.75%	6.00
Total Pilsner			4,920.00	13.24%	
Amber	Crowler	10.00	100.00	0.27%	10.00
Amber	Pint	760.00	4,560.00	12.27%	6.00
Total Amber			4,660.00	12.54%	
Stout	Crowler	12.00	120.00	0.32%	10.00
Stout	Pint	742.00	4,452.00	11.98%	6.00
Total Stout		754.00	4,572.00	12.30%	
Porter	Crowler	17.00	170.00	0.46%	10.00
Porter	Pint	690.00	4,140.00	11.14%	6.00
Total Porter			4,310.00	11.60%	
English Brown Ale	Crowler	16.00	160.00	0.43%	10.00
English Brown Ale	Pint	622.00	3,732.00	10.04%	6.00
Total English Brown Ale			3,892.00	10.47%	
TOTAL			**37,170.00**	**100.0%**	

This exercise had taken Mike most of a day to put together but it was time well spent. After this investigation he felt that they needed to examine their whole pricing structure and think about margin per brand and per pack type. This would give them a clearer idea of how much they needed to sell in order to cover the overhead, because they could think of it in terms of target quantities for each **stock keeping unit** (SKU).

> A **stock keeping unit** (SKU) is a product identification code that refers to a specific brand in a specific pack type. Thus, the SKU encompasses both the product together with the size and format in which the product is sold.

Mike knew most of the brewers in town, and Wagener Brewing's owner, Trae, was known to be the most business-minded of them all. Wagener had been a successful brewery for about seven years, and Mike asked if Trae would be willing to give him some pointers on costing decisions. Mike explained that he would like to see specific numbers, and even though Happy Hour Brewing Co.'s income statement was accurate, he needed more detailed information in order to make decisions. Trae understood Mike's frustrations and shared with him Wagener's journey of tracking inventory first on a clipboard, then a spreadsheet, and finally using inventory management software.

Trae explained that adopting the inventory management software had been a culture shift for the brewery—it wasn't an easy transition, but the payoff in terms of data made it worth the effort. Maintaining the integrity of the data entered into the software was the key to having it run smoothly. Trae felt that the time spent to input clean, accurate data was well worth it, because the output allowed him to forecast with precision and make detailed production plans for distributors. The sharper the data, the better the result.

> See chapter 6 for more information on finding the accurate cost of your beer.

Getting inventory management software was tempting, but Mike was realistic about how much time that would take to implement accurately. He decided to make that a goal for the next calendar year and to focus on doing the best job that he could with simple tools. Trae shared some templates with Mike to help him fine-tune the beer costing. Before sending them to Mike, Trae gave him a tutorial for how to use the spreadsheets.

First, Trae set up each SKU in Wagener's accounting system as an item. This allowed the brewery to invoice for the specific items that were sold, and to pull a sales by item report (table 1.9).

TABLE 1.9 SALES BY ITEM SUMMARY
WAGENER BREWING

	October 20XX		
	Qty	Amount	Avg Price ($)
Beers			
Short Street			
15.5_A (15.5 gallon keg of Short Street)	1.00	150.00	150.00
Total Short Street	1.00	150.00	150.00
Five Forks IPA			
5.16_A (5.16 gallon keg of Five Forks)	6.0	300.00	50.00
Total Five Forks IPA (barrel of Five Forks)	6.0	300.00	50.00
Roscoe Porter			
15.5_A	35.00	4,220.65	120.59
5.16_A	15.00	750.00	50.00
Total Roscoe Porter	50.00	4,970.65	99.41

TABLE 1.9 SALES BY ITEM SUMMARY (CONT.)
WAGENER BREWING

	October 20XX		
	Qty	Amount	Avg Price ($)
Timber Winter IPA			
15.5_A	26.00	3,175.64	122.14
15.5_B	4.00	455.72	113.93
Case_A	250.00	7,562.50	30.25
Case_B	105.00	3,144.75	29.95
Total Timber Winter IPA	385.00	14,338.61	74.07
Paradise			
15.5_A	20.00	3,000.00	150.00
Total Paradise	20.00	3,000.00	150.00
Good Nature			
15.5_A	3.00	450.00	150.00
Total Good Nature	3.00	450.00	150.00
Good Nature_Barrel			
15.5_A	0.40	60.00	150.00
Case_A	10.00	302.50	30.25
Total Good Nature_B	10.40	362.50	90.13
Abundance IPA			
15.5_A	75.00	9,288.75	123.85
15.5_B	4.00	455.64	113.91
5.16_A	19.00	950.00	50.00
Case_A	241.00	7,290.25	30.25
Case_B	210.00	6,289.50	29.95
Total Abundance IPA	549.00	24,274.14	69.60
King Street Single Hop Red			
15.5_A	26.00	3,022.50	116.25
15.5_B	2.00	227.82	113.91
5.16 Wholesale_B	1.00	50.00	50.00
5.16_A	10.00	500.00	50.00
Case_A	333.00	10,073.25	30.25
Case_B	85.00	2,545.75	29.95
Total King Street Single Hop Red	457.00	16,419.32	65.06
Icebreaker Imperial IPA			
15.5_A	10.00	1,500.00	150.00
Case_A	18.00	544.50	30.25
Total Icebreaker Imperial IPA	28.00	2,044.50	90.13
TOTAL	**1,509.40**	**66,309.72**	**98.43**

Notes: _A and _B denote different sales territories; _Barrel, barrel-aged; Case, 24× 12 oz. cans; 5.16, 5.16 gal. keg; 15.5, 15.5 gal. keg.

See chapter 7 for examples of product costing reports available from brewery-specific inventory management software.

First, the dates of the report are set to a defined period, usually to last month, and then the report is exported to a spreadsheet program. The next step is to delete all the extraneous rows so that it's just the raw data (table 1.10).

A column is added for "Barrel Equivalent," which shows the total barrels of each item sold in a month. Finally, data is sorted by brand so that all sales of a single brand are together (table 1.11).

TABLE 1.10 SALES BY ITEM SUMMARY
WAGENER BREWING

		October 20XX		
		Qty	**Amount**	**Avg Price ($)**
Short Street Pale Ale	15.5_A	1.00	150.00	150.00
Five Forks IPA	5.16_A	6.00	300.00	50.00
Roscoe Porter	15.5_A	35.00	4,220.65	120.59
Roscoe Porter	5.16_A	15.00	750.00	50.00
Timber Winter IPA	15.5_A	26.00	3,175.64	122.14
Timber Winter IPA	15.5_B	4.00	455.72	113.93
Timber Winter IPA	Case_A	250.00	7,562.50	30.25
Timber Winter IPA	Case_B	105.00	3,144.75	29.95
Paradise	15.5_A	20.00	3,000.00	150.00
Good Nature	15.5_A	3.00	450.00	150.00
Good Nature_Barrel	15.5_A	0.40	60.00	150.00
Good Nature_Barrel	Case_A	10.00	302.50	30.25
Abundance IPA	15.5_A	75.00	9,288.75	123.85
Abundance IPA	15.5_B	4.00	455.64	113.91
Abundance IPA	5.16_A	19.00	950.00	50.00
Abundance IPA	Case_A	241.00	7,290.25	30.25
Abundance IPA	Case_B	210.00	6,289.50	29.95
King Street Single Hop Red	15.5_A	26.00	3,022.50	116.25
King Street Single Hop Red	15.5_B	2.00	227.82	113.91
King Street Single Hop Red	5.16_B	1.00	50.00	50.00
King Street Single Hop Red	5.16_A	10.00	500.00	50.00
King Street Single Hop Red	Case_A	333.00	10,073.25	30.25
King Street Single Hop Red	Case_B	85.00	2,545.75	29.95
Icebreaker Imperial IPA	15.5_A	10.00	1,500.00	150.00
Icebreaker Imperial IPA	Case_A	18.00	544.50	30.25

Notes: _A and _B denote different sales territories; _Barrel, barrel-aged; Case, 24× 12 oz. cans; 5.16, 5.16 gal. keg; 15.5, 15.5 gal. keg.

TABLE 1.11 SALES BY ITEM SUMMARY
BARREL EQUIVALENT
WAGENER BREWING

		October 20XX		
		Qty	Amount	Barrel Equivalent
Short Street Pale Ale	15.5_A	1.00	150.00	0.50
Five Forks IPA	5.16_A	6.00	300.00	1.00
Roscoe Porter	15.5_A	35.00	4,220.65	17.50
Roscoe Porter	5.16_A	15.00	750.00	2.50
Timber Winter IPA	15.5_A	26.00	3,175.64	13.00
Timber Winter IPA	15.5_B	4.00	455.72	2.00
Timber Winter IPA	Case_A	250.00	7,562.50	16.69
Timber Winter IPA	Case_B	105.00	3,144.75	7.01
Paradise	15.5_A	20.00	3,000.00	10.00
Good Nature	15.5_A	3.00	450.00	1.50
Good Nature_Barrel	15.5_A	0.40	60.00	0.20
Good Nature_Barrel	Case_A	10.00	302.50	0.67
Abundance IPA	15.5_A	75.00	9,288.75	37.50
Abundance IPA	15.5_B	4.00	455.64	2.00
Abundance IPA	5.16_A	19.00	950.00	3.17
Abundance IPA	Case_A	241.00	7,290.25	16.09
Abundance IPA	Case_B	210.00	6,289.50	14.02
King Street Single Hop Red	15.5_A	26.00	3,022.50	13.00
King Street Single Hop Red	15.5_B	2.00	227.82	1.00
King Street Single Hop Red	5.16_B	1.00	50.00	0.17
King Street Single Hop Red	5.16_A	10.00	500.00	1.67
King Street Single Hop Red	Case_A	333.00	10,073.25	22.24
King Street Single Hop Red	Case_B	85.00	2,545.75	5.68
Icebreaker Imperial IPA	15.5_A	10.00	1,500.00	5.00
Icebreaker Imperial IPA	Case_A	18.00	544.50	1.20

Notes: _A and _B denote different sales territories; _Barrel, barrel-aged; Case, 24× 12 oz. cans; 5.16, 5.16 gal. keg; 15.5, 15.5 gal. keg.

The next step involves the production spreadsheet. Wagener's production spreadsheet was set up so that each brand and batch had its own tab. The brand tabs include detailed recipes, and each ingredient line of the recipe is linked to another tab that lists ingredient costs (table 1.12). The result is that the recipe has an estimated cost (table 1.13). One critical detail is to update the unit cost of all ingredients each month.

Of course, not all ingredients will have a change to cost each month, but it is important to update for any changes so that pricing is as accurate as possible. The added advantage, Trae said, was that the exercise kept him close to the numbers and helped him identify vendors with whom he needed to negotiate. The updated cost per brand (table 1.14) feeds into a summary tab that lists the updated costs of all SKUs.

TABLE 1.12 INGREDIENT COSTS
AS OF 6/1/20XX
WAGENER BREWING

Malts	Price per unit
2-Row	0.51
White Wheat	0.56
Chocolate	0.76
Munich	0.55
Biscuit	0.71
Cara Blond	0.73
Honey Malt	0.77
Cara Malt	0.83
Hops	
Centennial	9.90
Brewers Gold	9.00
Simcoe	13.40
Sterling	9.25
Azacca	13.25
Sabro	12.20
Sorachi Ace	13.85
El Dorado	10.85
Packaging	
keg collars	0.465
keg caps	0.10

TABLE 1.13 FIVE FORKS IPA RECIPE
WAGENER BREWING

Ingredient	Quantity	Cost
2-Row	900	459.00
White Wheat	200	112.00
Honey Malt	20	15.40
Azacca	12	159.00
Sabro	11	134.20
Sorachi Ace	9	124.65
El Dorado	10	108.50
Gypsum		
Calcium Chloride		
A24 Yeast		
Keg Collar	30	13.95
Keg Cap	30	3.00
TOTAL		**1,129.70**
Average Yield		**13.85 BBL**
Average Direct Cost per Barrel		**81.57**

TABLE 1.14 BRAND COST PER BARREL
WAGENER BREWING

Brand	Ingredients Cost per Barrel ($)
Short Street Pale Ale	79.87
Five Forks IPA	81.57
Roscoe Porter	84.52
Timber Winter IPA	89.22
Paradise	75.98
Good Nature	73.44
Abundance IPA	78.25
King Street Single Hop Red	81.37
Icebreaker Imperial IPA	104.03
Mobile canning costs per barrel	**83.04**

To continue the process, the summary of beer costs is copied into a new tab of the sales spreadsheet. The cost of mobile canning or bottling fees is factored in for packaged goods. Then the barrels sold is multiplied by the cost per barrel from the beer cost list (table 1.15).

Mike was impressed by the data and also daunted by the process. Trae admitted that it took several hours of undivided attention each month. But the upside is that Wagener had pretty good data for being such a small operation. Mike wholeheartedly believed that the detailed planning is what would help his brewery continue to grow even as the industry was getting more competitive.

Just when Mike felt sure that he understood the process, Trae added that he also accounted for labor, excise tax, and overhead in COGS. Mike already felt overwhelmed, but he was determined to at least understand the process. Trae explained that these expenses come straight from the income statement. To get the correct data it's important to separate brewery labor from other labor, and to allocate overhead expenses to the correct class. Mike knew that he and Erica had already discussed separating labor by class, so this might be less work than he first thought.

Trae showed Mike the COGS and Expenses portion of the income statement (table 1.16). The highlighted column in table 1.16 indicates that only the brewery portion of an expense should be allocated to COGS. Highlighted rows indicate the expense accounts that are considered part of COGS; in addition to the direct materials, these costs (excise tax, direct labor, and overhead) are part of the cost of beer.

TABLE 1.15 SALES BY ITEM SUMMARY WITH COST
WAGENER BREWING

				October 20XX			
		Qty	Amount	Barrel Equivalent	Ingredients Cost	Packaging Cost	Ingredients and Packaging Cost
Short Street Pale Ale	15.5_A	1.00	150.00	0.50	39.94	-	39.94
Five Forks IPA	5.16_A	6.00	300.00	1.00	81.57	-	81.57
Roscoe Porter	15.5_A	35.00	4,220.65	17.50	1,479.10	-	1,479.10
Roscoe Porter	5.16_A	15.00	750.00	2.50	211.30		211.30
Timber Winter IPA	15.5_A	26.00	3,175.64	13.00	1,159.86		1,159.86
Timber Winter IPA	15.5_B	4.00	455.72	2.00	178.44		178.44
Timber Winter IPA	Case_A	250.00	7,562.50	16.69	1,572.43	2,217.50	3,789.93
Timber Winter IPA	Case_B	105.00	3,144.75	7.01	708.58	931.35	1,639.93
Paradise	15.5_A	20.00	3,000.00	10.00	759.80	-	759.80
Good Nature	15.5_A	3.00	450.00	1.50	110.16	-	110.16
Good Nature_Barrel	15.5_A	0.40	60.00	0.20	14.69	-	14.69
Good Nature_Barrel	Case_A	10.00	302.50	0.67	132.07	88.70	220.77
Abundance IPA	15.5_A	75.00	9,288.75	37.50	2,934.38	-	2,934.38
Abundance IPA	15.5_B	4.00	455.64	2.00	156.50	-	156.50
Abundance IPA	5.16_A	19.00	950.00	3.17	247.79	-	247.79
Abundance IPA	Case_A	241.00	7,290.25	16.09	1,342.28	2,137.67	3,479.95
Abundance IPA	Case_B	210.00	6,289.50	14.02	1,180.30	1,862.70	3,043.00
King Street Single Hop Red	15.5_A	26.00	3,022.50	13.00	1,057.81	-	1,057.81
King Street Single Hop Red	15.5_B	2.00	227.82	1.00	81.37	-	81.37
King Street Single Hop Red	5.16_B	1.00	50.00	0.17	13.56	-	13.56
King Street Single Hop Red	5.16_A	10.00	500.00	1.67	135.62	-	135.62
King Street Single Hop Red	Case_A	333.00	10,073.25	22.24	1,892.36	2,953.71	4,846.07
King Street Single Hop Red	Case_B	85.00	2,545.75	5.68	544.88	753.95	1,298.83
Icebreaker Imperial IPA	15.5_A	10.00	1,500.00	5.00	520.15	-	520.15
Icebreaker Imperial IPA	Case_A	18.00	544.50	1.20	208.07	159.66	367.73
			66,309.72	195.30	16,763.01	11,105.24	27,868.25

TABLE 1.16 INCOME STATEMENT EXCERPT: COGS AND EXPENSE
WAGENER BREWING

	Administrative	Brewery	Taproom	TOTAL
Cost of Goods Sold				
Beer - Guest	0.00	0.00	602.68	602.68
Beer - House	(18,624.15)	0.00	18,951.75	327.60
Bottles	0.00	1,782.00	0.00	1,782.00
Brewing Ingredients	0.00	4,696.64	0.00	4,696.64
Discounts Given	0.00	0.00	3,598.15	3,598.15
Dishwasher Service	0.00	0.00	421.15	421.15
Excise Tax	0.00	339.82	0.00	339.82
Gas/Oxygen	0.00	0.00	881.59	881.59
Groceries	0.00	0.00	10,248.37	10,248.37
Liquor Sold	0.00	0.00	1,684.52	1,684.52
Merchandise	0.00	0.00	4,568.99	4,568.99
Merchant Discounts/Bankcard Fee	0.00	0.00	294.77	294.77
N/A Beverage Sold	0.00	0.00	278.50	278.50
Payroll COGS	0.00	1,841.76	8,309.97	10,151.73
Wine Sold	0.00	0.00	1,737.50	1,737.50
Total COGS	(18,624.15)	8,660.22	51,577.94	41,614.01
Gross Profit	0.00	13,931.93	72,962.06	33,893.99
Expense				
100% Deductible Meals	0.00	0.00	303.00	303.00
Bank Service Charges	6.00	0.00	0.00	6.00
Cash Under/Over	0.00	0.00	0.00	0.00
Computer and Internet Expenses	0.00	0.00	29.99	29.99
Dues and Subscriptions	295.00	0.00	0.00	295.00
Guaranteed Payment	5,000.00	0.00	0.00	5,000.00
Insurance Expense	0.00	210.50	2,294.36	2,504.86
Janitorial Expense	0.00	95.00	768.24	863.24
Kegs	0.00	5,760.00	0.00	5,760.00
License & Permits	75.00	0.00	0.00	75.00
Marketing	0.00	1,566.25	390.00	1,956.25
Merchant Fees	0.00	0.00	4,676.39	4,676.39
Office Supplies	116.24	0.00	95.69	211.93
Payroll	242.00	219.80	11,370.92	11,832.72

TABLE 1.16 INCOME STATEMENT EXCERPT: COGS AND EXPENSE (CONT.)
WAGENER BREWING

	Administrative	Brewery	Taproom	TOTAL
Postage and Delivery	49.00	0.50	0.00	49.50
Professional Fees	1,831.88	369.06	29.57	2,230.51
Rent Expense	0.00	3,593.04	3,593.04	7,186.08
Repairs and Maintenance	0.00	255.31	356.34	611.65
Small Equipment	0.00	0.00	1,612.66	1,612.66
Small Wares	0.00	0.00	416.52	416.52
Supplies	50.00	726.08	3,216.17	3,992.25
Utilities	69.90	1,104.57	2,069.45	3,243.92
Total Expense	7,735.02	13,900.11	31,222.34	52,857.47

> See Chapter 6 for more information on how to correctly allocate payroll expense.

Trae explained that the final step was to apply these costs to each beer, allocating the labor, excise tax and overhead by volume sold. He added a column for these expenses, a column for total cost, and finally a column for margin per beer (table 1.17).

The amounts in the Labor, Excise Tax, OH (overhead) column in table 1.17 are calculated by taking the total of labor, excise tax, and overhead for the brewery ($10,094.15; *see* table 1.16 for relevant entries under Brewery) and multiplying it by the percentage of total barrel equivalent for each item. For the SKU "Short Street Pale Ale 13.2_A," it would be

Labor, Excise Tax, OH = (Excise Tax + Payroll COGS + Utilities) × (SKU Barrel Equivalent/Total Barrel Equivalent)

$$= (647.82 + 8341.76 + 1104.57)$$
$$\times \left(\frac{0.4258}{186.84} \right)$$
$$= 10094.15 \times 0.00227896$$
$$= 23.00$$

EXPERT ADVICE

What Mike was learning, without realizing it, is the concept of breakeven. When a company understands its breakeven cost, which can be expressed in units and/or dollars, it can be a game changer. This information is a powerful tool to help managers set and achieve goals. In my experience, many business owners have said that the greatest benefit to

knowing the breakeven amount is having a target for what they need to sell to cover costs. So, instead of having no goal and hoping for the best after the month closes, or hearing a goal of "we need to sell 100,000 dollars this month," more specific measurements such as "we need to sell 200 half-barrel kegs, 300 pony kegs, and 7,000 pints in the taproom" is a much more specific goal. The managers I have met in the beer industry do not, in general, love to crunch the numbers. Putting revenue goals in terms that are more relevant to the day-to-day operations of those who are responsible for achieving those goals can be transformative for your business.

> See chapter 6 for instruction on how to calculate a breakeven point.

After being open for six months, the Happy Hour Brewing Co. owners were getting to know their business. At this point they had been able to successfully enter and reconcile the last three months of data. The days were long, and most of the work to run the financial side of the business was happening after-hours at their kitchen table. Even so, Mike and Erica were self-disciplined enough to sit down and review the financial reports each month. It's funny, just a few months ago they felt like they didn't know what they were doing, and they even dreaded the idea of having to sit down and look at the reports. But at this point, with a few months of following Charles's suggested method for reviewing reports, the couple were really starting to see the value

TABLE 1.17 SALES BY ITEM SUMMARY
WAGENER BREWING

			Qty	Amount	Barrel Equivalent	Ingredients Cost	Labor, Excise Tax, OH	Total Cost	Margin ($)	Margin (%)
						October 20XX				
Short Street Pale Ale	15.5_A		1.00	150.00	0.50	39.94	25.84	65.78	84.22	56%
Five Forks IPA	5.16_A		6.00	300.00	1.00	81.57	51.69	133.25	166.75	56%
Roscoe Porter	15.5_A		35.00	4,220.65	17.50	1,479.10	904.49	2,383.59	1,837.06	44%
Roscoe Porter	5.16_A		15.00	750.00	2.50	211.30	129.21	340.51	409.49	55%
Timber Winter IPA	15.5_A		26.00	3,175.64	13.00	1,159.86	671.91	1,831.77	1,343.37	42%
Timber Winter IPA	15.5_B		4.00	455.72	2.00	178.44	103.37	281.81	173.91	38%
Timber Winter IPA	Case_A		250.00	7,562.50	16.69	1,572.43	862.81	2,435.24	5,127.26	68%
Timber Winter IPA	Case_B		105.00	3,144.75	7.01	708.58	362.38	1,070.96	2,073.79	66%
Paradise	15.5_A		20.00	3,000.00	10.00	759.80	516.85	1,276.65	1,723.35	57%
Good Nature	15.5_A		3.00	450.00	1.50	110.16	77.53	187.69	262.31	58%
Good Nature_Barrel	15.5_A		0.40	60.00	0.20	14.69	10.34	25.03	34.97	58%
Good Nature_Barrel	Case_A		10.00	302.50	0.67	132.07	34.51	166.59	135.91	45%
Abundance IPA	15.5_A		75.00	9,288.75	37.50	2,934.38	1,938.19	4,872.56	4,416.19	48%
Abundance IPA	15.5_B		4.00	455.64	2.00	156.50	103.37	259.87	195.77	43%
Abundance IPA	5.16_A		19.00	950.00	3.17	247.79	163.67	411.46	538.54	57%
Abundance IPA	Case_A		241.00	7,290.25	16.09	1,342.28	831.75	2,174.03	5,116.22	70%
Abundance IPA	Case_B		210.00	6,289.50	14.02	1,180.30	724.76	1,905.06	4,384.44	70%
King Street Single Hop Red	15.5_A		26.00	3,022.50	13.00	1,057.81	671.91	1,729.72	1,292.78	43%
King Street Single Hop Red	15.5_B		2.00	227.82	1.00	81.37	51.69	133.06	94.76	42%
King Street Single Hop Red	5.16_B		1.00	50.00	0.17	13.56	8.61	22.18	27.82	56%
King Street Single Hop Red	5.16_A		10.00	500.00	1.67	135.62	86.14	221.76	278.24	56%
King Street Single Hop Red	Case_A		333.00	10,073.25	22.24	1,892.36	1,149.26	3,041.62	7,031.63	70%
King Street Single Hop Red	Case_B		85.00	2,545.75	5.68	544.88	293.35	838.23	1,707.52	67%
Icebreaker Imperial IPA	15.5_A		10.00	1,500.00	5.00	520.15	258.43	778.58	721.42	48%
Icebreaker Imperial IPA	Case_A		18.00	544.50	1.20	208.07	62.12	270.20	274.30	50%
				66,309.72	195.30	16,763.01	10,094.15	26,857.16	39,452.56	59%

Notes: _A and _B denote different sales territory; _Barrel, barrel-aged; Case, 24× 12 oz. cans; 5.16, 5.16 gal. keg; 15.5, 15.5 gal. keg.

in looking at the data on a regular basis. Mike didn't look forward to it, but he did always come away understanding a little bit more about why the month had turned out the way it did and gaining an idea or two of how to tweak results for the coming month. As her knowledge of finance and accounting grew, Erica looked forward to the opportunity to dive into the reports. It was clear that the ideas were starting to connect, and she was seeing the broader picture of the business.

Erica would stay at that kitchen table well after the official review was over. Mike relaxed by watching TV for an hour or so before going to bed, but Erica was stuck on the idea of doing more with the financial information. She couldn't help but think about the future and project the financial results into the future. Questions about the business would come to her. "What would our numbers look like if we got just five more people in the door each hour?" "Can we afford to hire another bartender?" "Should we raise our pint prices by 25 cents?" In the past, these thoughts would come and go without her paying any real attention to them. But now, with a greater understanding of how the numbers worked, Erica was able to take those thoughts one step further and consider the possible results. This new confidence was exciting because she felt more empowered to manage the business. She also realized that this was just the beginning and if she followed this path of learning and understanding

the levers that affected her business, she could actually run the company one day! A silly joke, because of course she and Mike already ran the company. But, sometimes, the pair couldn't help but feel that they were in a reactive phase, with the company being just a series of events that happened while they watched, instead of being the clearly directed organization that they hoped it would be. Little did they know that this feeling would come and go for the rest of their careers as business owners.

As the days went by, Erica kept running through some of these business questions and she started to create projections. She was returned to the idea of raising the pint prices because it was the easiest financial modeling to prepare. By raising the price per unit sold the extra amount would fall straight to the bottom line. It was a small increase and would help them cover their loan payments. The drawback was that Erica and Mike were afraid higher prices would alienate consumers and the whole endeavor would backfire. Erica had discussed this with Mike, and he was interested but hesitant. Erica decided to present her projections to Mike the next time they sat down to review the books. She also wanted to have another meeting with their CPA, Charles. It had been a few months since they met with Charles, and now that they had several months of revenue on the books Erica wanted to know his opinion on how they were doing.

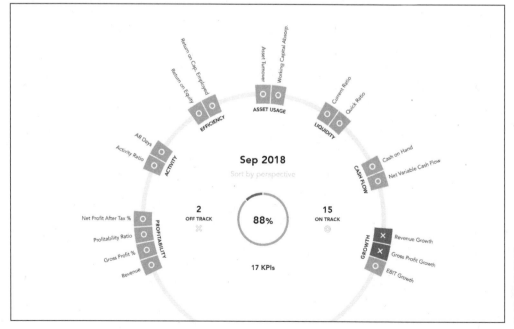

Figure 1.2. Key performance indicators relevant to the Happy Hour Brewing Company. Image courtesy of Fathom Applications Pty Ltd, www.fathomhq.com.

Charles had requested a copy of the couple's latest financial reports a week before their meeting so that he could get familiar with the numbers. He used these to compile a presentation of their financial results, demonstrate how the business compared to peer benchmarks, explain key ratios, and suggest key performance indicators that would help Erica and Mike keep a finger on the pulse of Happy Hour Brewing Co.'s health.

> See chapter 3 for a discussion of key ratios.

Charles opened the presentation, not with pages of numbers, but with colorful graphics that helped Erica and Mike see, quite literally, the state of the business.

EXPERT ADVICE

We all learn in different ways—listening, seeing, reading, doing—and it's important when searching for an advisor to find someone who can communicate in a way that you can understand. As a business owner, you will discuss vitally important topics with your CPA, and you will need to clearly understand the information and advice they give.

Mike and Erica found it quite refreshing to look at their data visually, and to start with a high-level analysis of whether their bussiness was on track where it should be. The opening graphic displayed seventeen **key performance indicators** (KPIs) that measure different elements of the brewery's health (fig. 1.2). They were grouped into different aspects: profitability, activity (how quickly they convert assets into profit and cash), efficiency, asset usage, liquidity (the relationship of cash or near cash assets to other long-term assets), cash flow, and growth.

Each KPI was green and marked with O or red and marked with X to indicate whether it met the target. The target was based on the company's budget. Mike and Erica were able to clearly see if the goals of each month had been met relative to what they had planned. Opening with this information helped set the stage for the rest of the conversation. Mike and Erica could immediately identify if there were critical areas of the business that were starting to slip and needed to be shored up.

As Mike and Erica went through the KPI information, Charles explained each KPI by defining it, describing what it indicated, how it was measured, and what direction was considered a positive move. The meeting

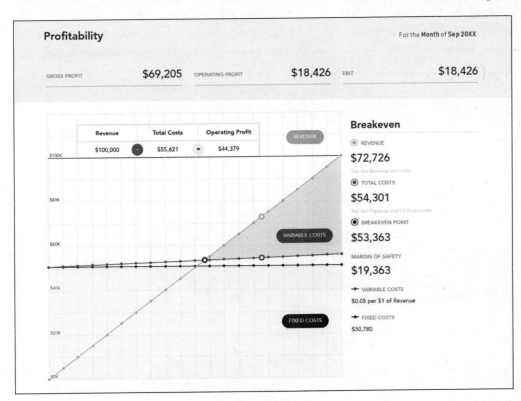

Figure 1.3. Graph summarizing the profitability KPI, showing revenue and costs. Image courtesy of Fathom Applications Pty Ltd, www.fathomhq.com.

was strengthening the couple's knowledge of finances, and they were learning information that would help them become sharper business owners.

Next, Mike and Erica looked at the business profitability. Charles presented graphs that clearly showed revenue and costs and broke out those costs between fixed and variable (fig. 1.3).

What was refreshing about this approach is that the actual financial reports were the last thing covered. By the time they got to the reports, Mike and Erica had seen all aspects of their financial health explained in a way that was intuitive to them. When the financial reports were presented, it was much easier to digest the information that was in those reports. Having a KPI dashboard made Mike and Erica confident that they could maintain an understanding of their finances.

After their meeting with Charles, the couple turned to their financial reports, beginning with the balance sheet. They noticed that cash was up 10% from last month and inventory was 8% lower. There had been no change to fixed assets. The accounts payable balance was up 20% from last month and credit cards were up 5%. The long-term loan was down, but just barely. This was because repayments were split between interest and principal, with most of the money going to interest. Each month they were only paying down a few hundred dollars in loan principal.

Erica analyzed the findings: lower inventory was good because it suggested that inventory was moving more quickly and the time to turn inventory into sales—and cash—was shorter than it had been in previous months. She noted that high inventory levels tie up cash on the balance sheet, so it's preferable to keep the levels low and keep moving the product as quickly as possible (fig. 1.4).

On the liabilities side, the increase in accounts payable and credit card debt made sense because they had just received a bill for chemicals that was in accounts payable, and they had purchased hops on the credit card. This prompted Mike to inquire about how the purchase of hops had been treated. Prior to opening, the purchase of hops had been recorded to COGS and then had to be moved to the balance sheet, so he wanted to make sure they were not making that mistake again.

Erica confirmed that the balances were correct. She showed him the inventory adjustment that Shannon had taught her to make as part of the month-end close. The inventory adjustment made on the last day of the month moved some of the cost out of COGS and back on to the balance sheet, bringing the inventory balance in agreement with the value of the inventory count (fig. 1.5).

Erica's process was to take inventory count at the end of the month and multiply the quantity of goods

Figure 1.4. Having a high inventory ties up cash and is tatamount to having cash on a shelf unused. Lower inventory levels usually indicate that inventory is moving and turning into sales and more cash.

ACCOUNT	DEBIT	CREDIT
Inventory:Work in Process	1,111.06	
Inventory:Finished Goods	4,195.30	
Inventory:Finished Goods:Serving Tanks	577.48	
Inventory:Raw Materials		720.61
Brewing Ingredients		5,163.23

Figure 1.5. Example of an inventory adjustment journal entry to reconcile inventory balance with value of the inventory account. Note that raw materials and brewing ingredients will eventually move to the debit column as they become beer.

on hand by the cost of each ingredient (table 1.18). That is how she arrived at the current inventory balance at the end of the month. Then, to adjust what was on the balance sheet, she put the other side of the entry into COGS.

See chapter 2 for a discussion of double-entry accounting, and chapter 3 for an explanation of the relationship between inventory and cost of goods sold.

Erica was really getting a handle on the financials. And the more she learned, the more fun it became to review the numbers. She proudly dove into the analysis of the income statement. Sales were up again,15% from last month, yet COGS were up 17% from last month. Erica noted that, because the increase in COGS was higher than the increase in sales, it was something to dig into. If COGS also grew by 15% that would make sense because sales were up 15%. Because it grew at a higher rate than sales, it suggested that the brewery was not controlling costs properly, or that the sales mix was moving toward more expensive beers to brew. She and Mike dove into the detail and saw that the grain and hops accounts looked reasonable, but Other Additions was unusually high. Mike was able to quickly identify the cause: he had experimented with a couple of different yeast strains last month. They were one-off purchases and expensive. That unusual cost was driving the increase in COGS. Because of this, Mike agreed to discuss with Erica when he was thinking of performing similar experiments in the future to ensure that they had the budget available to pay for the higher costs.

Erica went back to the income statement and continued her analysis. Most of the expenses were similar to last month, except for insurance, which was high because she had made a quarterly payment that covered December through February. She and

TABLE 1.18 INVENTORY COUNT AS OF 12/31/20XX

Malts	Price per unit	Quantity on hand 12/31/20XX	Value
2-Row	0.51	500	255.00
White Wheat	0.56	250	140.00
Chocolate	0.76	200	152.00
Munich	0.55	400	220.00
Biscuit	0.71	450	319.50
Cara Blond	0.73	400	292.00
Honey Malt	0.77	500	385.00
Cara Malt	0.83	300	249.00
Hops			
Centennial	9.90	88	871.20
Brewers Gold	9.00	66	594.00
Simcoe	13.40	176	2,358.40
Sterling	9.25	22	203.50
Azacca	13.25	176	2,332.00
Sabro	12.20	88	1,073.60
Sorachi Ace	13.85	66	914.10
El Dorado	10.85	132	1,432.20
Packaging			
keg collars	0.465	50	23.25
keg caps	0.10	40	4.00
			11,818.75

Mike decided that it would be a good idea to spread the insurance expense over the three months that it covered. Erica went back and allocated two-thirds of the insurance expense to Prepaid Expenses on the balance sheet, which would be recognized as an expense on the income statement in January and February.

The concept of Prepaid Expenses is related to accrual accounting. See chapter 2 for an introduction to this concept.

Mike was excited to see the business grow. He estimated that if they continued the trend of increasing sales by 15% each month that the brewery would hit $500,000 in revenue by year end! Erica grinned because she was one step ahead of Mike. She had compiled projections based on the assumption that they raise pint prices by 25 cents (tables 1.19 and 1.20).

TABLE 1.19 PROJECTION FOR REMAINDER OF YEAR WITH CURRENT PRICES
UNADJUSTED INCOME STATEMENT

	Actual	Actual	Actual	Actual	Actual	Actual
	Month 1	**Month 2**	**Month 3**	**Month 4**	**Month 5**	**Month 6**
Ordinary Income/Expense						
Income						
Draft Sales	39,650.76	36,130.00	41,527.75	33,882.94	38,423.75	40,745.00
Packaged Beer					1,318.00	2,897.00
Merchandise Sales	440.00	496.00	496.00	294.00	454.00	572.00
Total Income	40,090.76	36,626.00	42,023.75	34,176.94	40,195.75	44,214.00
Cost of Goods Sold						
Beer - Guest	825.41	447.89	277.94	601.66	602.68	708.39
Beer - House	7,930.15	7,226.00	8,305.55	6,776.59	7,684.75	8,149.00
Mobile Packaging					3,802.00	
Excise Tax	198.25	180.65	207.64	169.41	192.12	203.73
CO_2	766.02	857.64	844.65	792.35	881.59	582.67
Merchandise	151.33	169.00	167.33	102.00	154.00	190.67
Payroll COGS	168.62	1,882.51	1,990.20	3,902.15	3,985.00	4,203.35
Total COGS	10,039.79	10,763.69	11,793.31	12,344.16	17,302.14	14,037.80
Gross Profit	30,050.97	25,862.31	30,230.44	21,832.78	22,893.61	30,176.20
Expense						
Guaranteed Payment	0.00	0.00	0.00	2,500.00	2,500.00	3,000.00
Insurance Expense	1,122.09	1,122.09	1,122.09	1,122.09	1,122.09	1,122.09
Interest Expense	0.00	0.00	0.00	0.00	0.00	0.00
Marketing and Advertising	1,144.00	1,732.09	485.25	361.50	185.25	3,178.00
Office Supplies	370.57	265.50	163.61	548.86	211.93	164.20
Payroll	0.00	1,866.76	2,013.66	1,984.28	2,175.25	2,782.06
Professional Fees	3,205.00	1,000.00	3,347.00	800.00	705.00	0.00
Rent Expense	6,235.00	6,235.00	6,235.00	6,235.00	6,235.00	6,235.00
Repairs and Maintenance	58.37	108.00	657.00	920.60	446.84	108.00
Taxes						
Local	0.00	0.00	200.00	0.00	0.00	0.00
State	0.00	0.00	150.00	0.00	0.00	0.00
Property Taxes	0.00	0.00	0.00	0.00	0.00	0.00
Total Taxes	0.00	0.00	350.00	0.00	0.00	0.00
Utilities	7,391.98	6,827.34	5,777.89	5,971.70	6,258.64	7,210.46
Other Expenses	2,673.52	2,607.21	2,308.32	2,407.86	4,059.58	2,047.60
Total Expense	22,200.53	21,763.99	22,459.82	22,851.89	23,899.58	25,847.41
Net Ordinary Income	7,850.44	4,098.32	7,770.61	(1,019.12)	(1,005.97)	4,328.79
Net Income	**7,850.44**	**4,098.32**	**7,770.61**	**(1,019.12)**	**(1,005.97)**	**4,328.79**

TABLE 1.19 PROJECTION FOR REMAINDER OF YEAR WITH CURRENT PRICES (CONT.)

UNADJUSTED INCOME STATEMENT

Actual	Projected	Projected	Projected	Projected	Projected	Projected
Month 7	**Month 8**	**Month 9**	**Month 10**	**Month 11**	**Month 12**	**TOTAL**
42,590.25	40,000.00	36,000.00	44,000.00	34,000.00	30,000.00	456,950.45
4,366.00	4,500.00	4,500.00	5,000.00	4,800.00	5,200.00	32,581.00
515.00	420.00	420.00	420.00	420.00	420.00	5,367.00
47,471.25	44,920.00	40,920.00	49,420.00	39,220.00	35,620.00	494,898.45
379.46	350.00	350.00	350.00	350.00	350.00	5,593.43
8,518.05	8,000.00	7,200.00	8,800.00	6,800.00	6,000.00	91,390.09
	3,512.00			3,800.00		11,114.00
212.95	200.00	180.00	220.00	170.00	150.00	2,284.75
1,234.85	850.00	850.00	850.00	850.00	850.00	10,209.77
171.67	143.33	143.33	143.33	143.33	143.33	1,822.67
3,876.56	4,000.00	4,000.00	4,000.00	4,000.00	4,000.00	40,008.39
14,393.54	17,055.33	12,723.33	14,363.33	16,113.33	11,493.33	162,423.10
33,077.71	27,864.67	28,196.67	35,056.67	23,106.67	24,126.67	332,475.35
3,000.00	3,500.00	3,500.00	3,500.00	3,500.00	3,500.00	28,500.00
1,122.09	1,122.09	1,122.09	1,122.09	1,122.09	1,122.09	13,465.08
1,249.00	1,250.00	1,250.00	1,250.00	1,250.00	1,250.00	7,499.00
2,008.69	0.00	2,000.00	2,000.00	3,000.00	0.00	16,094.78
275.52	285.00	285.00	285.00	285.00	285.00	3,425.19
3,008.06	3,842.00	3,842.00	3,842.00	3,842.00	4,520.00	33,718.07
0.00	400.00	1,200.00	300.00	1,200.00	300.00	12,457.00
6,235.00	6,235.00	6,235.00	6,235.00	6,400.00	6,400.00	75,150.00
608.00	415.00	415.00	415.00	415.00	415.00	4,981.81
0.00	0.00	0.00	0.00	0.00	0.00	200.00
0.00	0.00	0.00	0.00	0.00	0.00	150.00
0.00	0.00	0.00	5,000.00	0.00	0.00	5,000.00
0.00	0.00	0.00	5,000.00	0.00	0.00	5,350.00
7,136.23	6,744.70	6,744.70	6,744.70	6,744.70	6,744.70	80,297.74
4,462.12	2,785.22	2,944.51	4,092.06	4,221.36	4,376.81	38,986.18
29,104.71	26,579.01	29,538.30	34,785.85	31,980.15	28,913.60	319,924.85
3,973.00	1,285.66	(1,341.63)	270.82	(8,873.48)	(4,786.93)	12,550.50
3,973.00	**1,285.66**	**(1,341.63)**	**270.82**	**(8,873.48)**	**(4,786.93)**	**12,550.50**

TABLE 1.20 PROJECTION FOR REMAINDER OF YEAR WITH PRICE INCREASE TO PINTS
INCOME STATEMENT ADJUSTED FOR PRICE RAISE

	Projected Month 8	Projected Month 9	Projected Month 10	Projected Month 11	Projected Month 12	Projected TOTAL
Ordinary Income/Expense						
Income						
Draft Sales	41,800.00	37,620.00	42,845.00	35,530.00	31,350.00	462,095.45
Packaged Beer	4,500.00	4,500.00	5,000.00	4,800.00	5,200.00	32,581.00
Merchandise Sales	420.00	420.00	420.00	420.00	420.00	5,367.00
Total Income	46,720.00	42,540.00	48,265.00	40,750.00	36,970.00	500,043.45
Cost of Goods Sold						
Beer - Guest	350.00	350.00	350.00	350.00	350.00	5,593.43
Beer - House	8,000.00	7,200.00	8,800.00	6,800.00	6,000.00	91,390.09
Mobile Packaging	3,512.00			3,800.00		11,114.00
Excise Tax	200.00	180.00	220.00	170.00	150.00	2,284.75
CO_2	850.00	850.00	850.00	850.00	850.00	10,209.77
Merchandise	143.33	143.33	143.33	143.33	143.33	1,822.67
Payroll COGS	4,000.00	4,000.00	4,000.00	4,000.00	4,000.00	40,008.39
Total COGS	17,055.33	12,723.33	14,363.33	16,113.33	11,493.33	162,423.10
Gross Profit	29,664.67	29,816.67	33,901.67	24,636.67	25,476.67	337,620.35
Expense						
Guaranteed Payment	3,500.00	3,500.00	3,500.00	3,500.00	3,500.00	28,500.00
Insurance Expense	1,122.09	1,122.09	1,122.09	1,122.09	1,122.09	13,465.08
Interest Expense	1,250.00	1,250.00	1,250.00	1,250.00	1,250.00	7,499.00
Marketing and Advertising	0.00	2,000.00	2,000.00	3,000.00	0.00	16,094.78
Office Supplies	285.00	285.00	285.00	285.00	285.00	3,425.19
Payroll	3,842.00	3,842.00	3,842.00	3,842.00	4,520.00	33,718.07
Professional Fees	400.00	1,200.00	300.00	1,200.00	300.00	12,457.00
Rent Expense	6,235.00	6,235.00	6,235.00	6,400.00	6,400.00	75,150.00
Repairs and Maintenance	415.00	415.00	415.00	415.00	415.00	4,981.81
Taxes						
Local	0.00	0.00	0.00	0.00	0.00	200.00
State	0.00	0.00	0.00	0.00	0.00	150.00
Property Taxes	0.00	0.00	5,000.00	0.00	0.00	5,000.00
Total Taxes	0.00	0.00	5,000.00	0.00	0.00	5,350.00
Utilities	6,744.70	6,744.70	6,744.70	6,744.70	6,744.70	80,297.74
Other Expenses	2,830.22	2,985.01	4,063.19	4,259.61	4,410.56	39,114.81
Total Expense	26,624.01	29,578.80	34,756.98	32,018.40	28,947.35	320,053.48
Net Ordinary Income	3,040.66	237.87	(855.31)	(7,381.73)	(3,470.68)	17,566.87
Net Income	**3,040.66**	**237.87**	**(855.31)**	**(7,381.73)**	**(3,470.68)**	**17,566.87**

According to their POS data, the brewery sold about 2,000 pints per week. By adding 25 cents, that put them even with the price per pint of the closest bar and added $2,000 to the bottom line each month. See the difference in gross profit for projected months in table 1.19 (current prices) and table 1.20 (increased prices). They thought of how they could make that extra revenue work for them, such as paying down debt a little quicker. The revenue increase was over $24,000 per year that Mike and Erica didn't currently have, and which they could use to really make some headway on liabilities. Mike felt they had set their prices lower than they should have been at the opening just to give an incentive to come into the taproom. Happy Hour Brewing Co. had a steady crowd—Mike felt that the taproom had developed a loyal group of patrons and if customers were to go anywhere else for a beer they would be paying more. Betting that the business would not see a drop off in sales, Mike and Erica decided to increase prices the next week.

The increase in price was great, but Mike had greater plans. Erica could see that something was on his mind and asked for his thoughts. Mike suggested that they consider a larger system to increase production and any excess capacity could be used to start producing beer to distribute. Erica's initial reaction was to question whether they were ready for that. Mike laid out the options: self-distribution or third-party distribution. Their state allowed self-distribution up to 7,000 barrels. Erica immediately started rattling off the logistic considerations. Kegs: would they buy or lease? If buying, they would need to buy at least 100 more kegs to begin. Leasing required less capital to begin but was more expensive per unit. Leasing did, however, offer a fast fix if they didn't currently have the cash to buy cooperage. Sales: they would need a salesperson. Ideally that would be Mike, because they knew he would be the best ambassador for the product. Was it responsible to put that onto his plate too? Pickup of empty kegs, keeping track of all of their customers. The list of logistical considerations was growing. Distribution was going to add complexity to the production plan, but it had the potential to bring in a lot more revenue.

Erica's mind went back to the economics of the business. If they signed with a third-party distributor,

the distributor usually would take 30% of the **price to retailer** for themselves. This was an industry-standard charge to handle the placement of a brand in the market. Of course, if Mike and Erica self-distributed then they would keep that 30%. Most breweries in their area charged $150 per half-barrel keg to retailers. The difference in profit for selling the beer in the Happy Hour Brewing Co. taproom versus in a wholesale environment was dramatically different. Each half-barrel keg holds 124 pints (15.5 gal.) and would normally lose about four pints to foaming and overpouring. Happy Hour Brewing Co. was charging—now, after the recent price raise—$6 per pint. So that same half-barrel keg in the taproom would realize $720. Same beer, same cost, but $570 more gross revenue if sold in the taproom.

EXPERT ADVICE

Mike and Erica are surprised at the cost of selling beer through a distributor, and there are even more expenses that they have not yet considered. Working with a distributor may require significant marketing expenses. Examples include cost of promotional beer, promotional giveaways (t-shirts, coasters, etc.), distributor incentives, and POS materials.

The numbers were sobering, and Erica questioned why they were even considering distributing. Mike felt that they had the capacity to brew more than could be sold in their taproom. He wanted to find an outlet to sell all the beer they could produce to maximize their investment. This meant starting distribution or opening a new taproom. Mike also noted that, if they self-distributed, then they could keep the margin dollars they would otherwise give away to a distributor. Distribution opened the door to scaling, too.

Mike and Erica considered options. Was there any guarantee of how much they could sell? Will they know how much needs to be produced? If their beer becomes a hit on the wholesale front, then will they need to buy more tanks and more kegs? And they hadn't even broached the subject of distributing their packaged beer.

Erica and Mike decided to create a projection of revenue and cost before deciding on distribution. They started with sales assumptions for the first three months.

Mike felt comfortable that they could get fifteen distribution accounts in the first month, another ten in the second, and ten again in the third month. Because the number of breweries had increased so much in their area, there would be competition for sales. Mike knew from talking to others in the industry that new distribution accounts were more likely to want sixtel kegs than half-barrel kegs, because that gave them the opportunity to rotate through more beers. For their projections, Erica and Mike assumed one-third of sales would be half barrels and the rest would be sixtels. They set a sales price of $150 for a half barrel and $85 for a sixtel.

Mike felt sure that they had enough capacity to make and sell beer wholesale in addition to retail sales in the taproom. The biggest constraint was going to be time. Just how much time would it take to create those sales? Mike and Erica assumed one win for every five accounts visited. Based on their original assumptions, that meant that Mike needed to visit five accounts every two days for the first month. If each account takes a half hour to an hour to visit, then he was looking at half of his day, every other day, taken up with sales. It was doubtful that they could afford for Mike to spend that much time on sales. They considered having Tom, their part-time bartender, help out with sales. Tom was a younger guy and was eager to contribute more to the business. Mike knew that Tom's very limited experience in the industry meant Mike would have to train Tom from the ground up. While Mike and Erica were hesitant to have someone other than Mike represent their beer to outside accounts for the first time, they decided to try to find 10 hours of sales work that could be moved off of Mike and onto Tom. Tom's extra hours would be an additional expense, but it was necessary if Happy Hour Brewing Co. wanted to move into self-distribution.

Mike and Erica continued to list other expenses needed if they did distribution themselves. Mike could use their truck for deliveries, which would save them from buying a vehicle for the business, but increased maintenance and gas would be a new expense. Accounting time would go up because they would be creating invoices and tracking payments for the distribution accounts. At some point they would need to add marketing to support sales, but decided to leave that on the back burner as an expense to be added later. Tap handles were a must if they wanted to convince local taprooms to carry their beer.

Tom's extra payroll would be $200 per week, including payroll tax. Erica and Mike budgeted $150 per week for vehicle expenses. An order of 100 kegs would be about $10,000 even if they could find some used kegs. They would need a keg washer, which would cost around $7,000. And they calculated, based on a minimum order of four dozen, a tap handles cost of $30 each plus maybe $500 setup fee. The grand total was a $12,000 one-time cost for the initial order of kegs, the keg washer, and tap handles, and a recurring $1,400 per month for vehicle costs and extra payroll. Erica drew up the first revenue projection. The cost for the first three months would be roughly $23,200, while the projected revenue for the same period would only be $15,935 (table 1.21).

Although the first quarter was projected to be a loss, it was due to one-time costs. The numbers looked like they could clear over $7,000 revenue in future quarters. It was looking like an easy decision. However, as Erica looked over the calculations again she realized they had not factored in COGS on the beer. The brewers had enough time to make the additional beer they were planning on selling, so there would be no additional payroll for production labor. To factor

TABLE 1.21 PROJECTED REVENUE FOR INITIAL THREE MONTHS SELF-DISTRIBUTION

	Number of Accts	Number of kegs sold to account	Number of half-barrels	Number of sixtels	Half-barrel revenue	Sixtel revenue	Total revenue
Month 1	15	2	10	20	$1,500	$1,700	$3,200
Month 2	25	2	16	34	$2,400	$2,890	$5,290
Month 3	35	2	23	47	$3,450	$3,995	$7,445
Total Units			49	101	$7,350	$8,585	$15,935
Total Barrels			24.5	16.8			

TABLE 1.22 CASH FLOW ANALYSIS FOR INITIAL THREE MONTHS SELF-DISTRIBUTION

	Month 1	Month 2	Month 3	Total
Incremental Revenue	$3,200	$5,290	$7,445	$15,935
Incremental Direct Costs	($724)	($1,188)	($1,681)	($3,593)
Other Incremental Expenditures	($20,400)	($1,400)	($1,400)	($23,200)
Net Cash Flow	($17,924)	$2,702	$4,363	($10,858)

COGS, Erica used the average cost per barrel from the production spreadsheet. Of course, the total will vary depending on the style, but on average they spent $78.50 per barrel in ingredients. They added another $8.50 per barrel for water, utilities, and excise tax. That totaled $3,593.10 in additional COGS, as shown in "Incremental Direct Costs" in table 1.22.

Erica and Mike reviewed the numbers again and had to admit that without the tap handles and kegs, the margin was attractive. Even if they continued to only sell a low volume each quarter, and they kept the first quarter customers buying at the same level, the price increase would result in more than $24,000 of additional margin over the course of a year. The extra profit would allow them to get out of debt faster. They brainstormed the best way to pay for the extra start-up costs if they decided to go down this path. The easiest option was to deplete the $10,000 in their savings account and put the other $2,000 on a credit card. Erica wasn't comfortable with such drastic measures; cash flow had stabilized and Erica had finally gotten to the point where she could sleep at night. If they went back to walking a tightrope of finances, the stress would come back.

It was too late to pull Mike back in. He had seen the future (and the margin). One glance at the numbers and he was determined to make it happen. After a couple minutes of consideration, Mike suggested that they sleep on it. Erica felt sure that he was going to find a way to make distribution happen.

See chapter 7 for more information on the financial differences between self-distribution and third-party distribution.

Several days came and went with no mention of wholesale sales. Saturdays were Erica and Mike's day to think and talk business, and that afternoon they sat down and looked at the reports for the week. The taproom was up 10% from last week, and it was the fifth straight week of increasing sales. The cash balance had increased $2,000 and the accounts payable was down from last week. All great indicators of a solvent, growing business. They were feeling pretty confident about the business. Mike confessed that he had not been able to shake the idea of taking the brewery to the next level. Because of their consistent growth and fiscal responsibility, their financial foundation was getting stronger each week. Aside from the financial success, their staff was becoming more self-sufficient and both he and Erica were starting to have more time for working on additional business projects.

Erica was almost certain that Mike was going to lobby to begin self-distribution, so she was surprised when that turned out not to be the message at all. Although there was a lot of upside in self-distribution sales, Mike had seen that the margin on retail sales in the taproom was even stronger—he was curious what it would look like if they opened a second taproom.

Mike presented to Erica some projections for a second taproom. Erica was floored. First, Mike actually broke out a spreadsheet—that had to be a first in the whole time that she had known him. It also meant that Mike was pretty excited about this idea to go to that far with analyzing the data. Second, she was amazed at the audacity of the idea. How in the world did Mike think they would be able to manage a second taproom? They barely had their arms around the first one. But she was intrigued enough to look at the projections with him.

Mike had put together a rough estimate of financial performance for the first year, which showed a substantial increase in income for the second year. Mike explained that the brewery currently used about 50% of its production capacity. They could handle production for a second taproom with the current equipment. That helped minimize capital expenditures for the second location. Based on his research, Mike estimated the build-out would cost about $160,000. Other expenses would put the initial investment at about $200,000. The projections showed Happy Hour Brewing Co. would be able to recoup all of the start-up costs within a year and a half, and after that plenty of money would flow to the bottom line. Mike shared his analysis with Erica (table 1.23).

TABLE 1.23 SECOND TAPROOM PAYBACK ANALYSIS

Capital expenses	
Leasehold Improvements	$160,000
Computers	$3,000
Architect Fees	$5,000
Furniture and fixtures	$30,000
Total capital expenses	$198,000
Kegs	$5,000
Rent - prior to opening	$6,000
Payroll - prior to opening	$4,000
Utilities - prior to opening	$6,000
Smallwares	$4,000
Legal fees	$3,000
Total start-up costs	$226,000
Monthly net income from second location	
Estimated revenue	$47,000
Cost of beer	($8,000)
Mobile canning	($3,000)
Additional excise tax	($100)
Taproom labor, payroll tax, benefits	($4,500)
Rent	($6,500)
Utilities	($4,000)
Other expenses	($8,000)
Estimated net income	$12,900
Number of months to pay back investment in second location: 18	

Erica was impressed with the work Mike had put in to the projections. Of course, she had several questions. First, how to get the cash to start the project. Second, were they popular enough to demand a second taproom. And finally, were they ready to

take this on, on a personal and brewery level? Erica felt like they were just starting to steer the business into calmer waters—she wasn't sure if they should change tack now.

Putting in more money of their own was not an option for Erica and Mike. To raise the additional capital, they could either go back to the bank and ask for more or bring in investors. Erica was excited about the possibility of expanding, but it was hard to believe that other people might be interested in buying into their dream. They continued to talk about the possibilities well into the night and agreed to keep the conversation going. The data certainly supported a financial benefit of a second taproom. It was a pivot from their original discussion of self-distribution, but another business lesson they were learning is that they often ended up on paths they didn't expect at first.

It had been a few weeks and Mike couldn't shake his interest in a second location. He knew he had to fully vet the idea for Erica to be on board. His pitch must be clear and compelling. Mike decided to write a budget to prove to her (and to himself) that he'd really thought this through and that it made sense for the business. The goal of producing a budget felt unattainable to him, but it was an important step.

See chapter 8 for more information on budgeting.

Mike began by pulling the financial reports for the first six months of the existing taproom and putting them into a spreadsheet. Line by line, Mike examined the income statement to see how each account might change month over month. There were certainly things that would be different for the second taproom. The learning curve would be shorter (at least he hoped it would) and profitability should come more quickly.

Mike considered the relevant factors in the first line item: Sales. Over the first six months the sales should be greater because they would charge the same price for beers as they did in the first location. That would increase the revenue for the first six months versus the original taproom because they had discounted pint prices when Happy Hour Brewing Co. first opened so that they could attract customers. Now that the brewery was an established brand, Mike didn't see the need to start with a discounted sales price. The quantity of beer sold should also increase because Mike planned to tweak their sales mix. He felt that he'd developed a better understanding of what to offer in the taproom, having found a balance between offering new, interesting beers and session-able standards that would encourage people to stay longer. Additionally, the new taproom would heavily promote beer to go. Mike had heard from several of his peers that sales of six-packs and bottles out of the taproom was quite lucrative. The owner of one of the more successful breweries in town told Mike that he felt like the to-go sales had also increased brand awareness, and had been an important driver of wholesale sales, should Mike ever reconsider starting distribution. Finally, sales would increase due to the location of the new taproom. Fortunately for Happy Hour Brewing Co., the state's liquor laws allowed a taproom to operate without producing the beer on site. Without the need for a large brewery space, Mike knew they could afford a more optimal location with less square footage.

Of course, Mike was a long way from knowing where the actual location would be, but he had enough information to know that it would be in a densely populated neighborhood with a large amount of foot traffic and few other competing taprooms. What's more, the neighborhood would have plenty of food options close by that could be brought into the taproom.

If there was one thing Mike had learned in his years in the brewing business, is was that it is difficult to keep people consuming beer without a food offering. Yet food was a giant pain to produce. As Mike saw it, there were a few options: the simple approach was to invite patrons to bring in food from nearby food trucks or restaurants; the complex approach was to go full bore and open a restaurant. Mike wanted to stick to the business model he knew had worked for Happy Hour Brewing Co. He kept it simple, deciding not to prepare any food in-house, but ensuring patrons had easy access to it by choosing a location near to several food outlets. Even

better, if he could find a location with nearby food outlets that were not serving beer, he could create a symbiotic relationship.

In sum, budgeting sales would come down to a few factors:

- operating hours
- retail square footage
- sales price per unit
- quantity sold per customer visit (also referred to as "per person average" or "PPA" in the restaurant world)

Now with more experience, this was Mike's chance to do it over and heed the lessons from his first time around. The operating hours would be tighter, focusing on their prime selling hours: 4 p.m. to 10 p.m. Tuesday through Thursday; 4 p.m. to midnight Friday; noon to midnight Saturday; and noon to 10 p.m. Sunday.

The original taproom was 1,000 sq. ft. and there were a few nights when customers would have to stand and wait for a table to clear out. If doing a second taproom, and all other factors being equal, Mike could do a few hundred more square feet. On the other hand, sometimes having a lot of people in a smaller space made the taproom feel popular. Mike knew that ultimately it would come down to the real estate available when he was ready to pull the trigger. For the purposes of this budget, he would leave it the same at 1,000 sq. ft.

One boon for Mike in this budget exercise was the availability of real-world data from the existing taproom. Erica had used the POS system reports to pull information from the original taproom about numbers of patrons per hour, the average number of beers purchased per ticket, and the average dollar of revenue per ticket. Other important input came from the experience Erica had behind the bar. She had picked up on a pattern: when customers started their purchase with a big beer (i.e., a beer over 7% ABV) they were more likely to have a lower total ticket amount, but a higher likelihood of purchasing beer to go. Erica reasoned that if customers started big they may be less inclined to keep drinking due to the large amount of alcohol in the first beer, yet the same customer was more likely to pick up a six-pack to take home. Customers who started

TABLE 1.24 SALES BUDGET FOR SECOND TAPROOM

	Actual	Actual	Actual	Actual
	Month 1	**Month 2**	**Month 3**	**Month 4**
Year One revenue from Taproom 1	$40,090.76	$36,626.00	$42,023.75	$34,176.94
Less: revenue earned outside of Taproom 2's operating hours	$4,000.00	$4,500.00	$4,540.00	$4,440.00
Additional revenue if we had charged $6 per pint from the beginning	$3,153.71	$2,838.73	$1,357.55	$1,016.39
Draft revenue subtotal	$39,244.47	$34,964.73	$38,841.30	$30,753.33
Average ticket	$14.50	$15.20	$16.25	$18.45
Number of customer turns	2,707	2,300	2,390	1,667
Difference in average ticket from sampler tray group vs big beer drinkers	$7.00	$7.00	$7.00	$7.00
Increase in number of sampler tray drinkers	30%	30%	30%	30%
Incremental revenue from shifting customers to sampler trays*	$5,683.68	$4,830.65	$5,019.49	$3,500.38
Draft revenue subtotal	$44,928.15	$39,795.38	$43,860.80	$34,253.71
Adjustment in sales for established brand	$898.56	$795.91	$877.22	($229.50)
Draft revenue total	$45,826.71	$40,591.29	$44,738.01	$34,024.21
Packaged beer revenue	$4,400.80	$3,898.03	$4,296.25	$3,267.39
Total revenue	$50,227.51	$44,489.32	$49,034.26	$37,291.60

* Number of customer turns × Difference in average ticket from sampler tray group vs big beer drinkers × Increase in number of sampler tray drinkers

with the lighter beers (<4.5% ABV) ordered more beers than other patrons, but the ticket amount was the lowest. Of the light beer drinkers, 40% stayed for three or more beers, and 15% stayed for four or more beers; however, they were less likely to purchase any to-go beer. Surprisingly, the highest revenue-producing customers was those customers who started with a sampler tray. These customers seemed to follow one of two courses of action: start with a sampler, order a full pint, and then purchase beer to go; or start with a sampler and stay for two to three full pints. Either route produced the highest ticket amount of all customer profiles.

Erica confirmed with the other bartenders that they had noticed similar purchasing behavior. By analyzing data from the POS system and combining that with anecdotal evidence from bartenders, Erica developed a strategy to increase sales. She and Mike trained the bartenders to lead with a suggestion of a sampler tray, and to price it just low enough to encourage a large proportion of customers to choose it. Since implementing this strategy a few months ago, Erica and Mike had seen an increase in the average ticket.

Given all of this data, Mike had a lot to work with for his sales projections (table 1.24). He took the revenue from the prior 12 months and isolated only the hours that the new taproom will be open. He assumed that full sales price will be charged for those items, and added an increase for the 30% of clients that can be encouraged to buy a sampler tray. His final formula was as follows:

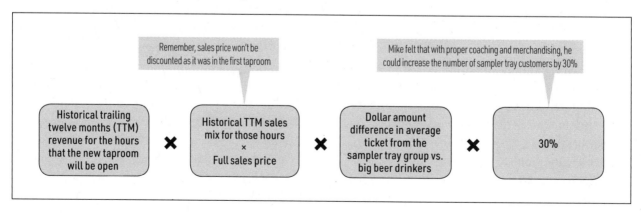

TABLE 1.24 SALES BUDGET FOR SECOND TAPROOM (CONT.)

Actual	Actual	Actual	Projected	Projected	Projected	Projected	Projected	Projected
Month 5	**Month 6**	**Month 7**	**Month 8**	**Month 9**	**Month 10**	**Month 11**	**Month 12**	**TOTAL**
$40,195.75	$44,214.00	$47,471.25	$46,720.00	$42,540.00	$48,265.00	$40,750.00	$36,970.00	$500,043.45
$4,640.00	$4,260.00	$6,000.00	$4,500.00	$4,500.00	$4,500.00	$4,500.00	$4,500.00	$54,880.00
$1,278.08	$1,452.78	$1,594.40	$1,561.74	$1,380.00	$1,628.91	$1,302.17	$1,137.83	$19,702.29
$36,833.83	$41,406.78	$43,065.65	$43,781.74	$39,420.00	$45,393.91	$37,552.17	$33,607.83	$464,865.74
$22.00	$19.35	$17.88						
1,674	2,140	2,409	2,479	2,232	2,570	2,126	1,903	26,597
$7.00	$7.00	$7.00	$7.00	$7.00	$7.00	$7.00	$7.00	
30%	30%	30%	30%	30%	30%	30%	30%	
$3,515.96	$4,493.76	$5,058.05	$5,205.79	$4,687.16	$5,397.48	$4,465.07	$3,996.08	$55,853.55
$40,349.78	$45,900.54	$48,123.70	$48,987.53	$44,107.16	$50,791.39	$42,017.25	$37,603.90	$520,719.29
($270.34)	($307.53)	($322.43)	($328.22)	($295.52)	($340.30)	($281.52)	($251.95)	($55.62)
$40,079.44	$45,593.01	$47,801.27	$48,659.31	$43,811.65	$50,451.09	$41,735.73	$37,351.96	$520,663.67
$3,848.88	$4,378.36	$4,590.42	$4,672.82	$4,207.29	$4,844.88	$4,007.94	$3,586.96	$50,000.00
$43,928.32	$49,971.36	$52,391.69	$53,332.13	$48,018.93	$55,295.97	$45,743.67	$40,938.91	$570,663.67

Doing this math, Mike was able to calculate an annual total of revenue for the second taproom. The final adjustment he made was to increase the first three months by 2% each and lower the remaining 9 months by two-thirds of a percent. Mike felt that this would compensate for the fact that the original taproom had slow sales at the beginning because no one knew the brand. But now, being an established brand and having a taproom in an area where the neighborhood was clamoring for a new brewery, he didn't think the second taproom would have the same lag in initial sales.

Mike also considered sales of packaged beer. Several colleagues had reported that taproom sales of packaged beer accounted for a few thousand dollars of revenue each month. Mike added this to his revenue projection for a second taproom and set a goal of $50,000 for additional packaged beer sales in the first year from the second taproom. In his sales model he apportioned the revenue across all months (table 1.24).

The next step was to expand that master sales chart into a production plan. Using his spreadsheet software, Mike made a chart of the beer sales in barrel equivalents by brand for each location in separate tabs. The brands were in the rows and the months were in the columns. Then Mike made a third tab and combined the totals of beer sold for both locations into one chart.

With a lot of tweaking, Mike was able to stack production to maximize efficiencies at his production facility. Moreover, he realized that by almost doubling his production he may be able to negotiate a lower purchase price for goods from his vendors, and therefore increase his margins. As part of his production planning, Mike analyzed his recipes to assess if any ingredients could be substituted for something that was used more universally in his brews, which would again improve his buying power and lower his COGS. The final piece of analysis was to review historical sales by brand and weed out any underperforming beers, or beers that were grossly over budget. The whole production planning process took Mike the better part of a weekend, but he felt much more prepared for the coming year *and* he had total COGS that were 3% less than last year. Unless they ran into unexpected expenses, that saving should all fall to the bottom line.

With raw materials budgeted for, the next big COGS item was labor. There were two big categories of labor to consider: production labor and bar staff. Originally, Mike thought that a second taproom wouldn't require any additional labor because the existing brewery staff had enough available time, but as he put together the

TABLE 1.25 SECOND TAPROOM BUDGET FOR FIRST YEAR
MONTHLY SALES AND COGS

	Projected Y2 Month 1	Projected Y2 Month 2	Projected Y2 Month 3	Projected Y2 Month 4	Projected Y2 Month 5	Projected Y2 Month 6
Ordinary Income/Expense						
Income - Taproom 1						
Draft Sales	47,650.30	43,419.23	49,905.97	40,718.82	46,175.74	48,113.73
Packaged Beer	7,926.23	7,222.43	8,301.45	6,773.24	7,680.95	8,003.32
Merchandise Sales	678.00	771.00	786.00	465.00	717.00	918.00
Income - Taproom 2						
Draft Sales	39,650.76	36,130.00	45,680.53	37,271.23	42,266.13	44,819.50
Packaged Beer	7,347.44	6,695.03	8,464.78	6,906.51	7,832.08	8,305.23
Merchandise Sales	698.00	781.00	796.00	465.00	737.00	938.00
Total Income	103,950.74	95,018.69	113,934.73	92,599.80	105,408.90	111,097.79
Cost of Goods Sold						
Beer - Guest	1,650.82	895.78	555.88	1,203.32	1,205.36	1,416.78
Beer - House	17,460.21	15,909.85	19,117.30	15,598.01	17,688.37	18,586.65
Mobile Packaging	9,638.45	11,424.48	9,321.35	10,570.55	11,079.15	11,574.72
Excise Tax	436.51	397.75	477.93	389.95	442.21	464.67
CO_2	1,532.04	1,715.28	1,689.30	1,584.70	1,763.18	1,165.34
Merchandise	236.00	267.00	272.00	165.00	249.00	316.00
Payroll COGS	7,133.81	7,133.81	7,133.81	7,133.81	7,133.81	7,847.19
Total COGS	38,087.83	37,743.94	38,567.57	36,645.34	39,561.08	41,371.33
Gross Profit	65,862.91	57,274.75	75,367.16	55,954.46	65,847.82	69,726.45

production plan he realized that was wishful thinking. Mike did the calculations and figured he would need one and a half additional full-time equivalent employees. The additional hours would be split between brewer tasks (which was paid at $18 per hour) and cellar tasks (which was paid at $14 per hour), so Mike used a blended rate of $16 per hour for budgeting purposes. The final portion of COGS that needed to be sorted out was excise tax. Mike could easily calculate this based on the additional barrelage of the second taproom—another major hurdle passed. Mike had his monthly sales and COGS budget (*see* table 1.25).

The next thing to be considered were the operating expenses for the second taproom. Mike began by taking existing expense information for the first taproom and carefully considered each account type. Would that be needed for the second taproom? If an account type was needed, would be it be more or less than the amount for the first taproom? What were the factors driving the amounts? He created the following chart:

Account	Relevant expense for taproom v2?	Amount % increase/ decrease from taproom v1	How is the expense allocated across the months?
Expense 1			
Expense 2			
Expense 3			

Using this analysis, Mike calculated the annual amounts of the expenses and then allocated them to each month appropriately. Some expenses would be equal each month, like rent. Others would be about the same amount for the second taproom, but unknown as to when in the year the expense would land, like repairs and maintenance. In order to budget for such expenses, Mike decided to copy the budget from the first taproom and put the same amount of expense in the same months for the second taproom as it had occurred for the first. Finally, some expenses would not repeat, for example, registration with the secretary of state's office,

TABLE 1.25 SECOND TAPROOM BUDGET FOR FIRST YEAR (CONT.)
MONTHLY SALES AND COGS

Projected Y2 Month 7	Projected Y2 Month 8	Projected Y2 Month 9	Projected Y2 Month 10	Projected Y2 Month 11	Projected Y2 Month 12	TOTAL
49,847.63	44,800.00	39,600.00	48,400.00	37,400.00	33,000.00	529,031.43
8,291.74	7,452.11	6,587.13	8,050.94	6,221.18	5,489.28	88,000.00
832.50	580.00	580.00	620.00	660.00	660.00	8,267.50
47,590.25	41,800.00	37,620.00	45,980.00	35,530.00	31,350.00	485,688.39
8,818.66	7,745.71	6,971.14	8,520.28	6,583.85	5,809.28	90,000.00
842.50	590.00	580.00	640.00	660.00	680.00	8,407.50
116,223.28	102,967.82	91,938.27	112,211.22	87,055.03	76,988.56	1,209,394.82
758.92	700.00	700.00	700.00	700.00	700.00	11,186.86
19,487.58	17,320.00	15,444.00	18,876.00	14,586.00	12,870.00	202,943.96
10,321.71	9,179.64	11,219.56	8,669.66	7,649.70	7,649.70	118,298.67
487.19	433.00	386.10	471.90	364.65	321.75	5,073.60
2,469.70	1,700.00	1,700.00	1,700.00	1,700.00	1,700.00	20,419.54
287.50	203.33	203.33	216.67	230.00	230.00	2,875.83
7,847.19	8,203.88	8,203.88	8,203.88	8,203.88	8,203.88	92,382.79
41,659.78	37,739.85	37,856.87	38,838.10	33,434.23	31,675.33	453,181.25
74,563.50	65,227.97	54,081.40	73,373.11	53,620.81	45,313.23	756,213.57

but those were few and the amounts minimal. Those lines would stay at zero for the second taproom budget.

Through the process of creating a budget for the second taproom Mike had also created a budget for the first taproom. These were the tweaks he made:

- Changed the sales price for beer to the current amount for the whole year (they had raised their prices twice in the current year)
- Increased sales in the first five months of the budget versus the same period last year. When they first opened, the number of patrons built up slowly because people were still finding the taproom.
- Increased sales to account for the new focus on sampler trays that the bar staff was now promoting in the tasting room
- Adjusted COGS for changes to the beers that would be brewed. In the beginning, Mike had gone a little overboard experimenting with beer styles that were too expensive, not popular with patrons, or some combination thereof. COGS for

the first few months of operations had been too high, so by tweaking the beer offerings the business's COGS would be lower.

- Adjusted COGS for abnormal waste that occurred in the first two months of the first year. As the production team was getting used to the brewhouse, they had to dump a few batches. That was another learning curve cost that would not be repeated in year two.

By this point, Mike had been working on this budget for the better part of two weeks. He felt so much more prepared for the possibility of operating a second taproom after going through this budgeting process. It had forced him to really think through the entire next year of operations in advance—a rehearsal, of sorts. So far, the numbers were looking reasonable (table 1.26). Mike was hopeful that they might even be able to afford the replica of his grandad's bar, which they had forgone on the last taproom build-out.

TABLE 1.26 SECOND TAPROOM BUDGET FOR FIRST YEAR
MONTHLY SALES, COGS, AND EXPENSES

	Month 1	Month 2	Month 3	Month 4	Month 5	Month 6	Month 7	Projected Month 8	Projected Month 9	Projected Month 10	Projected Month 11	Projected Month 12	Projected TOTAL
Ordinary Income/Expense													
Income - Taproom 1													
Draft Sales	39,650.76	36,130.00	41,527.75	33,882.94	38,423.75	40,745.00	42,590.25	41,800.00	37,620.00	42,845.00	35,530.00	31,350.00	462,095.45
Packaged Beer					1,318.00	2,897.00	4,366.00	4,500.00	4,500.00	5,000.00	4,800.00	5,200.00	32,581.00
Merchandise Sales													
Hats	28.00	22.00	12.00	24.00	16.00	0.00	0.00	20.00	20.00	20.00	20.00	20.00	202.00
Shirt Sales	412.00	474.00	484.00	270.00	438.00	572.00	515.00	400.00	400.00	400.00	400.00	400.00	5,165.00
Merchandise Sales	440.00	496.00	496.00	294.00	454.00	572.00	515.00	420.00	420.00	420.00	420.00	420.00	5,367.00
Income - Taproom 2													
Draft Sales													
Packaged Beer													
Merchandise Sales													
Hats													
Shirt Sales													
Merchandise Sales													
Total Income	40,090.76	36,626.00	42,023.75	34,176.94	40,195.75	44,214.00	47,471.25	46,720.00	42,540.00	48,265.00	40,750.00	36,970.00	500,043.45
Cost of Goods Sold													
Beer - Guest	825.41	447.89	277.94	601.66	602.68	708.39	379.46	350.00	350.00	350.00	350.00	350.00	5,593.43
Beer - House	7,930.15	7,226.00	8,305.55	6,776.59	7,684.75	8,149.00	8,518.05	8,000.00	7,200.00	8,800.00	6,800.00	6,000.00	91,390.09
Mobile Packaging					3,802.00			3,512.00			3,800.00		11,114.00
Excise Tax	198.25	180.65	207.64	169.41	192.12	203.73	212.95	200.00	180.00	220.00	170.00	150.00	2,284.75
CO$_2$	766.02	857.64	844.65	792.35	881.59	582.67	1,234.85	850.00	850.00	850.00	850.00	850.00	10,209.77
Merchandise													
Hats	14.00	11.00	6.00	12.00	8.00	0.00	0.00	10.00	10.00	10.00	10.00	10.00	101.00
Shirts	137.33	158.00	161.33	90.00	146.00	190.67	171.67	133.33	133.33	133.33	133.33	133.33	1,721.67
Merchandise Sales	151.33	169.00	167.33	102.00	154.00	190.67	171.67	143.33	143.33	143.33	143.33	143.33	1,822.67
Payroll COGS													
Payroll COGS - Other	168.62	1,882.51	1,990.20	3,902.15	3,985.00	4,203.35	3,876.56	4,000.00	4,000.00	4,000.00	4,000.00	4,000.00	40,008.39
Payroll COGS	168.62	1,882.51	1,990.20	3,902.15	3,985.00	4,203.35	3,876.56	4,000.00	4,000.00	4,000.00	4,000.00	4,000.00	40,008.39
Total COGS	10,039.79	10,763.69	11,793.31	12,344.16	17,302.14	14,037.80	14,393.54	17,055.33	12,723.33	14,363.33	16,113.33	11,493.33	162,423.10
Gross Profit	30,050.97	25,862.31	30,230.44	21,832.78	22,893.61	30,176.20	33,077.71	29,664.67	29,816.67	33,901.67	24,636.67	25,476.67	337,620.35
Expense													
Bank Service Charges	21.00	5.00	5.00	5.00	6.00	6.00	6.00	20.00	20.00	20.00	20.00	20.00	154.00
Business Licenses	0.00	0.00	0.00	0.00	0.00	0.00	0.00	0.00	0.00	0.00	150.00	50.00	200.00
Telephone/Cable/Internet	297.55	258.00	220.14	279.90	256.25	285.45	285.36	285.00	285.00	285.00	285.00	285.00	3,307.65
Dues and Subscriptions	29.99	357.99	29.99	49.99	229.99	189.99	289.99	29.99	134.99	69.99	249.99	109.99	1,772.88
Guaranteed Payment	0.00	0.00	0.00	2,500.00	2,500.00	3,000.00	3,000.00	3,500.00	3,500.00	3,500.00	3,500.00	3,500.00	28,500.00
Insurance Expense													
General Liability Insurance	367.63	367.63	367.63	367.63	367.63	367.63	367.63	367.63	367.63	367.63	367.63	367.63	4,411.56
Worker's Compensation	754.46	754.46	754.46	754.46	754.46	754.46	754.46	754.46	754.46	754.46	754.46	754.46	9,053.52
Insurance Expense	1,122.09	1,122.09	1,122.09	1,122.09	1,122.09	1,122.09	1,122.09	1,122.09	1,122.09	1,122.09	1,122.09	1,122.09	13,465.08
Interest Expense	0.00	0.00	0.00	0.00	0.00	0.00	1,249.00	1,250.00	1,250.00	1,250.00	1,250.00	1,250.00	7,499.00
Janitorial Expense													
Laundry	0.00	0.00	0.00	172.58	160.38	195.07	95.67	150.00	150.00	150.00	150.00	150.00	1,373.70
Janitorial Expense - Other	311.91	521.51	190.09	643.47	202.86	312.46	545.70	400.00	400.00	400.00	400.00	400.00	4,728.00
Total Janitorial Expense	311.91	521.51	190.09	816.05	363.24	507.53	641.37	550.00	550.00	550.00	550.00	550.00	6,101.70
Landscaping	50.00	25.00	0.00	50.00	0.00	196.98	75.00	25.00	25.00	25.00	25.00	150.00	646.98
Licensing & Permits	0.00	324.00	0.00	0.00	75.00	0.00	105.00	0.00	125.00	125.00	0.00	0.00	754.00
Marketing and Advertising	1,144.00	1,732.09	485.25	361.50	185.25	3,178.00	2,008.69	0.00	2,000.00	2,000.00	3,000.00	0.00	16,094.78
Merchant Fees	1,002.27	915.65	1,050.59	854.42	1,004.89	1,105.35	1,186.78	1,168.00	1,063.50	1,206.63	1,018.75	924.25	12,501.09
Office Supplies	370.57	265.50	163.61	548.86	211.93	164.20	275.52	285.00	285.00	285.00	285.00	285.00	3,425.19
Payroll													
Wages	0.00	1,652.00	1,782.00	1,756.00	1,925.00	2,462.00	2,662.00	3,400.00	3,400.00	3,400.00	3,400.00	4,000.00	29,839.00
Payroll Taxes	0.00	214.76	231.66	228.28	250.25	320.06	346.06	442.00	442.00	442.00	442.00	520.00	3,879.07
Payroll	0.00	1,866.76	2,013.66	1,984.28	2,175.25	2,782.06	3,008.06	3,842.00	3,842.00	3,842.00	3,842.00	4,520.00	33,718.07
Postage and Delivery	0.00	0.00	0.00	0.00	49.50	7.50	291.76	50.00	50.00	200.00	200.00	50.00	898.76
Professional Fees													
Accounting	705.00	1,000.00	2,147.00	0.00	705.00	0.00	0.00	400.00	900.00	0.00	900.00	0.00	6,757.00
Legal Fees	2,500.00	0.00	1,200.00	800.00	0.00	0.00	0.00	0.00	300.00	300.00	300.00	300.00	5,700.00
Professional Fees	3,205.00	1,000.00	3,347.00	800.00	705.00	0.00	0.00	400.00	1,200.00	300.00	1,200.00	300.00	12,457.00
Rent Expense	6,235.00	6,235.00	6,235.00	6,235.00	6,235.00	6,235.00	6,235.00	6,235.00	6,235.00	6,235.00	6,400.00	6,400.00	75,150.00
Repairs and Maintenance	58.37	108.00	657.00	920.60	446.84	108.00	608.00	415.00	415.00	415.00	415.00	415.00	4,981.81
Smallwares	1,156.08	225.15	89.92	632.40	92.79	0.00	1,259.80	500.00	500.00	500.00	500.00	500.00	5,956.14
Brewery Supplies	54.50	56.25	606.42	0.00	158.17	0.00	606.42	220.00	220.00	220.00	220.00	220.00	2,581.76
Taproom Supplies	47.77	176.66	336.31	0.00	2,080.00	34.25	0.00	267.23	296.52	1,146.57	1,325.87	1,836.32	7,547.50
Taxes													
Local	0.00	0.00	200.00	0.00	0.00	0.00	0.00	0.00	0.00	0.00	0.00	0.00	200.00
State	0.00	0.00	150.00	0.00	0.00	0.00	0.00	0.00	0.00	0.00	0.00	0.00	150.00
Property Taxes	0.00	0.00	0.00	0.00	0.00	0.00	0.00	0.00	0.00	5,000.00	0.00	0.00	5,000.00
Total Taxes	0.00	0.00	350.00	0.00	0.00	0.00	0.00	0.00	0.00	5,000.00	0.00	0.00	5,350.00
Utilities													
Garbage Service	375.76	375.76	374.75	374.75	374.75	374.75	374.75	374.75	374.75	374.75	374.75	374.75	4,499.02
Natural Gas	3,673.63	3,267.28	2,231.56	2,483.18	2,793.42	3,188.55	3,098.76	3,000.00	3,000.00	3,000.00	3,000.00	3,000.00	35,736.38
Electricity	1,220.65	1,295.44	1,188.11	1,142.50	1,209.78	1,525.01	1,399.13	1,300.00	1,300.00	1,300.00	1,300.00	1,300.00	15,480.62
Security	34.95	34.95	34.95	34.95	34.95	34.95	34.95	34.95	34.95	34.95	34.95	34.95	419.40
Water	1,789.44	1,595.91	1,728.38	1,656.42	1,589.49	1,801.75	1,943.28	1,750.00	1,750.00	1,750.00	1,750.00	1,750.00	20,854.67
Utilities	7,094.43	6,569.34	5,557.75	5,691.80	6,002.39	6,925.01	6,850.87	6,459.70	6,459.70	6,459.70	6,459.70	6,459.70	76,990.09
Other Expenses													
Total Expense	22,200.53	21,763.99	22,459.82	22,851.89	23,899.58	25,847.41	29,104.71	26,624.01	29,578.80	34,756.98	32,018.40	28,947.35	320,053.48
Net Ordinary Income	7,850.44	4,098.32	7,770.61	-1,019.12	-1,005.97	4,328.79	3,973.00	3,040.66	237.87	-855.31	-7,381.73	-3,470.68	17,566.87
Net Income	**7,850.44**	**4,098.32**	**7,770.61**	**-1,019.12**	**-1,005.97**	**4,328.79**	**3,973.00**	**3,040.66**	**237.87**	**-855.31**	**-7,381.73**	**-3,470.68**	**17,566.87**

TABLE 1.26 SECOND TAPROOM BUDGET FOR FIRST YEAR (CONT.)
MONTHLY SALES, COGS, AND EXPENSES

	Projected Y2 Month 1	Projected Y2 Month 2	Projected Y2 Month 3	Projected Y2 Month 4	Projected Y2 Month 5	Projected Y2 Month 6	Projected Y2 Month 7	Projected Y2 Month 8	Projected Y2 Month 9	Projected Y2 Month 10	Projected Y2 Month 11	Projected Y2 Month 12	Projected Y2 TOTAL
Ordinary Income/Expense													
Income – Taproom 1													
Draft Sales	47,650.30	43,419.23	49,905.97	40,718.82	46,175.74	48,113.73	49,847.63	44,800.00	39,600.00	48,400.00	37,400.00	33,000.00	529,031.43
Packaged Beer	7,926.23	7,222.43	8,301.45	6,773.24	7,680.95	8,003.32	8,291.74	7,452.11	6,587.13	8,050.94	6,221.18	5,489.28	88,000.00
Merchandise Sales													
Hats	60.00	60.00	60.00	60.00	60.00	60.00	60.00	60.00	60.00	60.00	60.00	60.00	720.00
Shirt Sales	618.00	711.00	726.00	405.00	657.00	858.00	772.50	520.00	520.00	560.00	600.00	600.00	7,547.50
Merchandise Sales	678.00	771.00	786.00	465.00	717.00	918.00	832.50	580.00	580.00	620.00	660.00	660.00	8,267.50
Income – Taproom 2													
Draft Sales	39,650.76	36,130.00	45,680.53	37,271.23	42,266.13	44,819.50	47,590.25	41,800.00	37,620.00	45,980.00	35,530.00	31,350.00	485,688.39
Packaged Beer	7,347.44	6,695.03	8,464.78	6,906.51	7,832.08	8,305.23	8,818.66	7,745.71	6,971.14	8,520.28	6,583.85	5,809.28	90,000.00
Merchandise Sales													
Hats	80.00	70.00	70.00	60.00	80.00	80.00	70.00	70.00	60.00	80.00	60.00	80.00	860.00
Shirt Sales	618.00	711.00	726.00	405.00	657.00	858.00	772.50	520.00	520.00	560.00	600.00	600.00	7,547.50
Merchandise Sales	698.00	781.00	796.00	465.00	737.00	938.00	842.50	590.00	580.00	640.00	660.00	680.00	8,407.50
Total Income	103,950.74	95,018.69	113,934.73	92,599.80	105,408.90	111,097.79	116,223.28	102,967.82	91,938.27	112,211.22	87,055.03	76,988.56	1,209,394.82
Cost of Goods Sold													
Beer – Guest	1,650.82	895.78	555.88	1,203.32	1,205.36	1,416.78	758.92	700.00	700.00	700.00	700.00	700.00	11,186.86
Beer – House	17,460.21	15,909.85	19,117.30	15,598.01	17,688.37	18,586.65	19,487.58	17,320.00	15,444.00	18,876.00	14,586.00	12,870.00	202,943.96
Mobile Packaging	9638.45	11424.48	9321.35	10570.55	11079.15	11574.72	10321.71	9179.64	11219.56	8669.66	7649.70	7649.70	118,298.67
Excise Tax	436.51	397.75	477.93	389.95	442.21	464.67	487.19	433.00	386.10	471.90	364.65	321.75	5,073.60
CO_2	1,532.04	1,715.28	1,689.30	1,584.70	1,763.18	1,165.34	2,469.70	1,700.00	1,700.00	1,700.00	1,700.00	1,700.00	20,419.54
Merchandise													
Hats	30.00	30.00	30.00	30.00	30.00	30.00	30.00	30.00	30.00	30.00	30.00	30.00	360.00
Shirts	206.00	237.00	242.00	135.00	219.00	286.00	257.50	173.33	173.33	186.67	200.00	200.00	2,515.83
Merchandise Sales	236.00	267.00	272.00	165.00	249.00	316.00	287.50	203.33	203.33	216.67	230.00	230.00	2,875.83
Payroll COGS													
Payroll COGS – Other	7,133.81	7,133.81	7,133.81	7,133.81	7,133.81	7,847.19	7,847.19	8,203.88	8,203.88	8,203.88	8,203.88	8,203.88	92,382.79
Payroll COGS	7,133.81	7,133.81	7,133.81	7,133.81	7,133.81	7,847.19	7,847.19	8,203.88	8,203.88	8,203.88	8,203.88	8,203.88	92,382.79
Total COGS	38,087.83	37,743.94	38,567.57	36,645.34	39,561.08	41,371.33	41,659.78	37,739.85	37,856.87	38,838.10	33,434.23	31,675.33	453,181.25
Gross Profit	65,862.91	57,274.75	75,367.16	55,954.46	65,847.82	69,726.45	74,563.50	65,227.97	54,081.40	73,373.11	53,620.81	45,313.23	756,213.57
Expense													
Bank Service Charges	20.00	20.00	20.00	20.00	20.00	20.00	20.00	20.00	20.00	20.00	20.00	20.00	240.00
Business Licenses	0.00	0.00	0.00	0.00	0.00	0.00	0.00	0.00	0.00	0.00	300.00	100.00	400.00
Telephone/Cable/Internet	570.00	570.00	570.00	570.00	570.00	570.00	570.00	570.00	570.00	570.00	570.00	570.00	6,840.00
Dues and Subscriptions	295.48	295.48	295.48	295.48	295.48	295.48	295.48	295.48	295.48	295.48	295.48	295.48	3,545.76
Guaranteed Payment	4,000.00	4,000.00	4,000.00	4,250.00	4,250.00	4,250.00	4,500.00	4,500.00	4,500.00	4,750.00	4,750.00	4,750.00	52,500.00
Insurance Expense													
General Liability Insurance	735.26	735.26	735.26	735.26	735.26	735.26	735.26	735.26	735.26	735.26	735.26	735.26	8,823.12
Worker's Compensation	1,131.69	1,131.69	1,131.69	1,131.69	1,131.69	1,131.69	1,131.69	1,131.69	1,131.69	1,131.69	1,131.69	1,131.69	13,580.28
Insurance Expense	1,866.95	1,866.95	1,866.95	1,866.95	1,866.95	1,866.95	1,866.95	1,866.95	1,866.95	1,866.95	1,866.95	1,866.95	22,403.40
Interest Expense	2,500.00	2,500.00	2,500.00	2,500.00	2,500.00	2,500.00	2,500.00	2,500.00	2,500.00	2,500.00	2,500.00	2,500.00	30,000.00
Janitorial Expense													
Laundry	300.00	300.00	300.00	300.00	300.00	300.00	300.00	300.00	300.00	300.00	300.00	300.00	3,600.00
Janitorial Expense – Other	800.00	800.00	800.00	800.00	800.00	800.00	800.00	800.00	800.00	800.00	800.00	800.00	9,600.00
Total Janitorial Expense	1,100.00	1,100.00	1,100.00	1,100.00	1,100.00	1,100.00	1,100.00	1,100.00	1,100.00	1,100.00	1,100.00	1,100.00	13,200.00
Landscaping	100.00	100.00	300.00	100.00	100.00	300.00	100.00	100.00	100.00	300.00	100.00	300.00	2,000.00
Licensing & Permits	400.00	0.00	0.00	0.00	0.00	0.00	0.00	0.00	300.00	0.00	0.00	0.00	700.00
Marketing and Advertising	3,000.00	3,000.00	3,000.00	3,000.00	3,000.00	3,000.00	3,000.00	3,000.00	3,000.00	3,000.00	3,000.00	3,000.00	36,000.00
Merchant Fees	2,598.77	2,375.47	2,848.37	2,315.00	2,635.22	2,777.44	2,905.58	2,574.20	2,298.46	2,805.28	2,176.38	1,924.71	30,234.87
Office Supplies	741.14	531.00	327.22	1,097.72	423.86	328.40	551.04	570.00	570.00	570.00	570.00	570.00	6,850.38
Payroll													
Wages	7,000.00	7,000.00	7,000.00	7,350.00	7,350.00	7,700.00	7,700.00	8,050.00	8,050.00	8,050.00	8,050.00	8,050.00	91,350.00
Payroll Taxes	910.00	910.00	910.00	955.50	955.50	1,001.00	1,001.00	1,046.50	1,046.50	1,046.50	1,046.50	1,046.50	11,875.50
Payroll	7,910.00	7,910.00	7,910.00	8,305.50	8,305.50	8,701.00	8,701.00	9,096.50	9,096.50	9,096.50	9,096.50	9,096.50	103,225.50
Postage and Delivery	100.00	100.00	100.00	100.00	100.00	100.00	100.00	100.00	100.00	100.00	100.00	100.00	1,200.00
Professional Fees													
Accounting	0.00	2,000.00	3,500.00	0.00	2,000.00	0.00	0.00	2,000.00	0.00	0.00	2,000.00	0.00	11,500.00
Legal Fees	500.00	0.00	0.00	500.00	0.00	0.00	500.00	0.00	0.00	500.00	0.00	0.00	2,000.00
Professional Fees	500.00	2,000.00	3,500.00	500.00	2,000.00	0.00	500.00	2,000.00	0.00	500.00	2,000.00	0.00	13,500.00
Rent Expense	12,500.00	12,500.00	12,500.00	12,500.00	12,500.00	12,500.00	12,500.00	12,500.00	12,500.00	12,500.00	12,800.00	12,800.00	150,600.00
Repairs and Maintenance	116.74	216.00	1,314.00	1,841.20	893.68	216.00	1,216.00	830.00	830.00	830.00	830.00	830.00	9,963.62
Smallwares	2,312.16	450.30	179.84	1,264.80	185.58	0.00	2,519.60	1,000.00	1,000.00	1,000.00	1,000.00	1,000.00	11,912.28
Brewery Supplies	68.13	70.31	758.03	0.00	197.71	0.00	758.03	275.00	275.00	275.00	275.00	275.00	3,227.20
Taproom Supplies	95.54	353.32	672.62	0.00	4,160.00	68.50	0.00	534.46	593.04	2,293.14	2,651.74	3,672.64	15,095.00
Taxes													
Local	0.00	0.00	200.00	0.00	0.00	0.00	0.00	0.00	0.00	0.00	0.00	0.00	200.00
State	0.00	0.00	150.00	0.00	0.00	0.00	0.00	0.00	0.00	0.00	0.00	0.00	150.00
Property Taxes	0.00	0.00	0.00	0.00	0.00	0.00	0.00	0.00	0.00	7,500.00	0.00	0.00	7,500.00
Total Taxes	0.00	0.00	350.00	0.00	0.00	0.00	0.00	0.00	0.00	7,500.00	0.00	0.00	7,850.00
Utilities													
Garbage Service	751.52	751.52	749.50	749.50	749.50	749.50	749.50	749.50	749.50	749.50	749.50	749.50	8,998.04
Natural Gas	5,510.45	4,900.92	3,347.34	3,724.77	4,190.13	4,782.83	4,648.14	4,500.00	4,500.00	4,500.00	4,500.00	4,500.00	53,604.57
Electricity	2,136.14	2,267.02	2,079.19	1,999.38	2,117.12	2,668.77	2,448.48	2,275.00	2,275.00	2,275.00	2,275.00	2,275.00	27,091.09
Security	69.90	69.90	69.90	69.90	69.90	69.90	69.90	69.90	69.90	69.90	69.90	69.90	838.80
Water	2,326.27	2,074.68	2,246.89	2,153.35	2,066.34	2,342.28	2,526.26	2,275.00	2,275.00	2,275.00	2,275.00	2,275.00	27,111.07
Utilities	11,364.27	10,634.04	9,062.83	9,266.89	9,762.98	11,183.27	11,012.28	10,439.40	10,439.40	10,439.40	10,439.40	10,439.40	124,483.57
Other Expenses	4,491.31	2,489.41	3,425.97	2,880.28	6,158.77	1,883.98	4,893.11	3,424.94	3,983.52	5,183.62	5,842.22	6,863.12	51,520.24
Total Expense	48,990.41	47,647.41	49,756.96	48,008.54	51,661.74	46,429.60	51,240.38	50,727.79	49,286.37	58,736.47	53,695.07	52,715.97	608,896.71
Net Ordinary Income	16,872.50	9,627.35	25,610.19	7,945.92	14,186.07	23,296.85	23,323.12	14,500.18	4,795.03	14,636.64	-74.26	-7,402.74	147,316.86
Net Income	**16,872.50**	**9,627.35**	**25,610.19**	**7,945.92**	**14,186.07**	**23,296.85**	**23,323.12**	**14,500.18**	**4,795.03**	**14,636.64**	**-74.26**	**-7,402.74**	**147,316.86**

Although Mike had a good idea of how much a second taproom would cost, and what the reward would be, he and Erica would still need to find the capital to start the expansion. They would be in the same situation as when they originally opened the brewery. And, again, the only options were to either get a bank loan or take on an investor. The benefit was that now Happy Hour Brewing Co. had a history of profitable months, so the decision of whether to lend this second round of money would be based more on the company's performance and less on Mike and Erica's personal financial situation.

ONE MONTH LATER

Mike was set. He had run through the numbers a few more times to make sure all of the calculations were correct. He was ready to sit down with Erica and show her the full budget for his vision of expansion. What he was not ready for was a shock to the existing business. So far, Happy Hour Brewing Co. had not suffered major staff turnover, but that suddenly changed when his assistant brewer, Carson, submitted her notice. Mike was stunned. Carson was a pivotal employee. She had been his assistant brewer for the last seven months and he felt like they were just now finding their stride. She had carefully followed his tutelage and was making good beer, and she was working independently with few to no mistakes. Without her, Mike could not have taken so much time out of the day-to-day work in the brewery to write his budget for a second taproom. The talent pool of brewers in town was small, and there was stiff competition for those people. It would take a while to find the right person. There was an awkward moment when Carson first delivered the news and Mike tried to adjust. Luckily, Mike's professionalism quickly reasserted itself and he congratulated Carson on her new opportunity, wishing her well. Mike said he was sorry to lose her, and he meant it.

It was inevitable that one day the brewery would have to deal with employee turnover but knowing that fact didn't soften the blow for Mike. He shared the news with Erica as soon as he could. Erica was able to help Mike see the good side: the people he was training were contributing to the industry, and

that was a testament to his management skills. They would just have to roll with the punches.

That night, Erica and Mike were winding down over dinner and talking over their options. Mike was conflicted and feeling anxious. He had been ready to share his new vision for expansion with Erica during their weekly finance meeting, but now the idea of opening a second taproom seemed like too much. How could he think about expanding to an entirely new location when it would take him the better part of a year to get back to the same place of trust with someone new? In that moment, Mike decided to go ahead and share with Erica his ideas for a new location. He told her that he'd worked on a full budget for a new taproom, as well as a whole company budget for the next 12 months. Erica's jaw dropped. Mike knew she was astonished at his effort. The budget had been a ton of work to put together, but it was important to Mike that he vet the idea and prove to Erica that he had really thought it through. What was hard for Mike to believe was the part where he told Erica that he actually enjoyed it at the end! But now, in light of losing a key staff member, was the idea reasonable? The day's setback had been very discouraging.

Erica was genuinely proud of Mike for putting together a budget. She knew how much he disliked that kind of work. She encouraged him, acknowledging that the day felt like one step forward, two steps back, but that was just part of the process of being a business owner. She asked Mike to tell her more about the idea of a second taproom. Erica could tell that this idea was pulling at his entrepreneurial heartstrings, and if ever there was a time to muster up some of that energy, it was now.

Mike gave Erica the highlights, explaining that he had created a financial model that duplicated their existing taproom. Same square footage, same number of taps. The things that were different were higher prices from day one; fewer experimental brews that didn't sell well the first time around or were too expensive to make; and a sales strategy that would lead to higher average tickets per customer. Erica had never heard her husband talk like this. Mike—the man who avoided financials as much as possible—was talking like a seasoned CFO. He explained that the second taproom was planned to be just like their original taproom, but adjusted for a shorter learning curve. Mike believed the numbers looked good and it seemed to make sense. The couple would need some money for the capital purchases to get started, but they could be cash flow positive by the second month.

Erica was impressed that Mike was talking about the business in ways that she had never heard from him before. They agreed to go over the budget the next day. Mike was looking forward to showing her the details. Losing Carson was definitely a setback, but they could not lose focus on the end goal of spreading their business further. They couldn't let the day's speed bump derail their vision.

FOUR YEARS LATER

Mike was having fun. He had just finished the family Thanksgiving Day touch football game with his nephew, Justin, and they were heading in to get cleaned up. It was awesome to be able to spend a holiday with the family again. The Thanksgiving Day football game in the front yard had been a tradition at his uncle Fred's house for years, but Mike had missed all of the family Thanksgiving gatherings in recent memory. Being at his uncle's house made him realize how much he missed time with his family. Justin had just been a high school freshman the last time they played and now he had started college and was whipping Mike in football. It dawned on Mike that his ability to be with his family that day was a mark of success for him professionally. The brewery was entering its fourth year of business, and, for once, Mike didn't feel like every available moment had to be spent focused on running the business. He had been sprinting for 1,800 days—now there was enough foundation that he could stop and walk.

By this time, Happy Hour Brewing Co. had two taprooms that were busy and brought in a respectable amount of revenue. Operations were going smoothly, and Mike was starting to feel normal again. Sometimes he was unsure of how to handle this new phase, knowing what to do most of the time, but kind of feeling out of his element because the problems that did come up were new

and different. The pace of things was settling into a tempo that was unusual to him.

Mike was sensing the emergence from start-up phase to adolescence. The company was now at a minimum cruising altitude that didn't need constant hand holding. It was profitable, yet still had room to grow revenue. In the last year Erica had started working full-time at the brewery. The couple were still adjusting to a little tighter personal financial picture, but the ability for the brewery to pay them both a fair compensation was another sign of success.

Happy Hour Brewing Co. had expanded its personnel to include a taproom manager, who handled general manager duties for both locations, and had taken on a fantastic bookkeeper who worked in-house 10 hours a week. Mike and Erica had gone through a couple of bookkeepers who were not the right fit, for various reasons, but for the past nine months George had been helping them out in the role. Several years earlier, their CPA had told them that a strong bookkeeper was a great investment. They hadn't understood at the time, but now Mike and Erica were seeing the benefit of having accurate, timely reports that allowed them to react quickly to the data.

The plan to expand to a second taproom had manifested, and Mike and Erica felt good about the number of locations that they had. Two taprooms felt right. That number might increase in the coming years, but for now the couple were able to easily manage both locations. In a search for more revenue, wholesale distribution was beginning to look attractive. Over time they had incrementally added production space. Recently, when the return on assets ratio was reviewed, it was lower than it had been historically. Mike and Erica realized this meant that there was excess capacity. Opening another taproom was an option, but they felt that the next logical place for a third location would be in a town about 45 minutes away, and they just didn't have the bandwidth currently to commit to a physical footprint that large. The other option was, therefore, wholesale distribution.

See chapter 3 for a discussion of key ratios.

The brewery could distribute by itself or sign with a third-party distributor. Mike had canvassed his colleagues and, sure enough, there were a myriad of opinions. Some were die-hard self-distribution proponents, while others thought that they came out ahead by working with a distributor. Mike and Erica had considered self-distribution about three years earlier, but, in the end, they had decided to follow Mike's idea of expanding through another taproom instead. But now they were ready to revisit the idea because the business had several years of positive cash flow and a full-time manager. This meant that the startup capital and time commitment needed to start distribution were more readily available.

One thing Mike had learned in his short time as a business owner was that doing research on a major decision seemed to yield a better result. Another piece of wisdom he had gleaned from experience is that if you wait to have 100% assurance your approach is correct, it may never come. Mike did what he had done in the past, just begin by putting one foot in front of the other.

Mike started by asking his colleagues for distributor contacts. He got the names of three different companies and wrote a well-crafted, honest email. He identified himself and the brewery, and immediately identified his purpose: to find out if they had interest in representing his brand. He then gave a quick overview of the brewery's history supported by some key sales statistics. Finally, he closed with a deliberate ask for a 15-minute call at a specific time.

Three days and no response. Mike's impatience was getting the better of him, so he followed up with a phone call to each. After multiple attempts, Mike finally talked with all three distributors. Only one said that Happy Hour Brewing Co. probably wouldn't fit in their portfolio. The other two were interested enough to learn more—one hurdle crossed! Mike maximized those short 15 minutes, learning a lot about how the distributor relationship worked. Mike had a short list of questions and worked them into each conversation. He picked up a theme as he went: it's a crowded market; most distributors already have a crowded craft portfolio; they take a lot of your margin; and you have to be a proven brand already distributing to either demand a signing bonus or receive a share of marketing costs with the distributor.

Mike was a little discouraged after his conversations with third-party distributors. It seemed a high hurdle to enter into the distribution market, but the opportunity to make full use of their capacity and maximize their return on investment was very attractive. After discussing it with Erica and his key employees, Mike decided the brewery should begin self-distribution.

After the second quarter of distributing kegs, Mike and Erica were starting to feel the extra margin drop to their bottom line. Now they had two months of operating expenses in the bank instead of one. They were finding a rhythm with their sales team. And there was a symbiotic lift to sales in the taprooms as well. At the end of the first year of self-distribution, Happy Hour Brewing Co. had five employees in production and sales, five full-time equivalents as front of house employees, and 2.3 full-time equivalents in admin. In all, Mike and Erica had built a tidy little business. Their revenue was about $6.5 million annually and they were producing around 15,000 BBL.

Maybe it was the idle hands, but Mike and Erica started thinking about an exit. It happened on vacation, the first one they had taken in several years. As the waves lapped their feet, and the daiquiri started to sink in, Erica started daydreaming about the future. The brewery was almost seven years old. She asked Mike what he saw 10, 20 years down the road. Mike had no idea what he wanted specifically, but admitted that he didn't want to be working as hard as he had been. His long-term vision included having plenty of money, living somewhere warm, with a great house and a stacked investment portfolio. Erica admitted that running a brewery wasn't what she wanted to be doing long-term. They started talking about what their exit from the company might look like. There were many options: selling to a major domestic producer; buying another brewery to grow but hiring a CEO; or creating an employee stock ownership plan (ESOP) to give the company to employees. Erica mentioned a business transition consultant who spoke at one of her networking group meetings several months ago—contacting her would be an easy first step.

See chapter 10 for information on succession planning.

A couple of weeks later during their next Saturday financial review session, Erica brought up the topic again. She wanted to have an initial conversation with the business transition specialist because she and Mike had agreed that they did not want to run the brewery forever.

A few weeks later, the consultant, Rachel, came for a tour of the brewery. Rachel went over several different options with Erica and Mike for business transitions, and the one that made the most sense was transferring ownership to their head brewer and general manager. Both of those employees lived the Happy Hour Brewing Co. brand and came to work ready to give their best every day. No decisions were made on the spot, but a seed was planted for Mike and Erica.

It wasn't until 18 months later that the topic of exiting the business came up again. Distribution was going great, so great, in fact, that Mike and Erica were having trouble keeping up. They were being courted by distributors in their home market as well as neighboring metro areas, and there was also an opportunity to do a third taproom. All signs were pointing to them needing to ramp up to a new phase of their adolescence. After this next expansion of distribution and a third taproom they were well poised to have a business model that would serve them for years to come.

To jump to the other side of the business cycle canyon was going to ask a lot of their team. Mike and Erica felt like this would be the best time to introduce the idea of transferring ownership to a few of their key employees. It would motivate those employees and increase their commitment to the company, at a time when Mike and Erica could not afford to lose them. Mike couldn't help but think back to a couple of years ago when Carson put in her notice. Maybe if the business had had some kind of ownership transfer program in place at the time things would have turned out different.

Mike and Erica talked it over and decided to offer equity to their head brewer and taproom manager. Over the next three years those two employees were each granted 3% ownership. As the transition went into effect, Mike and Erica started to lean back from the operations bit by bit. As Happy Hour Brewing Co. grew, they also needed to hire a chief operating officer. And to attract the type of talent they really needed, it required an offer of ownership, so another 5% equity was granted to that position. After an exhaustive search, which involved hiring a headhunter, Happy Hour Brewing Co. brought on Selena as their COO. With patience and diligence, Mike and Erica had been able to find someone with the skill set and personality traits that were the right fit for the job.

Selena was bullish. She saw how well the company was performing and she had the energy to go after it. At the end of her third year, the company was solidly in the mature phase of its life cycle. Happy Hour Brewing Co. had signed with a number of third-party distributors and its annual production was 50,000 bbl., with six taprooms in two states. As for Mike and Erica, most of their time was spent as the face of the company. Mike was heavily involved in the beers they made, collaborations, and the brand strategy. Erica was focused on operations. She loved to geek out on her production plan. She had all the raw ingredients lined up for the next three years, and she worked closely with the sales manager to make sure the supply chain for beer would support his sales goals.

Then it happened.

Mike answered a call from Jordan at Hathaway Partners, an investment bank. Jordan explained that the bank had investors who had expressed interest in acquiring an operation like Happy Hour Brewing Co.. Mike was shocked. He wasn't even sure he knew what an investment bank was, but he knew what "acquire" meant. Waves of excitement, anxiety, and caution flooded him. What could it hurt to find out more? He and Erica agreed to have lunch with Jordan the following week.

Just like that, the ball was in motion. The buyer was a portfolio investment company who had been looking to get into the brewery space for years. According to

Jordan, desirable targets were few and far between, and this group had had their eye on Happy Hour Brewing Co. for the past few years, waiting to reach out until they saw a sustainable pattern of growth. The conversation between Jordan and Mike continued for a few months before they agreed on terms that were reasonable to both parties.

The deal would be structured so that the portfolio investment company owned 70% of the company. Mike and Erica chose not to dilute their key employees, so that meant that the entire 70% would come out of their ownership in the company. That meant, after the transaction, the couple's ownership would be reduced to 19%. The purchase price would be based on earnings before interest, taxes, depreciation, and amortization, or **EBITDA** for short. The chosen multiplier was 6. That is, the value of the brewery would equal six times its EBITDA. Thus, with Happy Hour Brewing Co.'s current EBITDA of $2.9 million, that translated to an enterprise value of roughly $17.5 million. Mike and Erica would be paid 70% of that price for 70% of the company, which translated to a $12.3 million payment.

EXPERT ADVICE

When a company is bought or sold a value must be agreed upon by the buyer and seller. There is no one right or wrong way to value a business and, in the end, the purchase price is simply where a willing buyer and seller meet.

It is common for a sales price to be measured by a multiplier of sales or EBITDA. There are several business valuation methods, which vary depending on industry.

The buyer also had limits on what liabilities it would assume. There was a total of $3.25 million in liabilities that Mike and Erica would be responsible for, and which would be paid using the proceeds of the sale. After taxes, this left $5.43 million in their pocket. It was a far cry from the $12.3 million Mike and Erica first imagined, but it was also more money than they had ever envisioned having.

- $12.3 million purchase price
- ($3.25 million) to pay off debt
- ($3.62 million) to taxes
- $5.43 million in pocket

Mike and Erica wrestled with this decision for months before they decided to proceed. Their responsibility in the business would subside and they would only help to set the vision, but they would still be business partners with the investment firm, albeit a firm of people they did not know. Mike and Erica spent innumerable nights debating whether to take the deal. They were giving up their baby. It would be a big lifestyle change, and they were sure that some of their colleagues would say that they had sold out.

The truth was, the money was really hard to ignore. Mike and Erica would still have almost a fifth of the ownership, so they could influence direction and continue to use the brewery as a creative and professional outlet, but this move also afforded them much more free time and an opportunity to check a few more items off their bucket list. Scared and excited, the couple agreed to the deal.

The transaction closed just after the company's tenth anniversary. After the dust had settled, Mike and Erica took another vacation. It was a final chance to cash in those credit card points that had racked up through purchases when building the company from scratch, a sustained period of hard work, dedication, and a commitment to excellence. This time, the couple went to a little fancier beach and stayed in a little fancier hotel. And those daiquiris? They had a little fancier umbrella.

2

INTRODUCTION TO FINANCIAL MANAGEMENT

No matter your trade, financial management is a critical component to running a healthy business. Understanding how to read financial reports helps managers make sensible investment and financing decisions. In a perfect world all business owners would understand **payback period**, **return on capital employed**, **earnings per unit**, **working capital**, profit planning, **standard costing**, and **ratio analysis**. But it's not a perfect world and most small breweries do not have technical experts in-house to guide them through these complex topics. In this book, I hope to combine the practical foundations with just enough of the sophisticated concepts to allow you to take an informed approach to financial management for your brewery.

There are some key points of accounting which must be understood in order to advance through the content of this book. The information in this chapter presents the framework for accounting. Let's begin at the beginning!

BASIC FINANCIAL STATEMENT INTRODUCTION

Before we explain the concept of debits, credits, journal entries, ledgers, and accounts, let's discuss account types.

Assets are resources owned by a company with economic value that are expected to provide future benefit. Examples include cash, accounts receivable, inventory, and fixed assets.

Liabilities are what the company owes to others. Examples include accounts payable, credit card liabilities, and loans.

Equity is the difference between assets and liabilities. It is made up of three things:
1. Owner contributions
2. Owner distributions
3. Accumulation of net income or loss

If an owner puts money into the company, then the equity goes up as well as the cash balance (an asset); likewise, if an owner takes a cash distribution from the company, equity goes down and the cash balance falls. If a company generates net income, that increases equity; likewise, if a company has a loss that decreases equity. A handy memory aid is

$$\text{Assets} = \text{Liabilities} + \text{Equity}$$
$$A = L + E \qquad\qquad \text{(Ale!)}$$

Revenue represents the sale of goods or services.

Cost of goods sold (COGS) is a type of expense account. It represents the outflow of resources associated with the revenues from the sale of finished goods. As the saying goes, it takes money to make money, and the cost of what the company sells is represented in the COGS accounts. Examples of COGS are raw materials, overhead, excise tax, and brewing labor. Note that throughout the text I will refer to expenses, which you should interpret as including COGS.

Operating expenses are outflows of resources not related to the production of goods or services sold. Examples of operating expenses are office supplies, sales expenses, and administrative payroll.

Gains and **losses** represent what the company makes when a fixed asset is sold. It's the amount of proceeds minus the **adjusted basis** of the asset. For example, if the company sells a keg washer for $5,000 and the adjusted basis is $3,000, then the gain is $2,000.

Assets, liabilities, and equity are permanent account types, meaning that the ledgers for these accounts accrue over years. Revenues, expenses, gains, and losses are temporary account types, because they accumulate a balance throughout the accounting period but are cleared out and rolled into the balance sheet as part of retained earnings at the end of the accounting period.

ACCOUNTING: GENERAL STRUCTURE OF TRANSACTIONS

Accounting is a double entry system. While it may sound redundant to have one piece of information entered twice, it is actually quite important because one part serves as a verification for the other. The terms for these two parts are *debits* and *credits*. One account will receive a debit entry, meaning the amount will be entered on the *left* side of that account. Another account will receive a credit entry, meaning the amount will be entered on the *right* side of that account. The key is to know which account should be debited and which account

should be credited (table 2.1). The abbreviation for debit is "dr" and credit is "cr."

TABLE 2.1 ACCOUNT TYPES AS THEY APPEAR IN DOUBLE ENTRY BOOKKEEPING

Account Type	Increase	Decrease
Assets	Debit	Credit
Contra-Assets	Credit	Debit
Liabilities	Credit	Debit
Equity	Credit	Debit
Revenue	Credit	Debit
Cost of Goods Sold (COGS)	Debit	Credit
Expenses	Debit	Credit
Gains	Credit	Debit
Losses	Debit	Credit

Below is an example of what a transaction looks like in an accounting entry. See that the debit is on the left side of the entry, and the credit is on the right side of the entry.

XX/XX/20XX

Account	Debit	Credit
Rent Expense	$10,000	
Checking Account		$10,000

Accrual Accounting versus Cash Basis Accounting

Accrual accounting records revenue when it is earned: expenses are matched to the period in which the expense occurred, not necessarily when the cash hit the bank account. **Cash basis accounting** records revenue and expenses in the period cash was received or paid out. For example, you create an invoice for $5,000 on the 30th of the month. You receive payment on the 10th of the next month. In accrual accounting, revenue will show up on the 30th. In cash basis accounting, revenue will show up next month on the 10th, which is when you receive payment. Accrual accounting represents the economic reality of a company, whereas cash basis accounting removes the effect of timing differences.

There is no right or wrong basis for accounting, and your choice will depend on how the financial reports (usually referred to as simply *financials*) will be used. Additionally, a company may choose to report using one method for financials and another method for the tax return. For example, internal management reports may use accrual accounting, while the tax return is prepared using cash basis accounting.

The accounting world has recognized that there should be standards that ensure comparability among companies' financial reports. The Financial Accounting Standards Board, a US governing body of accounting, was established in 1973 and created the Generally Accepted Accounting Principles (GAAP) standard. Financial reports prepared in compliance with GAAP give assurance to the user that financial items are measured and reported the same way across multiple companies. GAAP requires the use of accrual accounting.

In the opening narrative in chapter 1, Mike and Erica received help from the Small Business Development Center (SBDC) setting up their accounting software. Most accounting software will manage debiting and crediting accounts in the correct way, but understanding how accounts function within the system is critical to a basic understanding of finance. There will be times when a company needs to make adjustments to the books through the use of journal entries. A journal entry is a manual adjustment to accounts, and in this situation you will need to understand which side of the ledger (i.e., debit or credit) needs to be adjusted. Journal entries are structured as follows:

XX/XX/20XX

Account	Debit	Credit
Account 1	$X	
Account 2		$X

Description of the adjustment

EXAMPLE 1:
07/31/2019

Insurance Expense	$3,000	
Prepaid Expenses		$3,000

To recognize insurance expense for July 2019

In our example 1, expenses will increase because Insurance Expense has been debited, and assets will decrease because Prepaid Expenses has been credited. Prepaid Expenses is considered an asset because you have paid early for an expense not yet incurred. Notice that both sides of the journal entry equal each other. It is not possible to record a journal entry when the debits do not match the credits.

A **ledger** is a collection of transactions for one account. For example, the credit card ledger will include all credit card transactions for a specified period of time. When all account ledgers are grouped together that is called the general ledger. A general ledger includes all accounting data of a company for a period of time.

Chart of Accounts

A company organizes its financial data into **accounts** and the list of accounts is called the company's **chart of accounts**.

There is no one master chart of accounts used by every brewery because it depends on the company's size, complexity, and particular needs. The chart of accounts may list only a few dozen accounts or it may list hundreds. A company will construct and adapt its chart of accounts over time to meet its needs.

Within the chart of accounts the order of accounts always follows the same method: balance sheet accounts are first, followed by the income statement accounts. And within each of these sections there is also a particular order. The organization of every chart of accounts around the world is as follows:

- Assets
- Liabilities
- Partner Capital (Equity)
- Revenues
- Cost of Goods Sold (COGS)
- Expenses
- Gains
- Losses

It is important for the chart of accounts to be constructed in the most useful manner for a brewery's specific needs. For example, if a brewery produces beer to sell wholesale and also has a brewpub in which they serve their beer and food, then the chart of accounts should include accounts to clearly see the revenue and cost of both sides of their business, that is, wholesale and retail. Within the categories of revenues and expenses, accounts might be further organized by department (e.g., production, brewpub or taproom, sales and marketing, and administrative) and by location. A company's chart of accounts will expand in size as its operations grow. A small start-up's chart of accounts may be very simple, while a large regional brewery's will be much more complex.

> Appendix B includes a few examples of a chart of accounts.

An important lesson is that there is no one right way to set up your chart of accounts. Each business has its own needs, so a chart of accounts should be customized to make the financial reports more relevant for the user. Equally as important is understanding that the chart of accounts is flexible. There is no need to feel handcuffed to one chart. It is expected and encouraged to adjust the accounts as your business needs evolve.

One caveat: the addition of accounts should be made judiciously. Before adding, consider if there is already another account that will work. Or is there another way to record the information that will give you the detail you are seeking. For example, if you have a Marketing account and then you purchase an advertisement in the weekly entertainment guide, is it necessary to create a new Advertising account, or will Marketing suffice? The answer depends on a couple of factors: management's preference on how much detail they would like to see; how frequently advertising will occur; and whether the same person is responsible for the marketing budget and the advertising budget. As another example, let's assume that a company operates a production brewery and a taproom, and it has a class for each division in its accounting software. The use of classes allows the income statement to be separated into revenue or cost centers, for example, "brewery" class versus "taproom" class. In the chart of accounts, there is a Supplies account that has been used for

general office supplies, but the company recently bought paper towels for the taproom. Should the company add a Taproom Supplies account? My recommendation would be no. Instead, use the existing Supplies account and classify the paper towels to the taproom. When management looks at the income statement by class they will see one Supplies account with an amount in the admin class and an amount in the taproom class. This allows the company to keep a tidy chart of accounts and see the performance of each division. If a company chooses not to use classes then the chart of accounts will be larger because the accounts will need to show detail by cost center (e.g., Office Supplies and Taproom Supplies, not just Supplies).

EXPERT ADVICE

In Mike and Erica's story in chapter 1, the couple started reviewing their taproom activity separately from the brewery activity to help give more detail to the financial results. They found that this made the reports more useful. To separate the two activities, they utilized the class option in their accounting software package. The class option is usually a standard feature of accounting software, although it may be called "divisions" or "departments" depending on the software you use. Adding classes allows you to create divisions such as brewery, taproom, and administrative. When you activate classes, it allows you to keep the number of accounts focused, yet still have details available about your expenses. For example, you may have one Rent account, but you can allocate Rent to the brewery, the taproom, and a portion to admin. Classes can also be helpful when setting departmental budgets.

Some software also has a function available for locations. Locations allows you to parse the data in yet another way. Imagine that you have three taprooms, each with a small brewhouse to serve that one location. To build on our previous example of rent, you could have one Rent account, with the total expense allocated among classes, and then by location within each class:

Rent>Brewery>Location A	$2,000
Rent>Brewery>Location B	$2,200
Rent>Brewery>Location C	$1,700
Rent>Taproom>Location A	$1,500
Rent>Taproom>Location B	$1,400
Rent>Taproom>Location C	$1,300
Rent>Admin>Location A	$500
Rent>Admin>Location B	$400
Rent>Admin>Location C	$400

You can view the total expense:

	$11,400

Or you can view by class:

Brewery rent	$5,900
Taproom rent	$4,200
Admin rent	$1,300

Or you can view by location:

Location A rent	$4,000
Location B rent	$4,000
Location C rent	$3,400

I highly recommend having one person responsible for editing the chart of accounts. If multiple people have access rights to the accounting file that allow them to make direct changes to the chart of accounts, the list can get unwieldly. Instead, filter all suggestions through one person who is responsible for maintaining the chart of accounts.

EXPERT ADVICE
The Benefit of Using GAAP

GAAP is a common set of accounting principles, standards, and procedures that companies in the US must follow when compiling financial statements. Some banking agreements require financial statements be prepared in compliance with GAAP. Investors may require that the companies they invest in have GAAP-compliant financial statements. When filing required financial statements as a public company, those statements are required to be prepared in compliance with GAAP. GAAP provides a level of consistency for recording

transactions to enable those using the financial statements to analyze and extract useful information. Without a set of standards such as GAAP, financial statements would not be of much use to those outside the company.

Under GAAP, accrual accounting is the standard method accepted. The other options for financial reporting—cash basis, modified cash basis, and income tax basis—are referred to as other comprehensive basis of accounting (OCBOA). Financial statements may be presented under OCBOA methods, but they must be clearly marked as such so readers understand that they have been prepared using a non-GAAP method.

Not all breweries have the employees and/or resources to ensure their financial statements are GAAP-compliant. A nanobrewery or an early-stage brewpub may not have the expertise to prepare GAAP-compliant financial statements unless they have an investor group that requires them. However, consistency in accounting is important for analyzing results and making the financial statements useful for management decision-making. GAAP methodology is used as a basis to ensure consistency.

GAAP provides guidance on costs that should be included in COGS, which generally carries through to the cost assigned to inventory. New brewery owners often ask why using GAAP is important or considered common practice. The reason is that GAAP forms the backbone of financial reporting in the US, because it is the standard for financial statements prepared that is relied upon in business.

For more information see *Brewers Association Cost of Goods Sold Manual* (Boulder, CO: Brewers Association, 2018), https://www.brewersassociation.org/educational-publications/cost-of-goods-sold.

It is important for business transactions to be kept separate from personal transactions. In reality, most small businesses begin with the owner spending money from his or her own pocket, but you should quickly graduate to having a separate bank account and accounting records solely for business transactions. Only business-related expenses are allowed deductions. Thus, if there is any evidence of personal expenses included in your records the Internal Revenue Service (IRS) will disallow any expenses that are not clearly business related. Personal expenses on the company books may "pierce the corporate veil," which may result in owners personally held liable for the corporation's debt.

How you keep your accounting information is important, too. Accounting software has tremendous value beyond basic organization of transactions. As you learned earlier, accounting is a double entry system. You can enter a transaction once and the software will automatically post the entry to the second account. While it is *possible* to keep records in a simple spreadsheet it is not a scalable solution and is prone to error. Accounting software provides a certain level of basic diligence that is advisable for a business of any size.[1] Software also typically allows businesses to assign access to multiple users, with different levels of access and authority, which is an important part of setting **internal controls.**

Internal Controls

Internal controls is the process for assuring an organization's objectives in operational effectiveness and efficiency, reliable financial reporting, and compliance with laws, regulations, and policies. Strong internal controls include a separation of custody of assets, authority to direct the use of assets, and recording assets. This is sometimes difficult for start-ups because such organizations have a few people doing many different jobs. You can expect internal controls for a business to evolve over time.

In a small company, internal controls may mean that co-workers who are not in an accounting role help out with tasks. For example, the office manager opens the mail and makes copies of checks received; the bookkeeper records the receipt of payment in the accounting system; and the owner deposits checks at the bank.

Requiring a second level of authorization for certain types of transactions can add assurance to the records by proving that transactions have been seen and approved by someone with the appropriate authority. Requiring approval for payments over a certain amount (e.g., $5,000) can prevent unauthorized spending.[2] Along the same lines, requiring approval for expenses put on company credit cards can prevent unauthorized purchases by employees. Controlling access to different parts of the software accounting system by requiring each user to have a unique login can help reinforce the separation of duties and provides a way to audit the system to identify the source of questionable transactions.

Another simple internal control method is to perform hard counts of cash and inventory on a regular basis. The more liquid the asset, the more frequent the count should be. Cash on hand should be counted daily, and inventory should be counted monthly. This practice can reveal misappropriations quickly, allowing you to correct errors and tighten processes so that the issue does not get out of hand.

Uniquely numbered documents for invoices, checks, and purchase orders can help minimize confusion when keeping records. Having documents with a unique item number can be helpful when identifying past transactions.

Monthly bank and credit card reconciliations can ensure that balances in your accounting system match up with balances in those accounts. A **reconciliation** is a simply process of matching transactions in your system to the transactions that the bank or credit card shows. It ensures that everything that did happen is in the books, and that everything that is in the books did happen. It's amazing how frequently transactions get duplicated inadvertently.

---

[1] Common software packages include QuickBooks™, Xero™, Orchestrated Beer, Crafted ERP, and Vicinity Brew®. Each software package varies in its features and complexity.

[2] Expensify and Concur are two programs that can be used for approving purchases by employees on company credit cards.

3

BALANCE SHEET AND INCOME STATEMENT

There are three reports that make a complete set of financial statements: the **balance sheet**, the **income statement** (also known as the profit and loss statement), and the **statement of cash flows**.

BALANCE SHEET

The balance sheet reports the assets, liabilities, and partners' capital at a specific point in time, such as December 31, 20XX. The details in the balance sheet report show the financial health of a company at that moment in time. The balance sheet is often used by investors, lenders, or company owners to see what is *owned* versus what is *owed*.

The balance sheet is divided into two parts, or sides: assets, and liabilities and equity. Both sides of the balance sheet must always equal each other. Table 3.1 is an example of a simple balance sheet.

TABLE 3.1 EXAMPLE BALANCE SHEET

	Dec 31, Year 1	Dec 31, Year 2	Dec 31, Year 3
Assets			
Cash	83,090	268,439	32,264
Accounts Receivable	92,000	140,000	187,000
Inventory	15,000	18,000	22,000
Fixed Assets	177,910	422,349	533,344
Accumulated Depreciation	(92,090)	(244,439)	(355,434)
Total Assets	**275,910**	**604,349**	**419,174**
Liabilities			
Accounts Payable	22,000	60,000	47,000
Credit Cards Payable	12,000	12,000	9,000
Long Term Liabilities	212,868	501,306	302,000
Equity			
Retained Earnings	(370,958)	(568,957)	(638,826)
Paid-In Capital	400,000	600,000	700,000
Total Liabilities and Equity	**275,910**	**604,349**	**419,174**

Now let's review some of the major account groups on the balance sheet.

Assets

Assets include several account types: cash, which includes checking accounts, savings accounts, cash on hand, and money market funds; **accounts receivable** (AR), which is invoices for which the company has not yet been paid; **inventory**; and fixed assets.

Inventory

Inventory is the materials and product on hand that have not yet been sold. Breweries are manufacturing companies that buy ingredients (hops, malt, etc.), combine them together, and generate a finished good (draft beer or packaged beer). Inventory is one of the most confusing areas of accounting for brewers. In my experience, these are the two most common questions about inventory:

1. When spending money on raw ingredients, etc., why does that not go on the income statement as an expense?
2. Do I report inventory at the amount I paid for the goods, or at the price at which I will sell the finished beer?

Concerning the first question, it is common to see brewers record purchases of ingredients as **cost of goods sold** (COGS) in error. While it's true that purchases will ultimately end up in COGS, they initially go on the balance sheet as inventory, which is where they stay *until the beer that is made with those purchases has been sold.* When you buy ingredients, you are simply swapping one asset (cash) for another (ingredients). Figure 3.1 shows the flow of items over time from purchases, through the manufacturing process, and finally as a cost of sale.

The second question—how to value inventory—is answered by the cost principle of accounting. The cost principle requires that assets be recorded at the cash amount (or its equivalent) at the time that an asset is acquired. Therefore, inventory should be recorded on the balance sheet at the cost at which you paid for the materials, not the amount for which you will sell the beer.

Most companies keep different inventory accounts for the following: raw materials, work in process, finished goods, and packaging materials (if applicable). The Raw Materials account should cover basic ingredients: hops, malt, fruit, other edibles, additives, and other ingredients. Note that it is not advised to keep liquid yeast as an inventory item. Because it is challenging to find a consistent way to measure and value liquid yeast, most breweries expense yeast as it is purchased. Dry yeast in a package that can be counted, however, would be fine to keep in inventory.

Work in process, or WIP, includes inventory items that are currently in the production cycle. This includes any stage between mashing and final packaged goods. Most breweries include a WIP inventory account on their balance sheet to capture the value of beer in tanks and/or barrels. During inventory count, a brewer will measure the volume of beer in a tank by reading a sight glass on the side of the tank, then that volume, in barrels, is multiplied by the cost of the beer per barrel. Breweries should have a master recipe sheet that is updated periodically that dictates the recipe for each beer and the current unit cost of each ingredient. This ensures a reasonably accurate calculation of value. Inventory management software keeps track of WIP value automatically.

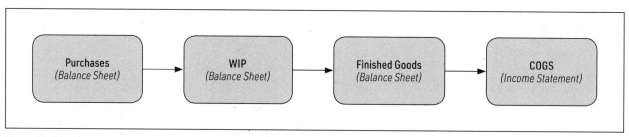

Figure 3.1. A business's purchases remain on the balance sheet until the finished goods made with those purchases are sold, at which point they are moved to the income statement as cost of goods sold.

EXPERT ADVICE

If you are using spreadsheets to manage your inventory, remember to periodically update the unit cost of your ingredients. This should be done quarterly to ensure that the value of your inventory is reasonably accurate. Setting aside time to review ingredient costs is also a good opportunity to audit prices from vendors, and a reminder to negotiate pricing and terms if needed. You may be surprised at the savings you can make by staying on top of vendor pricing and negotiating terms.

The other major component of inventory is finished goods. The Finished Goods account represents the value of beer after it has been kegged or packaged into bottles or cans. In addition to the cost of the liquid, you will also include the cost of packaging materials. For kegged beer, packaging materials will include keg collars, keg caps, keg leasing fees (if applicable), and single-use kegs (if applicable). For packaged beer, packaging materials will include bottles, crowns, labels, trays, boxes, cans, can ends, and can rings.

Fixed Assets (Capital Expenses)

The term fixed assets is synonymous with capital expenses. A fixed asset is a long-term asset, which means that it will not be converted to cash or be consumed within one year. Conversely, if a purchase is expected to convert to cash or be consumed within one year, then it is considered a **current asset**. Fixed assets are property, plant and equipment, and land. All categories of fixed assets, except for land, undergo **depreciation** over time. To **capitalize** an expense is to record it on the balance sheet as an asset and delay recognition of the full purchase price. This practice is an example of the **matching principle of accounting**. The matching principle states that all expenses must be matched in the same accounting period as the revenues they helped to earn.

Sometimes it's not practical to capitalize every purchase. For example, hoses may last a long time and be relatively inexpensive. Because it would be burdensome to depreciate each individual hose

over several years, most businesses adopt a de minimis policy, a Latin term that means too small or insignificant (lit. "concerning trifles"). A company adopts a de minimis accounting policy to establish a dollar amount threshold that determines whether a purchase is capitalized or expensed. As of this writing, the IRS has approved a de minimis amount of $2,500, meaning that the IRS allows you to expense in the year of purchase fixed assets costing less than $2,500.

EXPERT ADVICE

Should your company apply a de minimis policy? It depends on the goals of the company. For example, if a company's goal is to show as much profit as possible, then they may choose to capitalize every purchase (no matter how small the dollar amount) if it will not be consumed within a year. The trade-off is that the fixed asset list becomes very long and the time spent to calculate depreciation on every small purchase can be burdensome. On the other hand, employing a de minimis policy means that every purchase under the de minimis threshold will reduce net income even though it is a long-term asset. Net income will be lower using the de minimis approach, but calculating net income will be easier because you do not have to consider depreciation.

Once a business has chosen a policy it may not selectively apply this to assets. The rules must be applied the same for all purchases. This means that you may not choose to expense a $100 hose but capitalize a $100 computer accessory.

For tax purposes, $2,500 is the highest amount of de minimis allowed (as of the time of writing).

Every business is unique, so there is no one right way. Over the years, however, my experience has shown that adopting a de minimis policy at $2,500 is the best practical choice for smaller breweries. You should consult your own advisor and choose what is best for your situation.

For many categories of fixed assets, it makes sense that they are capital expenses: computers, equipment, machinery, vehicles, buildings, and land. In some situations, it can be confusing to determine how to categorize expenditures. Let's consider two tricky situations: deposits on equipment, and leasehold improvements.

Recording deposits on equipment. Deposits on equipment are not fixed assets. They should be recorded in a separate asset account until the equipment is received. Assume a company purchases a $30,000 fermentation vessel. Typically, this will be paid for with two checks, one for a 50% deposit and the second for the remainder plus freight. The first check should be recorded to your deposits account. I like to use Assets Not in Service, which is an Other Asset account. In this example, you would record the deposit for the fermentation vessel as a debit to Assets Not In Service for $15,000 and credit to cash for $15,000. The memo would note something along the lines of "payment 1 of 2 for 30 bbl. tank." Assume the second payment is made when the tanks are delivered and installed; in this case, let's assume that the second payment is $15,500, $500 of which is freight. Record the second check the same way as the first check. It's appropriate to put the entire $15,500 to the cost of the tank because freight and installation costs should be capitalized with the assets they support. The memo will note "payment 2 of 2 for 30 bbl. tank." Next, create a journal entry to move the full amount of the purchase out of Assets Not In Service and into Equipment. On the date that the equipment goes into service, debit Equipment for $30,500, credit Assets Not In Service for $30,500, and note "to recognize 30 bbl. tank placed in service."

05/01/20XX

Account	Debit	Credit
Assets Not In Service	$15,000	
Checking		$15,000

Payment 1 of 2 for 30 BBL tank

08/12/20XX

Assets Not In Service	$15,500	
Checking		$15,500

Payment 2 of 2 for 30 BBL tank

08/15/20XX

Equipment	$30,500	
Assets Not In Service		$30,500

To recognize 30 BBL tank placed in service

EXPERT ADVICE

Recording purchases as one amount (even though in reality they are paid with multiple cash outflows (e.g., down payment, progress payment, final payment upon delivery) offers many benefits. First, it provides a simplified fixed asset ledger—one line per item, as opposed to several lines that have to be added up. Second, it puts the fixed asset on the ledger at the date that it went in service, which makes the depreciation calculation more straightforward. Depreciation is allowed only when an asset has been placed in service. If you had a fixed asset ledger that included a $15,000 down payment in February even though the tank didn't arrive until June, then you would have to go through the notes to find the date that it was placed in service and add up the multiple checks to arrive at the full purchase price.

Recording leasehold improvements. Leasehold improvements are expenses for upgrades to your physical space. For example, if you rent a taproom location but need to build it out for its intended purpose as a bar, that is considered a leasehold improvement. The term leasehold improvement is synonymous with tenant improvement.

Depending on the project, leasehold improvements may be paid with a few large checks to contractors or, if you are doing it yourself, with several small expenses at the hardware store. There are also some intangible expenses that can be capitalized into the cost of the leasehold improvement project. Let's take the example of a brewery that has found a location for a new taproom and it now needs to account for the build-out. If the brewery needs to employ an architect to draw up plans, those costs will be capitalized as part of the taproom build-out. The same is true for any city or county permits that are required. In this case, let's assume the brewery owners chose to do the construction themselves, so they incurred dozens of trips to the hardware store and other miscellaneous small purchases. The best practice is to create a fixed asset account that is a subsidiary of the Leasehold Improvements account titled "Taproom Build-Out 20XX." As opposed to grouping a couple of payments into one transaction line (as described above for the purchase of tanks), here we recommend that you actually create an account for the single asset. Note that this is not normal for all fixed assets—it is not advisable to create an account any time that you want to record a purchase of a fixed asset. But in this case, it is appropriate because it gives you a reasonable way to collect all of the small expenses in one place. Large purchases will happen on an infrequent basis, so it will be easy to manage. In chapter 1, the owners set up multiple fixed asset accounts in their software that were tailored to their needs. They took the liberty of adjusting the chart of accounts so that they could see groups of large purchases, such as Brewery Equipment and Furniture and Fixtures.

Accumulated depreciation. Another indispensable part of the fixed asset section is the Accumulated Depreciation account. Its value is the cumulative total of all depreciation booked through the years for assets that a company owns. In a double entry system, the Accumulated Depreciation account holds the credit side of all of your depreciation journal entries. (Remember that Depreciation is an expense, and therefore that account holds the debit side of your depreciation journal entries.) Because depreciation represents the decrease in value of an asset over time due to wear and tear, we book, or record, accumulated depreciation as a negative amount with the fixed assets so that the financial statements represent the net value of fixed assets. Imagine if a company had a bunch of assets that were five years old with a total purchase price of $500,000. In reality, those assets are not worth the same amount after five years of use. Accumulated depreciation accounts for the decline in value so that the fixed assets are properly stated. The natural balance of Accumulated Depreciation is a credit, yet it is shown on the balance sheet next to fixed assets as a debit balance. In accounting this is called a **contra-account**, in this case a contra-asset account.

Liabilities

Liabilities represent amounts that a company is obligated to pay in the future. **Current liabilities** will be due within a year and long-term liabilities will be due at a point further than one year in the future. Examples of current liabilities are **accounts payable** (AP), credit cards, payroll liabilities, and the current portion of long-term debt. The current portion of long-term debt is the sum of the payments of a long-term liability that will be due within a year. Imagine that a brewery has a five-year loan with a bank. Payments for that loan will stretch over the five years; those payments that will be paid out over the next twelve months should be represented as a current liability, while the remainder should be a noncurrent liability.

EXPERT ADVICE

It is common for small businesses to have loans from an owner to a company, or a loan from a company to an owner. Before recording a transaction as such, be sure that the intention is to pay back the money to the lender. If the intent is simply to contribute cash to a company with no expectation of pay back, it should be recorded as a capital contribution. If you do record a loan between a company and its owner, be sure to draw up a promissory note. A promissory note is a written promise to pay someone in the future and usually contains terms of the loan, including the duration, repayment requirements, and interest rate. Any loan between a partner and a company should have a stated interest rate that is at or above the applicable federal rate, which is the interest rate set by the IRS, updated monthly, that is considered to be the minimum that the IRS will recognize as a legitimate interest rate for loans between related parties. An owner or partner is considered a related party to a business in which she is an investor. If the interest rate of your loan is lower than this rate, then it may result in the IRS changing its treatment of the loan and that could result in a taxable event.

Equity

Equity is the section of the balance sheet that shows what is left over after liabilities are subtracted from assets. Equity sections may include different accounts depending on the corporate structure of your company. We'll cover a few of the most common accounts.

Retained Earnings

Retained Earnings is the cumulative income over all periods minus any amounts that have been paid as dividends to owners. For example:

	Net Income	Retained Earnings
Year 1 income	$50,000	$50,000
Year 2 income	$150,000	$200,000
Year 2 dividends	$20,000	$180,000
Year 3 income	$200,000	$380,000
Year 3 dividends	$40,000	$340,000

Retained Earnings also includes net income for the period. At the end of every accounting period, net income is the "bottom line" of earnings. Net income gets *closed* to retained earnings. The following example illustrates what it means to close net income to retained earnings. In the chart above, the net income of $150,000 in Year 2 will be added to the existing retained earnings of $50,000 from Year 1. The new retained earnings is now $200,000 for Year 2 and the income statement has been wiped clean, so to speak, for the next period.

Capital

Opening a brewery is a capital-intensive project. Brewery owners have a choice of either raising the required funds from investors, borrowing the required funds from banks or other lenders, or some combination of the two. When owners contribute money to the brewery it is considered *capital*. Note that owners include individuals actively participating in the company as well as investors (silent partners); anyone who has a stake of equity, no matter how small, is an owner.

Capital can be thought of as a bank account. When money goes into the company the Capital account goes up, and when money is distributed out of the company to the owners the Capital account goes down. The brewery should keep track of capital in total as well as each individual partner's capital. Remember when the brewery owners in chapter 1 adjusted their chart of accounts (p. 5)? They created "Members Equity – Mike" and "Members Equity – Erica" capital accounts to see the value of each partner's ownership in the company.

As owners initially put in money, the capital accounts increase. As the partnership incurs years of income, that income will be allocated among partners, making the capital accounts go up. As the partnership incurs years of loss, the loss will also be distributed, making capital accounts go down. Finally, if there is a distribution (cash or property), the capital accounts will go down, as shown in this example:

		Capital balance
Year 1 initial contributions	$100,000	$100,000
Year 1 additional contributions	$75,000	$175,000
Year 2 contributions	$100,000	$275,000
Year 3 distributions	$10,000	$265,000
Year 4 distributions	$30,000	$235,000

The key is to remember that contributions make capital go up and distributions make it go down!

KEY RATIOS: BALANCE SHEET

Understanding the balance sheet is important, and sometimes business owners want to see a few select numbers that give them an idea of how the business is performing. Organizations use **key performance indicators** (KPIs) at multiple levels to evaluate their success at reaching targets. These metrics may be financial or non-financial. Some of the key ratios related to the balance sheet are the current ratio, quick ratio, AR days, AP days, and inventory turnover. In chapter 1, Mike and Erica reviewed several key metrics with their CPA (p. 32), and the experience helped them identify ratios that were indicators of the company's performance. These key performance indicators became a type of shorthand by which the owners could evaluate performance quickly.

Current Ratio

The current ratio is a measure of liquidity. This measure compares the totals of the current assets and current liabilities. The higher the current ratio, the greater the "cushion" between current obligations and the business's ability to pay them. Generally, a current ratio of 2 or more is an indicator of good short-term financial strength. In other words, the current assets of the business should be at least double the current liabilities.

$$\text{current ratio} = \frac{\text{total current assets}}{\text{total current liabilities}}$$

Quick Ratio

The quick ratio measures the availability of assets that can quickly be converted into cash to cover current liabilities. Inventory and other less liquid current assets are excluded from this calculation. The quick ratio is a measure of the ability to pay short-term creditors immediately from liquid assets. A quick ratio of 1:1 or more is considered "safe."

$$\text{quick ratio} = \frac{(\text{cash \& equivalents} + \text{accounts receivable})}{\text{total current liabilities}}$$

Accounts Receivable Days

The accounts receivable days , or AR days (also referred to as days sales outstanding ratio), is a measure of how long it takes for the business to collect the amounts due from customers. A lower number indicates that it takes the business fewer days to collect its accounts receivable. A shorter time to collect debtors has a positive impact on cash flow. A higher number indicates that it takes longer to collect its accounts receivable.

$$\text{accounts receivable days} = \frac{\text{accounts receivable}}{\text{average revenue per day}}$$

The average revenue per day is straightforward to calculate. For example, if sales were $300,000 in June, a month with 30 days, the average revenue is $10,000.

Accounts Payable Days

Accounts payable days, or AP days, is a measure of how long it takes for the business to pay its creditors. A stable higher number of days is generally an indicator of good cash management. However, while a longer time taken to pay creditors has a positive impact on cash flow, it can create strain with the suppliers. At the extreme, an excessively high AP days ratio could indicate a problem with sufficiency of working capital to pay creditors.

$$\text{accounts payable days} = \frac{(\text{average accounts payable} \times \text{days in period})}{\text{purchases in the period}}$$

Calculate the average accounts payable by taking the sum of the beginning period AP and end period AP divided by 2. The AP days can then be measured. For example, assume the average AP for June is $120,000 and total purchases are $150,000. Multiply the average AP by 30 days (June is a 30-day month) and divide the result by the total of your purchases: $3,600,000 divided by $150,000 equals 24. This means you're paying your bills on average in 24 days.

Inventory Turnover

Inventory turnover is a measure of how efficiently the business converts inventory into sales. A lower number of days is generally an indicator of good inventory management. A shorter time holding inventory has a positive impact on cash flow. But a low result can also mean there is a shortage of inventory. Conversely, a high result may indicate overstocking.

$$\text{inventory days} = \frac{\text{inventory} \times \text{month length}}{\text{total cost of goods sold}}$$

Industry Benchmarks for Key Ratios

Many brewers are interested in not only what their ratios are, but how they stack up to their peers. There is a dearth of financial benchmarking information available for breweries, regardless of size. One reason why it's difficult to compare financial performance of breweries is that there's no consistent way to categorize financial information across the industry. Public companies are required to publish financial data, but it's almost irrelevant for start-ups or small breweries because the size and structure of the publicly owned companies whose financial information is available is very different than a small brewery's financials.

EXPERT ADVICE

Benchmarks depend on company size, age, and business model, but, roughly speaking, a production brewery should aim for 60% COGS, 40% gross margin, and 10%–15% net income. Note that 60% COGS includes raw materials, packaging materials, direct labor, excise tax, and overhead.

If you are trying to identify comparable industry data, ask your state guild or professional service advisors who specialize in breweries of your size. Particularly, bankers and CPAs may have relevant data. For instance, our firm uses a business intelligence tool that allows us to compare the financial information of companies in the same industry and to segment the data by size of company. We can present industry data to clients and help them see how they are doing relative to their peers. One significant limitation is that the sample size is relatively small, but it's still a great resource because there's similarity in the financial results. We encourage all clients to measure COGS in the same way, so the financial reports of our clients will be measured comparably. Another advantage is that companies can see anonymously how they compare relative to the other companies in their peer group of similar size.

INCOME STATEMENT (PROFIT AND LOSS)

The income statement, also known as the profit and loss (P&L) statement, provides an overview of the company's performance over a period of time. It includes three major sections: revenue, cost of goods sold, and operating expenses (see table 3.2 for an example).

TABLE 3.2 EXAMPLE INCOME STATEMENT

	Year 1	Year 2	Year 3
Sales			
Wholesale	$251,185	$334.913	$446,551
Retail	$210,195	$280,260	$373,681
COGS			
Wholesale	$151,696	$202,261	$263,014
Retail	$40,155	$56,873	$75,830
Gross Profit	**$269,529**	**$356,039**	**$481,388**
Sales & Marketing Expenses	$83,679	$73,099	$81,911
Operating Expenses	$434,335	$300,728	$333,145
Earnings before Interest, Tax, Depreciation & Amortization (EBITDA)	**($248,485)**	**($17,788)**	**$66,332**
Depreciation	$92,090	$152,349	$110,995
Interest Expense	$30,383	$27,862	$25,206
Net Income (Loss)	**($370,958)**	**($197,999)**	**($69,869)**

The presentation of a company's income statement can greatly affect its usefulness. For example, consider adding a column that shows each line item as a percentage of total revenue. Reviewing an income statement by class or location is also helpful. A financial statement may be organized vertically or horizontally to facilitate management's use of the data. In vertical organization, each department or location will have its own set of expense accounts (table 3.3). In horizontal organization, each department or location will be represented in a separate class.

In the example in table 3.3, the performance of the brewery versus the taproom is visible, but must be extracted with additional analysis. By contrast, in a horizontal structure each department has its own class, which provides a more useful management report because readers can clearly see the departmental breakout (table 3.4).

Not all accounting systems have the ability to break out finances horizontally, but if your system does have that feature I highly recommend using it.

TABLE 3.3 EXAMPLE OF VERTICAL FINANCIAL REPORT STRUCTURE

Brewery Sales	$251,185
Taproom Sales	$210,195
Total Sales	**$461,380**
Brewery Ingredients	$53,722
Brewery Labor	$41,263
Excise Tax	$2,711
Brewery Overhead[a]	$54,000
Brewery COGS	**$151,696**
Taproom Purchases	$13,105
Taproom Labor	$7,050
Taproom Overhead[b]	$20,000
Taproom COGS	**$40,155**
Total COGS	**$111,851**
Sales and Admin Labor	$50,000
Rent	$4,800
Insurance	$3,600
Interest	$30,383
Other Expenses	$551,704
Total Expenses	**$640,487**
Net Income	**($370,958)**

Note: Uses Year 1 data from table 3.2.
[a] Brewery overhead includes a portion of rent, insurance, utilities and equipment rental.
[b] Taproom overhead includes a portion of rent, insurance and utilities.

Cost of Goods Sold (COGS)

Cost of goods sold (COGS) is a category of expenses that represents the cost of the beer, food, merchandise, and anything else that a brewery sells. It is defined in GAAP as the sum of the applicable expenditures and charges directly or indirectly incurred in bringing an article to its existing condition and location. It is understood to mean acquisition and production cost, and its determination involves many considerations. This category of expenses shows up on the income statement just below revenues and above operating expenses.

Costs are matched to a sale of beer based on the beer that is sold. Costs are moved from inventory on the balance sheet to the COGS section of the income statement, thus recognizing the cost of the inventory that was sold and resulting in a gross profit margin for that beer sold. Major classifications of costs accounted for under COGS are as follows:

Raw materials are recorded at the cost to purchase, including tax, freight, and storage fees.

Packaging materials includes cans, bottles, labels.

Labor includes the salaries and wages of those employees involved in brewing, production, and packaging. It also includes related costs such as benefits and payroll taxes.

Overhead includes the portion of utilities, rent, depreciation/amortization, insurance, property taxes, and supplies that relate to production.

Waste is the beer that is dumped or lost in production.

Excise taxes are levied on beer that has been determined as saleable.

Overhead costs can be difficult to identify for one individual unit of production. Some classes of expenses can be specifically traced to production, while others cannot. For example, it is easy to identify the depreciation on pieces of production-related equipment, or if a brewery uses flow meters on incoming water then identifying the correct breakout of water cost among departments is easy. For other expenses, choose a cost driver and apply a percentage of total cost based on the cost driver. One example of a cost driver is using square footage to allocate rent for each department. Applying overhead costs is a process that should continue to evolve over time as operations grow in size and complexity. The *Brewers Association Cost of Goods Sold Manual* provides examples of different methods for allocating overhead to COGS.

COGS is perhaps the biggest area of inconsistent reporting for breweries. Some companies report

TABLE 3.4 EXAMPLE OF HORIZONTAL FINANCIAL REPORT STRUCTURE

Account	Brewery	Taproom	Admin	Total
Sales	**$251,185**	**$210,195**		**$461,380**
Ingredients	$53,722			$47,722
Labor	$41,263	$7,050		$48,313
Excise Tax	$2,711			$2,711
Purchases		$13,105		$13,105
Overhead	$54,000	$20,000		$74,000
Total COGS	**$151,696**	**$40,155**		**$191,851**
Sales and Admin Labor			$50,000	$50,000
Rent			$4,800	$4,800
Insurance			$3,600	$3,600
Interest			$30,383	$30,383
Other Expenses	$201,548	$75,700	$274,456	$551,704
Total Expenses	**$201,548**	**$75,700**	**$363,239**	**$640,487**
Net Income	**($102,059)**	**$94,340**	**($363,239)**	**($370,958)**

Note: Uses Year 1 data from table 3.2.

only the raw materials of beer as COGS, others may include labor, and others again may include excise tax. Usually the choice of what to include depends on the size of the company. A smaller brewery may not have the staffing resources or experience to do this correctly. Other breweries may have no one other than a small ownership group who reviews the financial reports. In other words, a bank or investment group is not judging this performance of the business, therefore the owner may decide this level of detail isn't necessary in the financials. While this is understandable, it makes it difficult to compare breweries' financial reports. Fortunately, the release of the *Brewers Association Cost of Goods Sold Manual* marks a huge step forward for the brewing industry because it provides a common standard that, if all brewers use it, will allow comparability among financial statements.

The largest brewpubs and breweries generally follow and adhere to GAAP for their financial statements as a matter of necessity due to external reporting requirements. Smaller breweries may not be subject to the same reporting requirements and may not have the resources to comply with full GAAP-compliant accounting. For these reasons, accounting practices for COGS at smaller breweries may be modified as needed.

A best practice process for setting up a COGS system for all sizes of brewpub and brewery includes the following steps.

1. Identify the personnel—internal and, if needed, external—who will be able to account for COGS in accordance with GAAP.
2. Understand the reporting requirements of the investor group, board of directors/board of advisors, management, and lender(s).
3. Set up the general ledger to track costs in the proper categories.
4. Set up internal reporting to appropriately report COGS in accordance with GAAP and develop a process and rationale for costs to be split between departments.

5. Set up a detailed costing recipe or "bill of materials" (BOM) for each different beer.
   a. Periodically update the costing recipes or BOMs with current costs.
   b. Review costs with brewers and production and packaging personnel to ensure costs accurately reflect the efforts to make and package the beer.
6. Accurately perform physical inventory observations for all inventory on the specified reporting period.
7. Regularly analyze the costs, systems, and procedures of brewpub/brewery activities to ensure the current system continues to accurately reflect the cost of activities.

EXPERT ADVICE

The most critical process for a brewery to have in place is an effective physical inventory count, which should be performed at the end of each reporting period, usually monthly. *In fact, having a monthly log signed off by the individual completing the inventory counts is* **required** *by the TTB.*[1] Procedures that make accurate inventory counts easier include: conducting the count after production activities have been completed, since moving inventory is difficult to count accurately; assigning multiple employees to the counting process to double check and supervise the count; and providing inventory count sheets that enable multiple locations to be tracked for the same inventory item. Count sheets should have every inventoried item listed and a space for the person counting to write in the quantity that is there on hand. The person counting should go from shelf to sheet (not sheet to shelf), working their way systematically through the warehouse(s). This method minimizes the chance of something being missed.

Implement well-defined procedures that are documented and communicated with the count team to ensure consistency and accuracy from count to count. Assign one person or department the ultimate responsibility of reconciling differences and determining when the physical inventory count procedures are complete and production activities can resume.

---

[1] "Records Issue 2 – Inventory Records," TTB website, under "Common Compliance and Tax Issues Found During Brewery Audits," updated December 18, 2018, https://ttb.gov/beer/beer-tutorial.shtml#_Records_Issue_2.

Every brewery licensed by the TTB is required to complete compliance reports. The frequency of reporting varies depending on the brewery's level of production. For more information see the TTB's tutorial at https://www.ttb.gov /beer/beer-tutorial/shtml.

By spending time in advance to create sound processes, breweries and brewpubs can calculate COGS efficiently and provide valuable feedback for management. Breweries should consider the inventory process to determine at which stage costs should be included in inventory and the cost amount to include.

Each brewery and brewpub operator has a different set of circumstances that affect the operational and accounting decisions of the company, and not every inventory accounting system will be set up the same way. Breweries and brewpubs should decide the level of accounting detail they want or need. The goal of a brewery or brewpub's accounting function should be to provide the best information possible to enable management to make decisions about the company's operations and financial stability.

Management should also consider who else will be using the financial statements. Other financial statement users can include a board of directors/ board of advisors, investors, lenders, and potential investors or acquirers. Any one of these users could ask for financial statements on a GAAP basis and may even request a report from a third-party CPA to ensure the reports are in compliance with GAAP. The cost of using a third-party CPA to complete a compilation, review, or audit on financial statements will vary, but it will be lower if the internal financial statements are already kept on a GAAP basis.

Accounting for Inventory and COGS

There are several ways to measure inventory and COGS. More complex accounting methods will increase the amount of time, resources, and accounting systems necessary to manage. The benefit to using more complex accounting methods, if implemented effectively, is more detailed operational data to manage the brewery inventory and sales.

Periodic Inventory Systems

The simplest COGS accounting system is a periodic inventory system in which costs are recorded to the expense accounts during a given period. At the end of the period, the brewery or brewpub operator performs a physical inventory to confirm the amount of goods on hand. Then the inventory accounts on the balance sheet are adjusted via a journal entry to align the amount on the balance sheet with the count.

Periodic inventory systems have long been used and are effective. However, while the periodic inventory system may be the simplest system in principle, it is manual in nature, often involves a large number of spreadsheets, and is prone to error. Each business must understand that the manual process will potentially reduce the accuracy of reports.

Breweries should determine raw materials cost using the last cost for the malts, hops, and other ingredients (including freight and tax). The item cost should be updated each period to get accurate values.

The WIP value should be determined using recipe costs (updated for the last purchase) plus an allocation of labor and overhead. In practical terms, this means that the brewery is measuring the amount of liquid in a tank by using a sight glass or flowmeter. The labor and overhead is added to the value of the liquid by multiplying a standard cost times the number of barrels on hand. Standard cost of labor and overhead is the expected cost that will be required to create one barrel of finished goods. Because there are more materials and labor involved to bring beer from WIP to the finished good stage, the standard cost multiplier will be different for WIP than it is for finished goods. Note that finished goods may have different labor and overhead amounts applied based on packaging type.

A brewery or brewpub operator has many options for calculating the amount of brewing overhead to include in the standard cost. The most basic method takes the balance in the pool of overhead accounts for a given period. For example, if the total overhead balance is $50,000 for one month and production for that month is 200 barrels, divide the balance by production for the period. So, overhead per barrel equals $50,000/200, or $250 per barrel of beer produced. For this calculation, $250 of overhead would be applied to WIP inventory and for Finished Goods (FG). The appropriate conversion of costs would be applied for any FG in kegs, bottles, and/or cans.

This basic method is generic and can be modified to fit many systems. However, it does not take into account that different beers require different amounts of time to produce or different processes that impact production costs. Also note that costs change over time and, thus, standard costs also will fluctuate. Standard rates need to be reviewed and updated periodically.

Perpetual inventory systems

Perpetual inventory systems are the alternative to periodic systems; they utilize computer software to track inventory transactions as they occur in real time and are generally used by larger breweries. A perpetual inventory requires a software system that is updated for each transaction so the system can accurately give operational data for all areas of the operation. Perpetual inventory systems replace spreadsheets and incorporate production transactions into the general ledger. Transactions are recorded on an item-level basis and, as those transactions are completed,

POTENTIAL ISSUES IN ACCOUNTING FOR INVENTORY AND COGS

A number of issues can arise in tracking and accounting for inventory and COGS. Among them are lack of reliable data, general data availability, resource availability, and system limitations. Of these potential issues, data availability and reliability are the most significant. There are no substitutes for reliable data and, if a system does not provide data in a useful format, it cannot contribute to sound accounting.

Data reliability and availability issues are usually the result of system restrictions or capacity issues, which are sometimes attributable to process flaws that do not provide for proper data collection and analysis in the first place. Resource constraints can also be a major hindrance to accounting for inventory and COGS. Without an adequate accounting department and/or sufficient support staff, brewery or taproom operators can find it difficult to manage the day-to-day payables and invoicing processes, not to mention calculating and applying allocations for indirect costs to inventory.

Within a perpetual system, timely information is critical. Numerous issues can impact timing and slow the process down as well as create variances within the system. Below are some examples.

- Purchasing and receiving
  - Price: price differences between when the product is ordered and received can result in a variance.
  - Quantity: a mismatch between the quantity of a received shipment and the quantity ordered can delay receipt into the system.
  - Unit of measure: Using a different unit of measure (pounds, kilograms, gallons, etc.) from the one used by the software can impact the costing system.
  - Delayed landed fees: operators may not know processing fees and shipping costs at the time the product was ordered; these items should be included in the raw material price.
- Production orders
  - Duplication of production orders: one brew is started in the brewhouse but two brews are initiated within the software; this situation can result from system or operator error.
- Overhead application rates
  - Time-intensive beers
  - Special release beers or barrel-aged beers
  - Efficiencies (or inefficiencies) within the system
  - Production gains and/or losses
- Physical inventory count adjustments

All of the items above can create variances within the production software that affect inventory cost. Some can be prevented through training and a focus on accuracy. Other variances will be generated through regular operations. Tracking variances will assist the brewery in identifying changes within production activities that affect product costs, whether they are positive or negative to COGS.

ADDRESSING ISSUES

Overcoming obstacles to accounting for inventory and COGS begins with system and process design and function. With good planning and appropriate system set up, accounting for inventory and COGS can be a routine process rather than a burdensome endeavor.

- Adequate up-front training for all users of the system is key.
- Breweries should ensure the system has adequate controls to address potential issues. Internal or external technology support is a must.
- Timely detection of issues will help keep operations on track. To allow issues to be resolved quickly, operators can design systems to notify users of routine and/or actionable events that require attention.
- Analysis and review processes are required to:
    - regularly analyze operating benchmarks to help identify changes to the system that could improve results;
    - track trends;
    - focus on larger issues or areas that the brewery has control over.

Understanding cost flow and the system's capacity to track that flow enables brewery and taproom operators to maximize efficiencies in the accounting process. With processes designed to fit the cost flow and the use of automated systems where possible, even small accounting groups or individual accountants will be able to handle a much greater reporting load while providing high-quality, useful information. This comprehensive approach addresses both systems and resource constraints while providing useful data for decision-making. In certain instances, operators may need to hire additional staff or switch systems to better fit accounting needs; however, more often the first step is developing an understanding of the accounting environment to determine what solutions can be overlaid on current processes to address issues more cost effectively.

Source: *Brewers Association Cost of Goods Sold Manual* available on https://www.BrewersAssociation.org.

the software calculates the financial impact and inventory quantity impact of the transactions. The potential for having real-time inventory and financial data is appealing because it allows a company to be nimbler in its operations.

In a perpetual system, overhead is entered into the software as part of the total costs of WIP and finished goods. Therefore, the overhead entered is usually calculated with standard brewing overhead costs and budgeted production for the upcoming year. As overhead costs and/or production costs differ from budgeted amounts, the total amount of pooled overhead costs show a variance to the overhead costs applied. Because it is built on estimates and a number of variables in costs and production level, the variances fluctuate during the year. Significant variances should be analyzed to determine what generated them. However, determining an acceptable range in the overhead variances will reduce excess time spent analyzing amounts that are insignificant in the overall production process.

Although accounting for COGS can be a complex endeavor, utilizing well-designed processes and systems can greatly alleviate the difficulty in arriving at a reasonable COGS value. While no two breweries or brewpubs will ever have identical processes for recording COGS, implementing a process designed around best practices can greatly increase comparability across the brewing industry. As more managers in the industry start to adhere to the same measurement of financials, it will allow industry benchmarks to be more easily compiled. Brewpubs and breweries of similar size should have similar processes in place based on available resources and abilities to implement best practices. By developing a better understanding of COGS in the brewing industry, individual breweries and brewpubs can share performance percentages and get a better perspective on their own operations through benchmarking against comparable organizations.

Example Accounting for Inventory and COGS

The example in table 3.5 demonstrates how the purchase of goods flows through the financials, first through various stages of production on the balance sheet, and then onto the income statement as part of COGS.

A brewery purchased raw ingredients on February 20 for $5,000. On March 5 the ingredients are used in a batch of beer that is brewed. On March 20 the beer is kegged, and on April 2 the beer is sold for $15,000. The payment for the sale is received on May 2. Assume the beginning cash balance is $50,000.

Gross Profit

The difference between income and COGS is gross profit (also called gross margin).

Operating Expenses

Following gross profit is operating expenses. Operating expenses are those that are required to run the business, but not related to creating the product that is sold. Major categories include Sales and Marketing and General and Administrative.

Sales and marketing expenses

Sales and marketing expenses include the following:

- The salaries, payroll taxes, and benefits of sales and marketing employees
- Promotional items (give-away apparel, mugs, banners, etc.)
- Events such as festivals, promotions, and tastings

- On-site materials, such as tap handles, coasters, signs
- Advertising
- Promotion expenses (discounts)
  - If the promotion is a discount on beer, represent the revenue that would have been received as a contra-revenue account.
  - If the promotion is beer used for samples, move the COGS of the beer to a marketing account.

General and administrative expenses

General and administrative expenses include the following:

- The salaries, payroll taxes, and benefits of administrative employees
- General company insurance
- Legal and other professional fees
- Office supplies
- Interest expense
- Non-COGS utilities

Interest Expense

If a company carries a loan on the books, whether for a vehicle, bank loan, or any other interest-bearing instrument, it should break out the payments between principal and interest. The portion of payment related to interest should increase Interest Expense on the income statement and the portion related to principal should reduce the loan on the balance sheet.

TABLE 3.5 EXAMPLE OF TRANSITION FROM INVENTORY TO COGS

BALANCE SHEET						
	February 19	February 20	March 5	March 20	April 2	May 2
Cash	50,000	45,000	45,000	45,000	45,000	60,000
Accounts Receivable	0	0	0	0	15,000	0
Inventory: Raw Ingredients	0	5,000	0	0	0	0
Inventory: WIP	0	0	5,000	0	0	0
Inventory: Finished Goods	0	0	0	5,000	0	0
INCOME STATEMENT						
	February 19	February 20	March 5	March 20	April 2	May 2
Revenue	0	0	0	0	15,000	0
COGS	0	0	0	0	5,000	0
Gross Profit	0	0	0	0	10,000	0

Example Accounting for an Interest Expense

A brewery purchased a vehicle on June 10 for $25,000 (table 3.6). It paid $10,000 down and financed the remainder from the dealer. The payments are due the first of the month starting in August;, for purposes of this example, assume that the $600 payment is $500 principal and $100 interest. Assume the beginning cash balance is $50,000.

Depreciation

An asset is a resource with economic value that an entity owns or controls with the expectation that it will provide a future benefit. Fixed assets are items that are purchased for long-term use and are not likely to be converted quickly into cash. Fixed assets include large equipment items, such as tanks, and buildings and vehicles.

WHAT IS NOT A FIXED ASSET?

Inventory

Inventory is not a fixed asset because it is expected to be used in less than a year.

Items of small value (less than $2,500)

If a company has a de minimis accounting policy for expense items that cost less than $2,500, then those purchases are not considered fixed assets. This is an exception because by all other measures the item would be considered a fixed asset (e.g., kegs). Most breweries have a de minimis policy.

Fixed assets lose value with the passage of time due to wear and tear. In accounting, that reduction in value is recorded as depreciation. Every fixed asset falls into a certain class as defined by the Financial Accounting Standards Board (FASB), and each class has a defined useful life. Examples of asset classes are equipment, vehicles, furniture and fixtures, leasehold improvements, and software.

Classes and item types have assigned useful lives for the purposes of calculating depreciation. Most brewery equipment has a seven-year life.

Depreciation is a **non-cash expense**. **Amortization** is the same concept as depreciation but relates to intangible goods. Examples of intangible goods include architect fees, start-up expenses, and trademarks.

For over twenty years, the US government has created tax rules that allow taxpayers to write off fixed assets in the year of purchase. In other words, taxpayers do not have to take a portion of depreciation over several years; they may take it all in the beginning. While no tax legislation can be considered permanent, the options for accelerated depreciation have been in existence for a long time and are a major tool for business tax planning.

Because of these tax advantages a business may have two different numbers for a brewery's depreciation: book depreciation and tax depreciation. Book depreciation adheres to financial accounting rules,

TABLE 3.6 EXAMPLE OF PAYMENTS BETWEEN PRINCIPLE AND INTEREST FOR LOAN PAYMENT

BALANCE SHEET						
	Account Type	**June 9**	**June 10**	**July 31**	**August 31**	**September 30**
Cash	Asset	50,000	40,000	40,000	39,400	38,800
Vehicle	Asset	0	25,000	25,000	25,000	25,000
Vehicle Loan	Liability	0	(15,000)	(15,000)	(14,500)	(14,000)
INCOME STATEMENT						
		June 9	**June 10**	**July**	**August**	**September**
Revenue		0	0	0	0	0
COGS		0	0	0	0	0
Gross Profit		0	0	0	0	0
Interest Expense		0	0	0	100	100
Net Income		0	0	0	(100)	(100)

which ignores tax incentives. If a company chooses to record book depreciation in their own financials, and then takes advantage of accelerated depreciation on the tax return, there is a reconciliation on the return to show the difference between the two numbers. This is called a **book-to-tax difference**. Note that, for simplicity, most small breweries choose to make the depreciation on their books equal to tax depreciation. This practice does not adhere to GAAP.

For example, say a brewery owns a $16,000 truck with a useful life of five years. For book depreciation, the company will deduct a portion of the $16,000. On the tax return, the brewery may choose accelerated depreciation and will deduct the entire $16,000 in the year of purchase.

Table 3.7 shows an example of how to calculate book depreciation for an asset with a useful life of seven years. Assume that a company purchases a $30,000 tank with a seven-year useful life and a $10,000 salvage value.

TABLE 3.7 BOOK DEPRECIATION OF A FIXED ASSET WITH A SEVEN-YEAR LIFE

	Tank Value	Depreciation	Net Value
Date of Purchase	$30,000	0	$30,000
Year 1	$30,000	$1,429	$28,571
Year 2	$30,000	$2,857	$25,714
Year 3	$30,000	$2,857	$22,857
Year 4	$30,000	$2,857	$20,000
Year 5	$30,000	$2,857	$17,143
Year 6	$30,000	$2,857	$14,286
Year 7	$30,000	$2,857	$11,429
Year 8	$30,000	$1,429	$10,000

Each year the company will book as depreciation expense the amount shown in the Depreciation column. Most depreciation calculations follow a separate set of rules called the modified accelerated cost recovery system (MACRS). MACRS requires that one-half of a year's depreciation be taken in year one, as opposed to a full year. That is why the example in table 3.7 shows a Year 1 depreciation of $1,429 instead of $2,857.

Some small businesses choose to forego recording monthly depreciation, and instead will wait for their CPA to provide a journal entry for the year's depreciation after the tax return is prepared. In this situation, the company is recording depreciation that is equal to the tax amount, so there is no book-to-tax difference. GAAP rules require book depreciation, and therefore that is the preferred method of reporting.

Net Income versus EBITDA

Net Income and EBITDA are similar but different calculations. Net income is the bottom line, that is, the revenue after all expenses (table 3.8). **EBITDA** stands for earnings before interest, tax, depreciation, and amortization.

EBITDA is a measurement commonly used by business owners and investors because it allows an apples-to-apples comparison between companies. It also is a better broad indicator of the cash generated by the day-to-day business operations. Interest, taxes, depreciations, and amortizations can vary widely from company to company. For example, a brewery that does not use accelerated depreciation might appear to be a better investment due to a lower depreciation expense than if they used accelerated depreciation.

TABLE 3.8 EXAMPLE INCOME STATEMENT WITH EBITDA AND NET INCOME

	Year 1	Year 2	Year 3
Sales			
Wholesale	251,185	334,913	446,551
Retail	210,195	280,260	373,681
COGS			
Wholesale	151,696	202,261	263,014
Retail	40,155	56,873	75,830
Gross Profit	**269,529**	**356,039**	**481,388**
Sales & Marketing Expenses	83,679	73,099	81,911
Operating Expenses	434,335	300,728	333,145
Earnings before Tax, Interest, Depreciation & Amortization (EBITDA)	**(248,485)**	**(17,788)**	**66,322**
Depreciation	92,090	152,349	110,995
Interest Expense	30,383	27,862	25,206
Net Income (Loss)	**(370,958)**	**(197,999)**	**(69,869)**

Another example of business differences that affect EBITDA is interest. Consider a brewery funded with equity rather than debt. It will not have the interest expense that a brewery funded from debt will have.

For these reasons, EBITDA levels the playing field between different entities and provides a valuable measurement of operating performance.

KEY RATIOS: INCOME STATEMENT

Common key ratios related to the income statement are gross profit, EBITDA, and net income. These are generally expressed as a percentage relative to total revenue.

Gross Profit

Gross profit represents how much money remains to cover other operating expenses after covering the costs to manufacture a good. It may be expressed as a dollar amount or a percentage.

gross profit \$ = total revenue − total COGS

$$\text{gross profit \%} = \left(\frac{\text{total COGS}}{\text{total revenue}} \right) \times 100$$

EBITDA

EBITDA represents a company's profitability before factoring in interest, taxes, depreciation, and amortization. It is a helpful metric when comparing performance between different companies. It is also helpful for a high-level understanding of the cash-generating ability of an entity. EBITDA may be expressed as a dollar amount or a percentage.

EBITDA \$ = net income + interest + taxes + depreciation + amortization

$$\text{EBITDA \%} = \left(\frac{\text{net income + interest + taxes + depreciation + amortization}}{\text{total revenue}} \right) \times 100$$

Net Income

Net income is the "bottom line" and represents profitability after covering all expenses. This does not account for payment of debt principal, which may be a required cost but does not affect the income statement. Net income may be expressed as a dollar amount or a percentage.

net income \$ =
total revenue − total expenses (including COGS)

$$\text{net income \%} = \left(\frac{\text{net income \$}}{\text{total revenue}} \right) \times 100$$

WORDS OF WISDOM

What two or three KPIs do you find most useful when monitoring the success of your business?
Our various departments all have their own KPIs to help manage their specific department. From a CFO standpoint, I regularly monitor our product margins because I feel that is a KPI that needs to be actively monitored and managed. There is both a focus on pricing as well as our product costs. I also like to study revenue per barrel and operating costs per barrel to see how we are trending against historical figures. Our production team focuses on KPIs related to labor hours as compared to production levels, and yields compared to previous months/years.

Heather McCollum
CFO, Firestone Walker

4

CASH IS KING!

If you have ever run a business before, you understand that cash is the lifeblood of an organization. It's important to review historical periods to understand how cash is generated and spent, and even more important to look ahead to see how cash *will be* generated and spent. Future planning helps you foresee the cash required by your business on a day-to-day, month-to-month, and year-to-year basis.

The general principle of cash flow management is to shorten your cash conversion cycle. That is, speed up your cash inflows (e.g., payments from customers) and slow down your cash outflows (e.g., payments to vendors, purchase of inventory and equipment, loan repayments, etc.). To slow your outflows, consider negotiating or lengthening credit terms with your suppliers. Another way to affect cash flow is to manage your inventory effectively. By keeping minimum amounts of inventory, which can entail ordering little and often, you avoid having cash tied up in inventory. While you may have to forego bulk purchase discounts, it may be wiser to keep cash on hand. To speed up your cash inflows there are a few common practices that may help: billing regularly, chasing bad debt, securing a line of credit, and negotiating shortened payment terms with distributors.

CASH RESERVES

Remember the part in chapter 1's storyline when Erica was concerned about the business only having a small amount of cash on hand? It's a common concern for businesses of all sizes. How much cash *should* you have on hand? The amount will be different for every company, and it is influenced by factors such as industry sector, company size, and access to other capital. Of course, personal preference of the owner or manager is a factor as well.

In general, a business owner's cash reserves should cover three months of fixed costs. Fixed costs stay the same each month regardless of the level of production. Examples include rent, salaries, insurance, utilities, interest payments, and other similar costs. Debt service, that is, the amount you are required to pay in loan principal payments, should also be included in your calculation of required expenses. The idea is, if all sales stopped tomorrow, how much money would we need to keep working until sales come back online? Achieving cash on hand to cover three months of fixed costs may take a long time, but it should be your goal.

How do you start the good habit of setting aside cash for your reserves? I recommend having the money in a separate savings account so that it's less easy to dip into. And once you begin with a minimal amount set aside, keep building on it until you achieve the target amount of savings you identify as appropriate for your company. Set up a weekly or monthly sweep of funds into the account. You could choose to sweep, for example, 5% of that week's sales, or make it a flat dollar amount like $200 per week. The amount that you set aside is less important than the action of saving. It's a habit, and like all habits it requires self-discipline at first but then becomes easy.

Periodically, you should review your cash on hand to see if the cash reserves target needs to be increased. As businesses grow, so do their expenses. An early-stage brewery may have minimal fixed expenses, but as an organization grows the safety net of cash will be greater due to larger staff, rent, and full-scale operational costs.

STATEMENT OF CASH FLOWS

The **statement of cash flows** is a report that analyzes transactions in the past. It is the link between the balance sheet and income statement. The statement of cash flows shows you how money moves in and out of a company over a period of time. Many small business owners can be frustrated when they have no money in the bank, even though their income statement shows that income was made during a period. Studying the statement of cash flows can explain that quandary. There are several uses of cash that don't show up on the income statement. Consider the purchase of raw materials or tanks. Both purchases use cash, yet they affect only the balance sheet and not the income statement.

The statement of cash flows reports the impact on cash flow over a period of time from a company's operating, investing, and financing activities. It converts accrual accounting to cash basis accounting and shows how cash was used. The statement reflects how changes to account balances on the balance sheet affect cash.

Formatting the Statement of Cash Flows

In table 4.1, you can see that a statement of cash flows has three sections: operating, investing, and financing. The Operating Activities section includes basic operations involved in the making and selling of your product. The Investing Activities section represents transactions where money is invested back into the company, for example, buying fixed assets. The

TABLE 4.1 EXAMPLE STATEMENT OF CASH FLOWS

	Year 1	Year 2	Year 3
Cash Flow from Operating Activities			
Net Income	(370,958)	(197,999)	(69,869)
Depreciation	92,090	152,349	110,995
Increase in Accounts Receivable	(92,000)	(48,000)	(47,000)
Increase in Inventory	(15,000)	(3,000)	(4,000)
Increase in Accounts Payable and Credit Cards Payable	34,000	38,000	(16,000)
Net Cash Flow from Operating Activities	**(351,868)**	**(58,650)**	**(25,874)**
Cash Flow from Investing Activities			
Purchase of Fixed Assets	(177,910)	(244,439)	(110,995)
Net Cash Flow from Investing Activities	**(177,910)**	**(244,439)**	**(110,995)**
Cash Flow from Financing Activities			
Increase in Bank Loans	212,868	288,438	(199,306)
Capital Contributions	400,000	200,000	100,000
Net Cash Flow from Financing Activities	**612,868**	**488,438**	**(99,306)**
Net Increase in Cash	**83,090**	**185,349**	**(236,175)**
Cash at Beginning of Period	**0**	**83,090**	**268,439**
Cash at End of Period	**83,090**	**268,439**	**32,264**

Financing Activities section captures activities related to the financing of the operations, usually changes to bank loans or contributions/distributions.

Operating Activities

The Operating Activities section begins with net income or loss for the period and works through a reconciliation to arrive at the total cash from operations. The lines following the net income add back non-cash expenses (e.g., depreciation, amortization), and adjust for changes to inventory, other current asset accounts, and current liabilities. Any time that you increase inventory or other assets, it will result in a decrease to cash. For example, if a brewer buys $3,000 of hops then that transaction required cash, but that reduction in cash isn't included on the income statement because the purchase of hops is simply a swap of one asset, cash, for another, inventory.

If the hops were purchased with a credit card, or put on account to be paid later, then the amount of payables increases. Just as any increase to an asset makes cash go down, an increase to a liability makes cash go up. So, in the example of a $3,000 hop purchase just mentioned, you will see an adjustment down in cash for purchase of inventory and a corresponding cash adjustment *up* because the credit card liability or accounts payable liability has increased by $3,000. The expense, even though it is not yet paid, has been recorded as an expense and decreases net income. A cash flow statement may be prepared in the direct method or the indirect method. The indirect method is most common, so we will focus on that method. When preparing the statement via the indirect method, net income is the starting point and you reconcile back to the cash balance. Not all expenses on the income statement are cash expenses. Depreciation, for example, is an economic concept that represents the loss of value of assets over time, but it does not decrease cash. Therefore, it's a positive adjustment from net income to cash. Let's look at a few more examples to illustrate this point.

- A period-over-period increase in asset accounts makes cash decrease (and vice versa).
  - Example 1: Inventory increases from $1,000 to $2,000 period over period; this lowers cash because you had to purchase inventory.

  - Example 2: Accounts Receivable decreases from $20,000 to $15,000 period over period. This increases cash because you have collected more receipts from customers. If you have a $5,000 invoice to a client that is unpaid at the end of Month 1, then you have already recorded the sale on your income statement but you haven't received the cash. Then, if that payment is received in Month 2, it increases cash but it is not recorded on the income statement because you captured it in Month 1—the month it was earned.

- A period-over-period increase in liability accounts makes cash increase (and vice versa).
  - Example 3: Accounts Payable increases by $5,000; you have accounted for the Expenses on the income statement but not paid them, so cash goes up.

Investing Activities

The Investing Activities section includes activities that are intended to expand or improve the business. These are transactions not necessarily related to the current level of activity of the business, but, rather, they are purchases that will allow you to expand or improve operations. When you put in new tanks to expand capacity, you are investing in the business. The transaction hasn't hit the income statement because you have swapped cash for fixed assets, so you must account for the use of cash as an adjustment on the statement of cash flows. Likewise, if you upgrade to new equipment and sell the old equipment, then the proceeds received on the sale of the equipment show up in this section. For example, if you buy a new tank for $30,000, fixed assets increase and cash decreases; if you sell a tank for $10,000, fixed assets decrease and the proceeds received make cash go up by $10,000.

Financing Activities

The Financing Activities section is where you record money raised, paying back loans, and making distributions. If your brewery needs $300,000 for an expansion, you may raise that money in a few ways: borrow from a bank or other lender; raise it from new or existing investors; or pay for it yourself. Any time a loan increases or you receive money from investors, cash goes up. When you pay back the loan principal, or distribute profits to investors, cash goes down. For example, if $300,000 comes partially from a bank loan ($200,000) and partially from investors ($100,000), then the financing section will show an increase to cash from loan received and a second increase in cash to capital increase.

Calculating the Statement of Cash Flows

1. Net Cash Flow from Operating Activities
   a. Start with net income from the income statement
   b. Add in depreciation and other non-cash expenses
   c. Subtract Increase in Accounts Receivable
   d. Subtract Increase in Inventory
   e. Add increase in Accounts Payable and Credit Cards Payable
2. Net Cash Flow from Investing Activities
   a. Subtract purchase of Fixed Assets
   b. Add proceeds from the sale of Fixed Assets
3. Net Cash Flow from Financing Activities
   a. Add Increase in Loans
   b. Subtract payment of loan principal (the portion of loan payments related to interest expense is included in the income statement, and therefore is part of net income)
   c. Add Capital Contributions
   d. Subtract payments of distributions to owners
4. Net Increase in Cash is the sum of all three sections
5. Cash at End of Period is Net Increase in Cash plus Cash at Beginning of Period

CASH FLOW FORECASTING

While the statement of cash flows uses historical information to analyze how cash was used in a prior period, cash flow forecasting looks forward to plan for future needs. A cash flow template will help you plan smartly and should be customized to suit the needs of your own business. Use it on a regular basis and make it part of the normal financial review process. The regular analysis of finances is a non-negotiable part of owning the business. Some months you may review finances and not be surprised at all, but it is vitally important you stay attuned to the rhythm of the business's finances so that you can detect issues and opportunities as they arise.

The needs of a brewery constantly change, and your cash flow forecast will highlight any shortfalls in cash that will need to be bridged. Many established, viable, and even profitable businesses fail due to cash not being available when they need it most. Cash flow is especially important for a start-up because initial expenses must be carefully balanced with the resources available. Cash flow forecasts need to be honest, not hopeful. It's important to be as realistic as possible. You probably already have an income statement forecast, but a cash flow forecast will require building a balance sheet forecast.

Good cash flow management is critical to running a successful business. As a brewer, you may be passionate about your craft, but don't forget you're in business to make a profit—otherwise you simply have a hobby. It's a simple principle, but one that can occasionally become lost amid dreams of building a large presence. You won't be able to stay in business, however, unless you have cash.

There will probably be points in your business's life cycle when you must make a choice to expand. This may require a large investment in equipment. The lag time between spending money on an expansion and seeing the cash come in from the additional beer made can stress brewery finances. This means you should accumulate sufficient cash in your company's bank account to pay all the bills in the meantime, whether these relate to invoices from suppliers, employees' wages, rent, tax, or anything else. So, for a large capital build, not only do you need to raise enough money to build the new equipment, you also need to cover any additional operating cash requirements as you ramp up sales to cover this additional overhead. You can cover these cash requirements from a variety of sources, for example, retained earnings, loans, or investor contributions.

The Importance of Cash

Everyone loves cash, but few breweries focus specifically on improving cash flow. Positive cash flow is critical to ensure brewers can pay the bills, re-invest in the business, and take dividends. The first step is to keep an eye on metrics that measure cash flow. For example, the Days on Hand in inventory, or Accounts Receivable Days in accounts receivable.

Watch inventory levels. If not managed properly, they will suck the life out of your cash flow. A typical brewery may spend a significant amount on raw materials and packaging. Keeping on top of your inventory value has never been more important.

Keep on top of your Accounts Payable and determine if you are paying your invoices too quickly—the Average Payable Days calculation is a useful measurement. Review vendor payment terms—do your vendors give you 30 days to pay, but you're paying in 20? Examine your invoice approval and payment process. Who can approve a payment? Are they really looking at what money goes out?

You may want to consider establishing a line of credit with your bank to buffer cash in lean times, and also consider the benefits of leasing for large equipment needs. Leasing can take the stress off of cash flow and leverage the expertise of a leasing company.

Manage profitability. Identify what you need for profit and work backward from there. Beginning with the end in mind, you can create a Profit Plan. When you increase profit, you increase cash flow. Here is an example:

- $ Sales growth of 3.5% over prior year
- $ Margin 40% of sales
- $ Operating expense 30% of sales
- $ Profit 10% of sales

Hold regular weekly meetings to review actual results compared to the plan. Use these meetings as an opportunity to train and educate your team on how the financials work, and how they can make a big difference in achieving the profit goal.

Kary Shumway
Founder of Beer Business Finance

5

INTERPRETING FINANCIAL STATEMENTS

As you get more comfortable with financial terms and key ratios, you'll find that financial statements tell a rich story. You can trace the entire history of a company through its financial reports. The key is to understand what the accounts represent, and to have context for the data. Financial data for one period hold very little value compared with what you can learn from viewing trends over a range of time and across business lines. Learning how to interpret financial information is likely the most valuable skill that this book can provide to you. Yes, it's important to understand the mechanics of accounting and, yes, it is important to understand things like depreciation, but, in the long run, it's likely that someone else will be doing that work. One day you'll be in the position where financial reports are given to you, and you'll need to be able to understand and interpret them without being given the background data. This skill is critical for business owners, and it will serve you well in other aspects of life. The language of business is always relevant.

CHART OF ACCOUNTS

The first key to useful data is to organize the chart of accounts in a way that best serves the company's needs. Think about how you will want to see the information and who else will want to see the information. Here are a few points to consider:

- What are your revenue streams?
  - Production brewery
  - Taproom or brewpub

If you are only a production brewery with no retail activity, then you will only have a production department. If you have a retail component, it may be a taproom or a full-fledged restaurant, or perhaps both. In that case you would have one department for the retail channel (taproom or restaurant), a second department for the production activity, and a third department for sales and administration.

- Will you be holding any other managers accountable for results of the business? Remember to think long term. In the early stages, you—the owner-operator—may be in charge of all aspects of the company. As you grow, you may want to hire department heads who direct the activity of the department and therefore are held accountable for the financial results.
  - Will a restaurant manager receive bonuses for hitting certain targets, such as restaurant labor as a percentage of restaurant revenue?
  - Will the sales manager be given a budget to manage?

Chances are, you'll want to see the performance of each revenue stream separately. You will need to see the same expense but only for one part of the business. For example, there will be a need for brewery supplies and restaurant supplies to be kept separate. The mechanics of making the information display in a useful manner will depend on the accounting software that you are using. The guiding principle for setting up the chart of accounts is to have the fewest accounts possible to give you adequate detail. There are companies that, because of size of operation and detail desired by management, end up with hundreds of accounts. This can become unwieldy to manage and requires strict organization just to make sure the transactions are recorded to the correct account. Usually, the size of the chart of accounts has a direct correlation with the size of the business and size of its accounting department. I'll discuss two different common accounting scenarios.

The most common accounting set up that we encounter in our firm is a brewery that runs QuickBooks™ Online. QuickBooks has two ways to segment data: classes and locations. Normally, classes will be set up for Admin, Brewery, and Taproom/Restaurant. Locations will be used if there are different physical locations at different addresses, whether in the same city or different cities.

The class and location functions are very useful for segmenting data so that you can review the performance of each location on its own, and reports can be filtered to only show data pertaining to a particular class or location. Individual transactions are tagged with a class and/or location.

A major drawback of QuickBooks is that most versions of the software are not designed to provide a classified balance sheet, meaning that it does not have the ability to show separate columns for different cost centers; it can only classify income statements. QuickBooks Enterprise is, at the time of publication, the only version of the software that can provide a classified Balance Sheet, and Enterprise is only available in standalone desktop format (i.e., not online).

Another accounting software package commonly used by breweries is OrchestratedBEER, or "OBeer."

OBeer allows the use of divisions (fig. 5.1), which is similar to classes. A user can filter reports to only see divisions, so the outcome is materially the same as running a report by class in QuickBooks. However, at the transaction level, specific transactions can't be tagged with a particular division. The result is that you may end up with multiple accounts for the same kind of expense, but for different divisions. For example, you may have 60000-00 Supplies (Admin division), 60000-01 Supplies (Brewery division), and 60000-02 Supplies (Taproom division). When pulling reports, you can hide any accounts that have a zero balance, which is helpful to keep the data to a reasonable size. Unfortunately, this increases the tedium of data entry for the accounting team. You can see how easy it would be to choose the wrong account, and how the system will require a larger chart of accounts.

INTRODUCTION TO FINANCIAL STATEMENTS

In our fictional company in chapter 1, the owners were shown a financial analysis during a financial review that visually displayed how they were doing. Just a few simple calculations gave the owners a shorthand for understanding their business. Each key ratio and each financial statement tells a story.

Balance Sheet

The balance sheet shows the health of a company at a moment in time. In a *very* simple manner of speaking, assets are good, liabilities are bad, and equity is the difference between the two. Think of equity as the owners' skin in the game. While you can't see the performance of a company on a balance sheet, the net income (which *does* measure performance) is represented as part of the equity section.

The balance sheet in table 5.1 shows that assets exceed liabilities, the former being positive for both months. However, when you dig deeper, you see that the current ratio (current assets/current liabilities) is unhealthy. June's current ratio is 1:3.7 but, ideally, it should be 2:1.

The current ratio was introduced in chapter 3 on page 70.

- Internal Use Only - Some Divisions / Segments may not be shown -

Balance Sheet

December 31, 20XX (compared to June 30, 20XX)

ⓘ

Assets		12/31/20XX		6/30/20XX		Difference	%
Current Assets							
Bank Accounts:	$	525,185	$	782,044	$	(256,859)	(32.8%)
Accounts Receivable:	$	366,665	$	240,945	$	125,721	28.5%
Inventory:	$	290,262	$	228,040	$	62,222	27.3%
WIP:	$	33,425	$	1,377	$	32,047	999.9%
Total Current Assets:	$	**1,215,537**	$	**1,252,406**	$	**(36,869)**	**(2.9%)**
Long Term Assets							
Fixed Assets:	$	2,173,767	$	2,110,636	$	63,130	3.0%
Accumulated Depreciation:	$	(869,738)	$	(853,406)	$	(16,332)	(1.9%)
Total Long Term Assets:	$	**1,304,028**	$	**1,257,230**	$	**46,798**	**3.7%**
Total Assets:	$	**2,519,565**	$	**2,509,636**	$	**9,929**	**0.4%**

Liabilities		12/31/20XX		6/30/20XX		Difference	%
Current Liabilities							
Accounts Payable:	$	228,733	$	318,983	$	(90,250)	(28.3%)
Lines of Credit:	$	70,168	$	170,168	$	-	- %
Credit Card Liabilities:	$	1,699	$	2,157	$	(458)	(21.2%)
Payroll Liabilities:	$	7,041	$	37,870	$	(30,829)	(81.4%)
Other Tax Liabilities:	$	(81,205)	$	(30,452)	$	(50,752)	(166.7%)
Other Current Liabilities:	$	91,407	$	71,884	$	19,523	27.2%
Total Current Liabilities:	$	**317,844**	$	**470,610**	$	**(152,766)**	**(32.5%)**
Long Term Liabilities							
Notes Payable:	$	883,537	$	957,637	$	(74,100)	(7.7%)
Total Long Term Liabilities:	$	**883,537**	$	**957,637**	$	**(74,100)**	**(7.7%)**
Total Liabilities:	$	**1,201,381**	$	**1,428,247**	$	**(226,866)**	**(15.9%)**

Equity		12/31/20XX		6/30/20XX		Difference	%
Equity							
Equity:	$	817,560	$	832,860	$	(15,300)	(1.8%)
Period Closing Accounts:	$	(2,000)	$	(2,000)	$	-	- %
Total Equity:	$	**815,560**	$	**830,860**	$	**(15,300)**	**(1.8%)**
Profit Period:	$	**502,624**	$	**250,529**	$	**252,095**	**100.6%**
Total Equity:	$	**1,318,184**	$	**1,081,389**	$	**236,795**	**21.9%**
Total Liabilities and Equity:	$	**2,519,565**	$	**2,509,636**	$	**9,929**	**0.4%**

Figure 5.1. An example of an OrchestratedBEER balance sheet.

TABLE 5.1 BALANCE SHEET
JUNE 30, 20XX
CURRENT MONTH VS. PRIOR MONTH

	Jun 30, 20XX	May 31, 20XX	$ Change
ASSETS			
Current Assets			
Checking/Savings			
Checking	9,902.03	1,706.32	8,195.71
Total Checking/Savings	9,902.03	1,706.32	8,195.71
Total Current Assets	9,902.03	1,706.32	8,195.71
Inventory	17,291.85	18,662.20	(1,370.35)
Net Fixed Assets			
Brewery Equipment and Machinery	159,179.17	153,679.17	5,500.00
Leasehold Improvements	54,329.36	54,329.36	0.00
Start-Up Costs	6,804.00	6,804.00	0.00
Total Fixed Assets	220,312.53	214,812.53	5,500.00
TOTAL ASSETS	**247,506.41**	**235,181.05**	**12,325.36**
LIABILITIES & EQUITY			
Liabilities			
Current Liabilities			
Accounts Payable			
Accounts Payable	19,801.32	19,801.32	0.00
Total Accounts Payable	19,801.32	19,801.32	0.00
Credit Cards			
Credit Card	9,734.23	3,167.82	6,566.41
Total Credit Cards	9,734.23	3,167.82	6,566.41
Other Current Liabilities			
Payroll Liabilities	7,000.00	0.00	7,000.00
Total Other Current Liabilities	7,000.00	0.00	7,000.00
Total Current Liabilities	36,535.55	22,969.14	13,566.41
Long Term Liabilities			
Loans Payable			
SBA Loan	163,740.00	133,740.00	30,000.00
Total Loans Payable	163,740.00	133,740.00	30,000.00
Total Long Term Liabilities	163,740.00	133,740.00	30,000.00
Total Liabilities	200,275.55	156,709.14	43,566.41
Equity			
Members Equity	125,000.00	125,000.00	0.00
Retained Earnings	(2,069.99)	(2,069.99)	0.00
Net Income	(75,699.15)	(44,458.10)	(31,241.05)
Total Equity	47,230.86	78,471.91	(31,241.05)
TOTAL LIABILITIES & EQUITY	**247,506.41**	**235,181.05**	**12,325.36**

If a balance sheet's liabilities exceed the assets, then the company is in a weak financial position. This isn't to say that there's something wrong with a business that shows more liabilities than assets. In a start-up, it is natural for liabilities to exceed assets because a brewery is a highly capital-intensive operation. It takes a lot of money to get a brewery off the ground, and then even more time is needed for revenue to appear.

While a snapshot of the company's finances may show the company is leveraged (i.e., using debt to finance its operations), an accurate opinion can't be formed without considering what has come before and what is expected to come in the future. Period-over-period analysis of the balance sheet can help users get a sense of the company's progress and the health of its operations.

Income Statement

The income statement (or profit and loss statement) shows a company's performance over a period of time. The income statement answers the question, "Am I making money?" It seems to be the report that is most intuitively understood by business owners. Revenue is what you sold, expenses are what you spent, net income is what's left over. A positive net income number shows that the company made money during a period; a net loss number shows that a company lost money during a period. But this is just the beginning of the insights that can be gained from analyzing the data in an income statement.

The income statement tells the owner or manager if the economic engine that has been built is operating in an efficient, effective manner. By analyzing the relationship of costs to revenue, you can determine if you are spending too much on a certain line item. For example, a common benchmark is that food costs should not exceed one-third of food revenue. If the income statement shows a different result, then action should be taken. Back in chapter 1 (pp. 32–35), Mike and Erica met with their CPA to review income metrics such as revenue growth, net income as a percentage of revenue, and gross margin. These helped Mike and Erica understand if their business model was working.

Statement of Cash Flows

The statement of cash flows shows how money was accumulated or spent over a period of time. Cash is the lifeblood of an organization, so analyzing only the balance sheet and income statement is foolhardy. Consider a brewery that is profitable and popular. The growth is happening so quickly that the owners need to expand and buy more tanks to increase capacity. While the income statement looks good, and the balance sheet looks good, the owners are feeling pressure because most of the cash being generated on the income statement is going to pay for new tanks. The more beer there is to brew, the more bodies are needed. So, the company has hired two more people. Now the payroll expense has increased. The net income still shows a profit, but the ability to meet payroll is getting harder and harder. Every two weeks management is wondering if they are going to make it. Eventually, the cracks get larger and the company ends up with multiple employees leaving at once due to payroll being missed; the beer can't be brewed, orders dry up because the distributors can't count on the product being available. The company significantly contracts, a victim of its own success. Proper understanding of the cash flow and planning for future cash flow needs could have mitigated the negative effects of rapid growth.

Customizing Financial Reports

Context is critical when interpreting financial reports. Management needs to consider both a **vertical analysis** and a **horizonal analysis**. Vertical analysis means a comparison of accounts within one period. For example, Food Revenue and Food COGS, or Front of House Labor as a percentage of Restaurant (or Taproom) sales. Remember in the first chapter when Mike and Erica created revenue accounts for Beer: Packaged, Beer: Draft, Merchandise, and Food; and COGS accounts for Beer COGS: Packaged, Beer COGS: Draft, Merchandise COGS, and Food COGS (p. 9)? This was done to allow for vertical analysis. Horizontal analysis means a comparison of performance from one period to another: total revenue for the last quarter versus the quarter before, or gross margin by month for one quarter, for example.

Vertical analysis helps answer questions relating to whether you are spending too much on a certain account (e.g., "Is labor too high?"). Horizontal analysis helps identify trends the business is experiencing overall (e.g., "How much should we expect sales to dip in Q4 of the coming year?").

MONTHLY FINANCIAL REVIEW

You can't manage what you can't measure.

—Peter Drucker

One of the most important parts of the management of a company is to review the financial results regularly and methodically. This allows a company to see if they are performing according to plan. Every month a company should review the full set of financial reports: balance sheet, income statement, and statement of cash flows.

To be truly effective, the financial review session should occur at the same time each month, with the same information shared with the same managers. This should happen as quickly as possible after the month has been closed to maximize the opportunity to act on the results. Going back to our story in the first chapter, one of the most important things Mike and Erica's CPA did was to encourage them to look at their financial

reports on a regular basis. Consistency is key so that trends can be established and understood. Fundamentally, financial review is looking at what did happen, comparing it to what you wanted to happen, asking questions to understand why there is a difference between what you wanted versus what happened, and taking steps to adjust in order to meet the desired outcome.

Each month the leadership team should review a full set of financial reports and a few KPIs.

MONTHLY FINANCIAL REVIEW CHECKLIST

☐ Balance sheet comparative to prior period and prior year

☐ Income statement comparative to prior period and prior year

☐ Income statement by class or division for current period

☐ Statement of cash flows for current period

☐ Budget versus actual current period and year-to-date

☐ KPI review

☐ Establish action items and assign responsibility

WORDS OF WISDOM

How frequently do you review financial reports and what reports are most helpful?

I look at the cost of all of our beers. I also review restaurant numbers for costs, and I review all overtime and ask managers to keep it reasonable. P&L [income statement] reports each month and quarter. Weekly sales on both sides of business [brewery and restaurant]. Staying aware of what cash will be coming in and when is important. We pay bills one week and then payroll the next. At this time the numbers have gotten pretty large. It's very important to watch cash.

Do you use departmental budgets? Do you use them to hold department heads accountable?

Not at this time.

What two or three KPIs do you find most useful when monitoring the success of your business?

1. Cash—which way it is going, and if it's down, figure out why.
2. Cash flow modeling is helpful.
3. COGS—watching what it costs to make all of our products.

What do you know now that you wish you knew when you were starting your operation?

Real numbers. The process of writing a business plan and intelligently analyzing what might happen is very difficult. I have found areas where we were right on and areas where things did not work out and changes had to be made. Many assumptions were made—plans that you thought you would do that just were not practical.

John Harris
Ecliptic Brewing

INTERPRETING FINANCIAL STATEMENTS

Let's imagine that a brewery's income statement for the month of January shows a loss of $5,000. At face value this may seem to be a negative result, but when compared against the budget for January the company made $10,000 more that month than they budgeted. January is historically a very slow month for this brewery, and even in strong years it's expected to be a month in which the company loses money.

Additionally, let's assume that the January result is compared to the same month last year. This reveals that the prior year result for the month was a loss of $13,000. Again, through comparison, you see that the current year's loss of $5,000 is much better than normal.

Let's consider another example: the cash on the balance sheet is $300,000 at the end of January. This seems like a strong number, and you assume that this covers the desired margin of safety. But cash by itself has little meaning unless you consider how it is relevant.

> Margin of safety is introduced in chapter 4.

Thinking the brewery is in good health, you look at the current ratio. The current ratio measures liquidity by comparing current assets (in this case Cash, AR, and Inventory) to your current liabilities (assume AP and Credit Card Debt). Liquidity refers to how fast you can convert something to cash. For this example, you find that the combination of cash, AR, and Inventory totals $450,000, and AP and Credit Card Debt is $500,000. This makes the current ratio 0.9 ($450,000 / $500,000). We can see that the brewery is in a weak position because its ability to pay obligations as they come due is less than the amount of obligations that are on the books. (The desired current ratio is 2.) Thus, through comparison, this one number, the current ratio, provides useful information about your ability to make upcoming payments and purchases.

> See chapter 3 (p. 70) for more information on the current ratio.

How frequently do you review financial reports and what reports are most helpful?

We prepare a year-over-year comparative P&L [income statement] monthly and review it monthly; we also prepare a budget-to-actual report for the month ended and year to date. We prepare a quarterly cash flow report that is mostly used for internal accounting purposes versus for management review. I find the comparative P&L to be the most useful; and for month-end accounting procedures, I find a current month to prior month comparative analysis to be of most help in spotting accounting errors as well as identifying trends.

Heather McCollum
CFO, Firestone Walker

The exercise on pages 98 and 99 uses an example income statement that you might see in a brewery. The majority of this income statement was generated from typical company accounting software (in this case, QuickBooks). We added a few rows to track critical key performance indicators.

Period-over-Period Growth

Period-over-period growth measures the change in revenue in a certain time frame—in the case of the exercise on pages 98 and 99, quarters—relative to the control period. The control period is another period of time against which you'd like to compare the current period's performance. Examples would be February 2020 vs January 2020 (where January is the control period), or February 2020 vs February 2019 (where February 2019 is the control period). This can be adapted for any time frame (e.g., monthly, quarterly, annually). Period-over-period growth is an indicator of how quickly a company is expanding. The formula for quarter-over-quarter growth is

$$\text{period-over-period growth} = \left(\frac{\text{current period revenue} - \text{prior period revenue}}{\text{prior period revenue}}\right) \times 100$$

COGS %

The cost of goods sold percentage (COGS %) tells business owners how much of every dollar of revenue goes toward the cost of readying the beer to be sold. A lower value is desirable. The formula is

$$COGS\ \% = \left(\frac{current\ period\ COGS}{current\ period\ revenue} \right) \times 100$$

Production breweries should have a COGS % of around 60%.

Gross Profit %

The gross profit percentage tells business owners how much of every dollar of revenue is available for operating costs and profit. It can be thought of as the complement to COGS %. The money left over after COGS will cover any non-production payroll, rent, insurance, taxes, interest, sales, and marketing expenses. For gross profit %, a higher value is desirable.

There are two ways to calculate gross profit percentage:

$$gross\ profit\ \% = \left(\frac{current\ period\ gross\ profit}{current\ period\ revenue} \right) \times 100$$

or

$$gross\ profit\ \% = 100\% - COGS\ \%$$

Production breweries should have a gross profit percentage of around 40%.

Payroll %

The payroll percentage helps business owners measure whether they are over- or understaffed relative to revenue. The formula is

$$payroll\ \% = \left(\frac{current\ period\ total\ payroll\ expenses}{current\ period\ revenue} \right) \times 100$$

Best practice is to include wages and salaries, payroll taxes, bonuses, and employee benefits (e.g., health insurance and retirement plans) when calculating payroll percentage.

NOI %

The net operating income percentage (NOI %) shows management how much of each dollar of revenue the company made after all expenses were paid. The formula is

$$NOI\ \% = \left(\frac{current\ period\ net\ operating\ income}{current\ period\ revenue} \right) \times 100$$

Continued on page 98

EXERCISE Using what you have learned, try completing the numbers that should be in the marked fields below.

BREWERY XYZ | PROFIT AND LOSS
JANUARY 20XX–DECEMBER 20XX

	Jan–Mar, 20XX	Apr–Jun, 20XX	Jul–Sep, 20XX	Oct–Dec, 20XX	
Income					
Gross Receipts					
Sales of Merchandise Income	43,978.45	41,160.47	12,621.31	3,408.11	
Sales of Product Income	264,153.83	232,398.14	2,471.83	2,536.00	
Beer - Kegged		18,599.49	108,793.15	165,554.92	
Beer - Packaged		58,088.10	209,850.20	219,262.70	
Total Sales of Product Income	$ 264,153.83	$ 309,085.73	$ 321,115.18	$ 387,353.62	
Shipping, Delivery Income			2.77		
Taproom Income	95,898.51	134,976.77	167,619.09	199,069.31	
Uncategorized Income	346.94	911.54	8,662.49	710.61	
Uncategorized Income-1				1,571.00	
Total Income	$ 404,377.73	$ 486,134.51	$ 510,020.84	$ 592,112.65	
Quarter-over-Quarter Growth					Answers on page 100
Cost of Goods Sold					
Beer - COGS	154,710.32	80,836.73	2,217.63	3,261.51	
Beer - Kegged		3,752.88	22,132.75	34,742.28	
Beer - Packaged		23,292.03	77,714.63	80,706.24	
Beer - Work In Progress Loss		4,920.54	14,242.25	24,112.18	
Total Beer - COGS	$ 154,710.32	$ 112,802.18	$ 116,307.26	$ 142,822.21	
Merchandise - COGS	7,398.33	7,701.21	22,741.62	25,357.91	
Supplies & Materials - COGS	845.26	52.61	2,970.71	371.58	
Taxes Excise/TTB - COGS					
State Excise - COGS	5,324.90	7,490.00	399.55	8,336.51	
Total Taxes Excise/TTB - COGS	$ 5,324.90	$ 7,490.00	$ 399.55	$ 8,336.51	
Total Cost of Goods Sold	$ 168,278.81	$ 128,046.00	$ 142,419.14	$ 176,888.21	
COGS %	42%	26%	28%		Answers on page 100
Gross Profit	$ 236,098.92	$ 358,088.51	$ 367,601.70	$ 415,224.44	
Gross Profit %	58%	74%	72%		Answers on page 100
Expenses					
Advertising	151.01	1,120.00	13,325.07	10,758.77	
Advertising/Promotional	6,535.00	4,769.60	2,393.00	1,452.49	
Auto	18.50			150.00	
Gas	338.16	310.55	234.05	358.84	
Total Auto	$ 356.66	$ 310.55	$ 234.05	$ 508.84	
Bank Charges	521.26	0.00		(267.53)	
Commissions & fees	2,188.54	3,466.94	1,779.56	4,837.33	

	Jan–Mar, 20XX	Apr–Jun, 20XX	Jul–Sep, 20XX	Oct–Dec, 20XX
Conferences/Trade Shows		369.00	1,075.00	
Donation			125.00	425.00
Cash	710.00	260.00	2,965.00	1,360.00
Total Donation	**$710.00**	**$260.00**	**$3,090.00**	**$1,785.00**
Dues & Subscriptions	1,096.89	1,085.46	1,645.88	2,250.13
Guaranteed Payments	4,000.00	8,000.00	4,000.00	15,000.00
Insurance	4,596.04	3,183.24	2,270.07	3,567.07
Interest Expense	10,603.69	10,520.54	10,509.00	10,500.70
Job Materials				
Legal & Professional Fees	2,140.00	5,853.75	5,151.55	2,484.65
Meals and Entertainment	1,043.01	979.81	1,686.02	1,360.02
Meals and Entertainment - Onsite			121.94	773.46
Office Expenses	283.52	183.82	286.44	371.73
Other General and Admin Expenses		104.00		
Payroll Expenses				
Company Contributions				
Health Insurance	4,478.64	3,577.74	3,577.74	8,118.43
Total Company Contributions	**$4,478.64**	**$3,577.74**	**$3,577.74**	**$8,118.43**
Taxes	9,092.77	9,128.29	10,414.37	12,679.96
Wages	88,469.92	101,993.13	122,842.90	71,176.59
Total Payroll Expenses	**$102,041.33**	**$114,699.16**	**$136,835.01**	**$91,974.98**
Payroll %	**25%**	**24%**	**27%**	
Promotional		465.05	12.00	
QuickBooks Payments Fees	9.50	42.18	13.00	17.00
Refund			(21.00)	
Rent or Lease	17,641.15	35,074.89	39,143.09	37,654.81
Repair & Maintenance	9,136.41	5,114.63	8,052.66	2,758.54
Research	121.15	521.85	334.82	127.30
Shipping and delivery expense	1,088.18	1,694.61	463.93	641.07
Supplies	18,940.78	15,920.38	37,705.59	32,640.87
Taxes & Licenses	2,963.50	626.83	10,058.06	(2,960.63)
Travel	1,688.72	1,710.46	3,301.12	863.81
Utilities	18,252.80	20,934.62	31,230.17	32,394.85
Total Expenses	**$206,109.14**	**$237,011.37**	**$314,696.03**	**$251,495.26**
Net Operating Income	**$29,989.78**	**$121,077.14**	**$52,905.67**	**$163,729.18**
NOI%	**7%**	**25%**	**10%**	

Answers on page 101 (Payroll %)

Answers on page 101 (NOI%)

ANSWERS

BREWERY XYZ | PROFIT AND LOSS
JANUARY 20XX–DECEMBER 20XX

	Jan-Mar, 20XX	Apr-Jun, 20XX	Jul-Sep, 20XX	Oct-Dec, 20XX
Income				
Gross Receipts				
Sales of Merchandise Income	43,978.45	41,160.47	12,621.31	3,408.11
Sales of Product Income	264,153.83	232,398.14	2,471.83	2,536.00
Beer - Kegged		18,599.49	108,793.15	165,554.92
Beer - Packaged		58,088.10	209,850.20	219,262.70
Total Sales of Product Income	$264,153.83	$309,085.73	$321,115.18	$387,353.62
Shipping, Delivery Income			2.77	
Taproom Income	95,898.51	134,976.77	167,619.09	199,069.31
Uncategorized Income	346.94	911.54	8,662.49	710.61
Uncategorized Income-1				1,571.00
Total Income	$404,377.73	$486,134.51	$510,020.84	$592,112.65
Quarter-over-Quarter Growth		20%	5%	16%
Cost of Goods Sold				
Beer - COGS	154,710.32	80,836.73	2,217.63	3,261.51
Beer - Kegged		3,752.88	22,132.75	34,742.28
Beer - Packaged		23,292.03	77,714.63	80,706.24
Beer - Work In Progress Loss		4,920.54	14,242.25	24,112.18
Total Beer - COGS	$154,710.32	$112,802.18	$116,307.26	$142,822.21
Merchandise - COGS	7,398.33	7,701.21	22,741.62	25,357.91
Supplies & Materials - COGS	845.26	52.61	2,970.71	371.58
Taxes Excise/TTB - COGS				
State Excise - COGS	5,324.90	7,490.00	399.55	8,336.51
Total Taxes Excise/TTB - COGS	$5,324.90	$7,490.00	$399.55	$8,336.51
Total Cost of Goods Sold	$168,278.81	$128,046.00	$142,419.14	$176,888.21
COGS %	42%	26%	28%	30%
Gross Profit	$236,098.92	$358,088.51	$367,601.70	$415,224.44
Gross Profit %	58%	74%	72%	70%
Expenses				
Advertising	151.01	1,120.00	13,325.07	10,758.77
Advertising/Promotional	6,535.00	4,769.60	2,393.00	1,452.49
Auto	18.50			150.00
Gas	338.16	310.55	234.05	358.84
Total Auto	$356.66	$310.55	$234.05	$508.84
Bank Charges	521.26	0.00		(267.53)
Commissions & fees	2,188.54	3,466.94	1,779.56	4,837.33

Side formulas:

$$16\% \quad \left(\frac{592,112.65-510,020.84}{510,020.84}\right) \times 100$$

$$5\% \quad \left(\frac{510,020.84-486,134.51}{486,134.51}\right) \times 100$$

$$20\% \quad \left(\frac{486,134.51-404,377.73}{404,377.73}\right) \times 100$$

$$30\% \quad (\$176,888.21 / \$592,112.65) \times 100$$

$$70\% \quad (\$415,224.44 / \$592,112.65) \times 100$$

	Jan-Mar, 20XX	Apr-Jun, 20XX	Jul-Sep, 20XX	Oct-Dec, 20XX
Conferences/Trade Shows		369.00	1,075.00	
Donation			125.00	425.00
Cash	710.00	260.00	2,965.00	1,360.00
Total Donation	$710.00	$260.00	$3,090.00	$1,785.00
Dues & Subscriptions	1,096.89	1,085.46	1,645.88	2,250.13
Guaranteed Payments	4,000.00	8,000.00	4,000.00	15,000.00
Insurance	4,596.04	3,183.24	2,270.07	3,567.07
Interest Expense	10,603.69	10,520.54	10,509.00	10,500.70
Job Materials				
Legal & Professional Fees	2,140.00	5,853.75	5,151.55	2,484.65
Meals and Entertainment	1,043.01	979.81	1,686.02	1,360.02
Meals and Entertainment - Onsite			121.94	773.46
Office Expenses	283.52	183.82	286.44	371.73
Other General and Admin Expenses		104.00		
Payroll Expenses				
Company Contributions				
Health Insurance	4,478.64	3,577.74	3,577.74	8,118.43
Total Company Contributions	$4,478.64	$3,577.74	$3,577.74	$8,118.43
Taxes	9,092.77	9,128.29	10,414.37	12,679.96
Wages	88,469.92	101,993.13	122,842.90	71,176.59
Total Payroll Expenses	$102,041.33	$114,699.16	$136,835.01	$91,974.98
Payroll %	25%	24%	27%	16%
Promotional		465.05	12.00	
QuickBooks Payments Fees	9.50	42.18	13.00	17.00
Refund			(21.00)	
Rent or Lease	17,641.15	35,074.89	39,143.09	37,654.81
Repair & Maintenance	9,136.41	5,114.63	8,052.66	2,758.54
Research	121.15	521.85	334.82	127.30
Shipping and delivery expense	1,088.18	1,694.61	463.93	641.07
Supplies	18,940.78	15,920.38	37,705.59	32,640.87
Taxes & Licenses	2,963.50	626.83	10,058.06	(2,960.63)
Travel	1,688.72	1,710.46	3,301.12	863.81
Utilities	18,252.80	20,934.62	31,230.17	32,394.85
Total Expenses	$206,109.14	$237,011.37	$314,696.03	$251,495.26
Net Operating Income	$29,989.78	$121,077.14	$52,905.67	$163,729.18
NOI%	7%	25%	10%	28%

16%
(91,974.98/
592,112.65)
×100

28%
(163,729.18/
592,112.65)
×100

6

FINDING BREAKEVEN AND COSTING BEER

BREAKEVEN

Breakeven is the point at which the gross profit of your sales for a period will cover all other operating expenses for the period. Every incremental sale after the breakeven point will result in net income. Breakeven may be expressed in dollars or as units sold. Note that the term breakeven is different than contribution margin. In chapter 1, Mike and Erica ran an analysis of how much they would need to sell in order to cover fixed costs, which is related to contribution margin. Contribution margin is revenue per unit less variable costs per unit. Breakeven, on the other hand, takes into account all expenses, regardless of whether they are fixed or variable, and helps managers understand how many units need to be sold before making a profit.

$$\text{Breakeven (\$)} = \frac{\text{operating expenses}}{\text{gross profit percentage}}$$

$$\text{Breakeven (units)} = \frac{\text{operating expenses}}{\text{gross profit dollars per unit}}$$

For example, assume that you sell a product for $10 per unit and it costs you $7 per unit. Therefore, your gross profit is $3 per unit, or 30%. Assume your operating expenses for a month are $400. Let's apply that to the formulas above:

Breakeven expressed in dollars

$$\text{Breakeven (\$)} = \frac{\$400}{30\%}$$
$$= \$1,334$$

Revenue	$1,334
COGS	($934)
Gross Margin	$400
Operating Expenses	($400)
Net Income	$0

Breakeven expressed in units

$$\text{Breakeven (units)} = \frac{\$400}{\$}$$
$$= 134 \text{ units}$$

Revenue	$1,340
COGS	($934)
Gross Margin	$406
Operating Expenses	($400)
Net Income	$6

You can get even more granular by specifying how many units of each SKU you will need to sell to break even. Table 1.17 in chapter 1 shows a visual representation of the breakeven calculation that Trae shares with Mike using Wagener Brewing's financial data.

> A **stock keeping unit** (SKU) is a product identification code. An SKU in a brewery references a specific brand in a specific pack type.
>
> The "pack type" refers to the size and format in which a product is sold. Common pack types include half-barrel keg, 50-liter keg, quarter-barrel keg, sixth-barrel keg (also called a sixtel), 12×22 (twelve 22 fl. oz. bottles), 4×6×12 (four six-packs of 12 fl. oz. cans or bottles), and 6×4×16 (six four-packs of 16 fl. oz cans).

FINDING THE ACCURATE COST OF BEER

How do you find the true, accurate cost of your beer? This is an important question for every brewer. The accuracy of your data depends on how good your record keeping system is. As your staffing, resources, and record keeping systems evolve, so does your ability to accurately cost beer.

WORDS OF WISDOM

What do you know now that you wish you knew then?
It's wise to put a strong emphasis on taproom volume and activity. At 1,000 bbl. production, one needs to project at least 40%–50% of that volume to be pushed through the tasting room. If too much emphasis is placed on packaged beer (bottle or can) in the early stages, it can be a long hill to climb up. The product margin in the taproom is the lifeline in the first year, maybe for years to come, unless very generously funded with liquidity.

Focus on keg distribution before packaged. Margins on keg distribution (as opposed to bottles or cans) can be good enough to implement early on. Focus only on one or two territories early on, particularly your own locale. If the beer isn't well received locally, it will likely be hard to gain traction out of your home market.

Guard against being undercapitalized. Don't underestimate operating expenses: chemicals, pest control, security, janitorial service, operating supplies, music license fees (don't forget this if you play music in your taproom), boiler maintenance program (if using steam), CO_2 and tank rentals, and keg lease program, to name a few.

Don't skimp on developing a social media program. Also protect unique names and images with trademarks.

Richard Strauss
Columbia Craft

Brewpubs and Taprooms

The *Brewers Association Cost of Goods Sold Manual* contains a useful discussion on best practices in the brewery and brewpub or taproom, some of which is distilled here.[1]

Brewpub operations can vary greatly, and the combination of a service-based industry (the restaurant) and manufacturing-based industry (the brewery) adds complexity. Food sales most often account for the majority of a brewpub's business, so brewpubs commonly use accounting guidance from the National Restaurant Association, which has a suggested general ledger account list for standardizing restaurant financials.

A best practice is to transfer beer from the brewery operations to the brewpub at a wholesale cost. This allows a company to analyze their financial performance by class (i.e., brewery and brewpub/taproom) as if the transactions to the other department were at arm's length.

Breweries should account for taproom activities as a department classified within the Selling expenses category of the income statement. Taproom expenses are not COGS and should not be classified in the COGS category of the income statement.

Draft losses should be assigned to the correct department's COGS. If you have the ability to calculate draft losses that occur in production versus losses that occur on the taproom floor, then break out the expenses appropriately. In the taproom, losses are usually from

---

[1] *Brewers Association Cost of Goods Sold Manual* (Boulder, CO: Brewers Association, 2018), section 2, pp.8–14, https://www.brewersassociation.org/educational-publications/cost-of-goods-sold.

a few areas: foaming issues associated with the product or draft system, the pouring technique of taproom staff, or improper accounting of product by bar staff (e.g., not charging or ringing in beers).

As with draft losses, brewery or brewpub breweries should track and account for draft beer poured, free of charge, for employees in the taproom. Tracking employee beers will help isolate draft losses. Point of sale (POS) systems allow for employee beers to be accounted for, and, to get accurate results, an expectation should be established that all transactions are entered into the system regardless of whether or not the beer is sold.

Labor

One of the biggest costs that a brewery will incur is the cost of labor. If you have an operation with multiple departments (e.g., taproom and brewery), you should consider breaking out labor by department so that you have a clear idea of the expense of each. Let's go over how breaking out payroll by department works.

When using a payroll company, the money is removed from the checking account in one transaction, so all departments are lumped together; there's one withdrawal from the bank account for net pay and one withdrawal for payroll tax. This is where bookkeeping will require a little more attention to detail; it will be more a more complex bookkeeping entry but will result in useful data. The first step is to have the payroll company set up departments: Brewery, Taproom, Sales, and Admin. Every employee is coded to a department that allows for departmental totals on payroll reports.

For employees that split time between two departments the business has a couple of options. First, ask the payroll company if they can automatically distribute wages and payroll taxes across two departments. If that's not an option, then there may be a little extra work when adding those entries into your accounting system. The employee's wages and payroll taxes for each pay period will need to be manually calculated across the appropriate departments. Make sure to add in Sales and Admin payroll accounts, even if the owners/founders aren't getting paid yet. Remember that you are building the chart of accounts to meet needs now and in the future. Those accounts will be ready when you need them.

> See detailed information on the chart of accounts in chapter 2.

Setting up classes, or divisions, for Brewery, Taproom, Admin, and Sales will alleviate the need for four separate payroll and payroll tax accounts. However, there is one significant drawback in doing this: some of the labor is considered COGS and some is an operating expense. For instance, consider a brewer whose activities are a direct input into the beer that's sold. Likewise, wait staff and cooks' labor is directly tied to the sale of food. So, the problem is that some labor needs to show up in COGS while some labor is overhead and shows up in operating expenses. The use of classes won't put the expense in the proper area of the income statement.

TABLE 6.1 TEMPLATE FOR RECORDING PAYROLL VIA TWO TRANSACTIONS
TRANSACTION 1 – DEBIT PAYROLL LIABILITIES, CREDIT CASH

Account	Debit	Credit	Class	Description
Payroll Liabilities	$XXX		Admin	To record withdrawal for payroll
Cash		$XXX	Admin	To record withdrawal for payroll

TRANSACTION 2 – CREDIT PAYROLL LIABILITY, DEBIT PAYROLL BY DEPARTMENT

Account	Debit	Credit	Class	Description
Payroll	$XXX		Brewery	To record production payroll
Payroll Tax	$XXX		Brewery	To record production payroll taxes
Payroll	$XXX		Taproom	To record taproom payroll
Payroll Tax	$XXX		Taproom	To record taproom payroll taxes
Payroll Liabilities		$XXX	Admin	To record total payroll liabilities

Wages related to management staff of both the brewery and taproom will be part of Operating Expenses. It is important to realize that just because the brewery and taproom have their own COGS Labor accounts, not *all* the department's labor will be included in COGS.

> See Chapter 3 for a discussion of what goes into COGS.

To properly capture payroll expense, make two accounting entries. The first is a simple debit to payroll liability and a credit to cash. The second is a journal entry to credit payroll liability and debit the payroll by department. This is another step forward in your accounting knowledge, and once you master the payroll journal entry you will have become a bit more proficient with bookkeeping skills. Table 6.1 (previous page) is a template to record a journal entry. Use it each time when you do payroll.

Look at the department summary in table 6.2, using example data taken from an anonymous brewery. The amount shown as a credit to cash in the journal entry (table 6.1, transaction 1) equals the amount taken from the bank account. And that's how the bank activity gets into the system without recording an expense. Table 6.3 shows the two journal entries to be made to correctly record payroll by department. The original $980 of tip liability is recorded on the books as part of the sales entry for taproom revenue.

Taproom COGS

To accurately calculate taproom COGS, first make sure that the chart of accounts either has accounts that separate taproom COGS from production COGS or isolates the revenue and expenses as a separate class only for taproom activity. Taproom revenue accounts should include Beer: Draft, Beer: Packaged, and, if applicable, Food, Nonalcoholic (N/A) Beverages, Liquor, and Wine. Taproom COGS should include the cost of the beer (at arm's length cost), labor (including payroll tax and benefits), and overhead (rent, utilities, maintenance, etc.).

Breweries should use caution because the "sale" of the beer from the brewery to the taproom creates a

TABLE 6.2 SAMPLE PAYROLL REPORT, DEPARTMENT SUMMARY
CHECK DATE: 9/1/20XX

Department	Current Pay	
0100 - Taproom	**Employee**	**Employer**
Earnings Paid		
Regular Earnings	$3,267.55	
Declared Tips	$980.00	
Total Gross Pay/Hours	$4,247.55	
Taxes/Deductions Withheld		
Federal Withholding Tax	$467.23	
State Income Tax	$297.33	
Social Security	$263.35	$263.35
Medicare	$61.59	$61.59
Other Taxes	$21.24	$212.38
Total Net Pay	**$3,136.82**	**$537.32**
0200 - Brewery	**Employee**	**Employer**
Earnings Paid		
Regular Earnings	$4,725.32	
Salary Earnings	$4,000.00	
Total Gross Pay/Hours	$8,725.32	
Taxes/Deductions Withheld		
Federal Withholding Tax	$959.79	
State Income Tax	$610.77	
Social Security	$540.97	$540.97
Medicare	$126.52	$126.52
Other Taxes	$43.63	$436.27
Total Net Pay	**$6,443.65**	**$1,103.75**
COMPANY TOTALS	**Employee**	**Employer**
Earnings Paid		
Regular Earnings	$7,992.87	
Declared Tips	$980.00	
Salary Earnings	$4,000.00	
Total Gross Pay/Hours	$12,972.87	
Taxes/Deductions Withheld		
Federal Withholding Tax	$1,427.02	
State Income Tax	$908.10	
Social Security	$804.32	$804.32
Medicare	$188.11	$188.11
Other Taxes	$64.86	$648.64
Total Net Pay	**$9,580.46**	**$1,641.07**

TABLE 6.3 SAMPLE PAYROLL JOURNAL ENTRY

TRANSACTION #1

Account	Debit	Credit	Class	Description
Payroll Liabilities	$14,613.94		Admin	To record withdrawal for payroll
Cash		$14,613.94	Admin	To record withdrawal for payroll

TRANSACTION #2

Account	Debit	Credit	Class	Description
Payroll	$3,267.55		Taproom	To record taproom payroll
Payroll Tax	$537.32		Taproom	To record taproom payroll taxes
Payroll	$8,725.32		Brewery	To record production payroll
Payroll Tax	$1,103.75		Brewery	To record production payroll taxes
Payroll Liabilities		$14,613.94	Admin	To record total payroll liabilities
Tip Liability	$980		Admin	To record tips paid to employees

duplication within the system that must be manually reconciled to avoid "selling" the same beer twice or recognizing income that doesn't exist. Generally, you will see three classes: Brewery, Taproom, and Admin. The double transaction is corrected in the Admin class. Correcting the double transaction allows accurate reporting for each division, and accurate reporting for the entire enterprise. This approach applies to brewpubs as well. Transferring beer at a wholesale cost allows brewpubs to analyze bar costs on an apples-to-apples basis compared to the costs involved in buying another brewery's beer through a distributor.

TOOLS FOR COSTING

Most businesses rely on technology to some degree, regardless of the industry in which they operate. Software specific to the brewing industry is available that addresses unique considerations like inventory management, production planning, restaurant point of sale engagement, and product delivery logistics. As a company grows, its technology needs will evolve. Most breweries start with a basic tool such as Excel; as the operations become more complex the technology needs to adapt and serve those needs.

Planning and Start-Up Phase

At the planning and start-up stage, the tools for product costing may be basic. Usually the brewer develops recipe spreadsheets that have costs associated with each beer. A cost is calculated per batch, a yield is assumed, and the total cost of the batch is divided by the barrels that are expected to be yielded. If a brewer in this stage finds the time to go through a costing exercise, then the standard cost is applied to the beer sold. We saw this method being used in the chapter 1 story, when Mike was learning how to combine detailed recipes for each brand to the ingredients cost (tables 1.12 and 1.13 on p. 27). Using the advice he got from Wagener Brewing, Mike could take the total volume of, for example, IPA sold and apply the standard cost from the recipe spreadsheet (see table 1.15 for an example). The actual revenue of the IPA would be taken from the POS system, and in a separate spreadsheet he would have put in the assumed cost for the volume sold to arrive at the gross margin for that beer, as was shown for Wagener Brewing in table 1.17. This is a reasonable approach, but the results will not be accurate.

The cost in your recipe sheet represents your standard cost per batch. In other words, this is what it should cost if all of your assumptions actually occurred. Real life will be different than what you planned, and your true COGS will not match calculated COGS. Common reasons for this variance include yields that vary from what was predicted and fluctuations in the cost of ingredients. The more detailed your assumptions and the shorter period of time between updates to the recipe sheet, the closer your calculated cost will be to your actual cost.

This is not to dismiss the standard cost method of calculating COGS. The exercise is still helpful because it gives you a good idea of profitability, but you need to recognize its limitations. For start-up breweries, however, this may be the best option given the organization's available time and resources.

Adolescence

As a company evolves into adolescence, it is likely that the brewery will purchase basic inventory management software. Inventory management software allows a company to create a bill of materials for each item that is manufactured, and to trace those costs through to the sale of the product. There are a number of software products available to breweries. At time of publication this includes Ekos Brewmaster, OrchestratedBEER, Unleashed, BREWD, VicinityBrew, and BeerRun. Most allow you to pull reports that show the actual cost and profit margin not only by brand, but also by SKU and batch. This level of detail can be extremely helpful because you can identify specific issues in the production process that lead to loss or inefficiencies. From a financial perspective, it also allows

companies to see the profitability of each product. In today's highly competitive market, this level of detail gives brewers insight to help them make wise choices with their product mix.

An example of the type of report that can be generated by inventory software is shown in table 6.4.

Maturity

At a larger scale of production, when annual volume increases have slowed, the key to profitability is having a hawkish view of costs. At this stage, most brewers use software for production planning and materials resource planning (fig. 6.1). Prior to this point, production planning may have been done on a whiteboard or spreadsheet. The planning software may be modules built in to an existing software package, or it may be separate software that integrates with inventory management and accounting. The most integrated solution is to have one system that includes accounting, inventory management, production planning, and customer management. The efficiency of entering an item into the system only once saves time and guards against error. This is essential when the operation gets to a mature size.

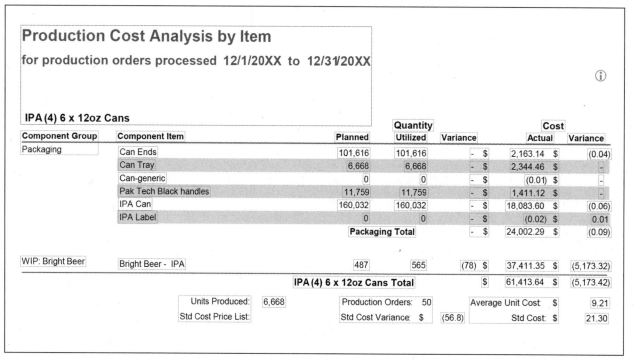

Production Cost Analysis by Item

for production orders processed 12/1/20XX to 12/31/20XX

IPA (4) 6 x 12oz Cans

Component Group	Component Item	Quantity Planned	Quantity Utilized	Variance		Cost Actual		Variance
Packaging	Can Ends	101,616	101,616	-	$	2,163.14	$	(0.04)
	Can Tray	6,668	6,668	-	$	2,344.46	$	-
	Can-generic	0	0	-	$	(0.01)	$	-
	Pak Tech Black handles	11,759	11,759	-	$	1,411.12	$	-
	IPA Can	160,032	160,032	-	$	18,083.60	$	(0.06)
	IPA Label	0	0	-	$	(0.02)	$	0.01
			Packaging Total	-	$	24,002.29	$	(0.09)
WIP: Bright Beer	Bright Beer - IPA	487	565	(78)	$	37,411.35	$	(5,173.32)
	IPA (4) 6 x 12oz Cans Total				$	61,413.64	$	(5,173.42)

Units Produced:	6,668		Production Orders:	50	Average Unit Cost	$	9.21
Std Cost Price List:			Std Cost Variance: $	(56.8)	Std Cost:	$	21.30

Figure 6.1. Excerpt of OrchestratedBEER Product Cost report.

TABLE 6.4 COPY OF BATCH - AVERAGE COSTS

Averages the cost per batch per product where the batch status is complete.

PRODUCT : WINTER ALE

Batch Number	Start Date	Batch Unit Cost	Batch Total Cost
123	1/2/20XX	$75.58	$2,849.23
456	1/7/20XX	$86.12	$6,123.09
789	1/28/20XX	$91.59	$3,251.57
			AVG $4,074.63
Winter Ale Totals		AVG $84.43	**SUM $12,223.89**

PRODUCT : IPA

Batch Number	Start Date	Batch Unit Cost	Batch Total Cost
012	1/4/20XX	$91.10	$4,243.30
			AVG $4,243.30
IPA Totals		AVG $91.10	**SUM $4,243.30**

PRODUCT : BLONDE ALE

Batch Number	Start Date	Batch Unit Cost	Batch Total Cost
345	1/28/20XX	$94.76	$2,274.26
678	1/16/20XX	$112.38	$3,798.42
901	1/9/20XX	$136.59	$1,516.17
			AVG $2,529.62
Blonde Ale Totals		AVG $114.58	**SUM $7,588.86**

PRODUCT : RED ALE

Batch Number	Start Date	Batch Unit Cost	Batch Total Cost
234	1/16/20XX	$76.62	$1,264.21
			AVG $1,264.21
Red Ale Totals		AVG $76.62	**SUM $1,264.21**

PRODUCT : PORTER

Batch Number	Start Date	Batch Unit Cost	Batch Total Cost
890	1/31/20XX	$63.43	$1,363.78
1234	1/23/20XX	$69.63	$3,001.09
			AVG $2,182.44
Porter Totals		AVG $66.53	**SUM $4,364.87**

PRODUCT : GOSE

Batch Number	Start Date	Batch Unit Cost	Batch Total Cost
5678	1/17/20XX	$73.61	$1,464.79
			AVG $1,464.79
Gose Totals		AVG $73.61	**SUM $1,464.79**
			AVG $2,831.81
Grand Totals		AVG $88.31	**SUM $31,149.91**

WORDS OF WISDOM

From my experience, maintaining open lines of communication and having a strong dedication to teamwork are two giant steps toward success. The goals for each department need to be respected and supported by all other departments. In order to accurately cost your product (goal of the accounting team), which leads to better visibility into pricing and, thus, meeting or exceeding margin expectations (goal of the sales team), you need strong communication and attention to detail by the brewers, cellarman, and packaging to ensure each bill of materials [costing recipe] is kept current and production is accurately tracked. Inversely, for inventory to steadily turn over and to avoid selling out of a product too quickly, or even having to dump out-of-date stock, the production team relies heavily on communication from the sales and marketing team and accurate inventory handling by the warehouse. One position is no more critical than another; they all need to be highly functioning to find long-term success. Make sure you are starting your road trip into this industry with fully inflated tires.

Mel Smith
Controller, Melvin Brewing (2016–18)

OPTIONS FOR GROWTH

A well-informed brewer who understands the specific elements of cost is better equipped to set prices appropriately. The first rule of pricing is to set prices so that you can reach breakeven. Beyond that, you should be able to price to achieve profit targets.

How much to charge is a complicated question. What is the competition doing? How much are people willing to pay? How are the beers marketed? In what channels are they sold? What volumes are you looking for with a particular SKU? There is no right answer that will work for all breweries. In this chapter, I'll go over a few fundamental considerations.

What is your sales strategy? Even this is not a clear question. There are several elements that make up a brewery's sales strategy:

- **Self-distribution versus third-party distribution**
  If selling your beer to accounts, will you be driving around to sell and deliver, or will you sign with a distribution company who will deliver the beer for you? (Please note that I did not say that the distributor would sell your beer for you. I believe that successful breweries do not put the responsibility to sell their beer in the hands of their distributor.

Distributor relationships are different for each brewery. The level of service will lie somewhere on a continuum between simply being a delivery mechanism for beer, and an indispensable business partner relationship.)

EXPERT ADVICE

Each state has different rules regarding self-distribution. At time of writing, most states allowed some form of self-distribution. Common limitations include a ceiling on the quantity that can be self-distributed or a minimum size of brewery that is allowed to self-distribute. The Brewers Association keeps a current list of state and local laws[1], which can help with the decision on whether self-distribution is right for your brewery.

- **Retail versus wholesale**
  Are you focusing on selling direct to consumers over your own counter, or are you selling wholesale to accounts (e.g., other bars, stores)?
- **Packaged versus draft**
  Are you offering your beer in bottles and cans, or just kegs?

---

[1]	https://www.brewersassociation.org/government-affairs/franchise-law-resources/

- **Restaurant versus taproom**
  If selling over your own counter, do you have a full restaurant or just a taproom with limited food options? The distinction usually hinges on what kind of food and level of service you are offering.

- **On-premises versus off-premises**
  On-premises sales means that the beer will be consumed on-site (your own taproom, or at another bar or restaurant). Off-premises sales means that the beer will be sold to-go and consumed off the premises of the seller (e.g., sold at a grocery or convenience store).

- **Contract brewing**
  Are you producing beer for someone else?

Almost every brewery's sales strategy has some combination of these elements. Think of these options as different stocks in an investment portfolio. If you have stock market investments, you would probably want to be well diversified: some blue chips, some emerging funds, large-caps, mid-caps, etc. Likewise, choose your go-to-market methods similarly so that you can diversify. In the discussion that follows I will talk about pricing tactics self- versus third-party distribution and retail versus wholesale, but in the real world these will not be siloed.

SELF-DISTRIBUTION VERSUS THIRD-PARTY DISTRIBUTION

There are pros and cons to both forms of distribution. Table 7.1 is a short, and certainly not exhaustive, list.

The biggest differentiators between the two models are, in self-distribution you will have more control over your product and you'll keep more of the margin, but you'll also have more expenses to execute the distribution. A common practice is for small breweries to start with self-distribution, build brand awareness, and within a few years transition to a third-party distributor who then may offer a payment to the brewery for distribution rights. Traditional wisdom would say that brands who get a bonus have a better chance of being represented well by the distributor, because the distributor has a vested interest in the brand.

TABLE 7.1 COMPARING SELF-DISTRIBUTION AND THIRD-PARTY DISTRIBUTION

SELF-DISTRIBUTION		THIRD-PARTY DISTRIBUTION	
Pros	**Cons**	**Pros**	**Cons**
Brewery keeps all margin – upwards of 30% that would go to the distributor. Brewery is in control of how your brand is merchandised in retail environments, and which accounts it is in.	Need employees to deliver beer. Difficult to scale due to logistics. Need to purchase delivery vehicle. All responsibility for delivering product rests with brewery. Difficult to get appointments with decision-makers.	Possibly will receive a signing bonus from the distributor. (These are increasingly rare and they are fully taxable.) Turnkey sales for supplier. Brewery will not be responsible for delivering the beer. Distributors can often provide detailed, useful data about depletions.	A large part of the PTR (price to retailer) stays with the distributor, usually 30%. Distributor management is a big job. Brewery is competing with all other craft brands in the distributor's book. Depending on state laws, the distributor may own the rights to distribute a brand for life. Very difficult to get out of contracts. Less strategic flexibility. Difficult to move to another distributor due to the buyout clauses or franchise law rules.

WORDS OF WISDOM

What should you know about self-distribution versus third-party distribution?

Be very aware of the margin impact. You'll pay a distributor 30% of the wholesale price to distribute your beer. You must have a good grip of your cost structure to know how much incremental sales this requires to be net neutral from a contribution perspective—it isn't 30%! Let's take an example using some round numbers.

Assume $150 keg prices [to retail], a marginal cost of $75 a keg, a Free on Board (FOB) of $100 with a distributor, and that you're currently selling 1,000 kegs a year. Self-distributing, you'll make $75 a keg × 1,000 kegs, so $75,000. By hiring a distributor you'll be making $25 a keg ($100 − $75) × 1,000 kegs, so $25,000. So, by giving away 33% of your price by using a distributor, you've given away 66% of your margin, which means you'll need to sell three times the amount you were selling when self-distributing to make the same total contribution. Therefore, the 33% loss of revenue by hiring a distributor means you have to brew (and sell!) three times the amount of beer you were selling while self-distributing to be net neutral.

	Distributor	Self-Distribution
Revenue	$100	$150
Cost	$75	$75
Margin per Unit	$25	$75
Units Sold	1,000	1,000
Total Margin	$25,000	$75,000

What should you know about on- versus off-premises sales?

Off-premises growth is very hard to grow when self-distributing. One-off drops are fine—we used to deliver once every six weeks to stores when self-distributing. Specialty grocery and bottle shops can work around that kind of schedule, but to expand into larger stores you need to be able to service multiple drops to stores per week, which most small breweries can't do. Therefore, if your brewery's goal is to grow off-premise sales, distributors can be a fundamental enabler of success.

Adam Robbings
Reuben's Brews

Just as the brewing industry has evolved rapidly since the turn of the century, so has the alcohol distribution industry. Distributors are merging or acquiring, and also restructuring their organizations. In the late 1990s the average distributor held less than 200 SKUs in its portfolio, which meant that each product got a decent share of attention. By the late 2010s the average distributor was handling over 1,000 SKUs (see table below). This dramatic increase results in less attention per brand, and a more intense fight for shelf space.

Year	Average SKU
1999	185
2003	200
2006	263
2008	470
2010	536
2012	657
2014	981
2016	1,025

Source: NBWA Distributor Productivity Report

RETAIL VERSUS WHOLESALE

Another sales strategy is to focus on retail sales. This is the taproom model where all beer is sold over your own counter, dock sales of kegs, or packaged beer to go. The benefit of the taproom retail model is that it's by far the most profitable, because your sales price is higher and the associated costs are lower. In a retail environment the raw materials cost of beer sold is about 20%. The drawback is that sales are limited to your location. Of course, brewers can always add additional taprooms and increase revenue, but each location has a ceiling of revenue caused by limitations such as retail square footage and hours of operation. Nonetheless, a taproom operator can do quite well.

What did you wish you knew about retail when you opened?

Be aware of POS systems that take a transaction fee. For small taprooms, we do lots of very small transactions. One taster here, one or two pints there. We didn't want to have a minimum order requirement, so when someone ordered a $2 taster and paid by card, that cost us around $0.50 with our original POS system. Obviously not sustainable! Systems with set percentage fees, like Square, are so much better for our business—the customer can get what they want, and we can survive the transaction fees.

Adam Robbings
Reuben's Brews

If you choose to scale your business by adding wholesale sales (either via a distributor or through self-distribution), then you will have larger revenues, but there's no guarantee that will translate to a larger net income on the bottom line. In order to increase your net income, you must attach margin to every product that you sell. Every unit must contribute to covering the cost of operating expenses. Without margin attached to each product, you will enter a cycle where you are spending more to make the beer than you can sell it for, and no money will flow to the bottom line. If appropriately priced, the volume you sell will translate to more income, but in order to be sure of that, the cost of each SKU must be carefully considered. Here is a common pricing model:

Revenue	
Less: (Variable Costs)	
Contribution Margin	
Less: (Fixed Costs)	
Net Profit	

Note that in this pricing model we designate costs as either variable or fixed. Variable costs are costs that increase in total as the quantity sold increases. Fixed costs are costs that stay the same regardless of the quantity sold, within a relevant range. Examples of variable costs include most COGS, such as raw materials and excise tax. Examples of fixed costs include all salaried employees (as opposed to hourly production employees), rent, and insurance.

Now let's apply real numbers to this model. We'll use example numbers from the sale of a case of four six-packs of 12 fl. oz. cans of IPA to a distributor:

Revenue	$20.95
Less: (Variable Costs)	($10.70)
Contribution Margin	$10.25
Less: (Fixed Costs)	($7.53)
Net Profit	$2.72

Here is a list of most types of expenses that should be considered as part of your variable costs:

Direct materials
Packaging materials
Hourly production employees
Utilities specific to production
Excise tax
Marketing cost
Hourly taproom or brewpub employees

Table 7.2 is a chart of pricing in a craft beer bar environment. In this chart we assume that the bar is buying a keg from a brewery or distributor.[2] You can see that the cost of draft beer is commonly 20% the sales price of a pint.

Contribution margin is a product's price minus all associated variable costs, resulting in the incremental profit earned for each unit sold. The total contribution margin generated by an entity represents the total earnings available to pay for fixed expenses and to generate a profit.

---

[2]   http://blog.bar-i.com/how-to-price-draft-beer

TABLE 7.2 PRICING AND MARGIN FOR CRAFT BEER IN BAR ENVIRONMENT

Cost per ½ BBL keg	Cost per 14.5 oz. serving	Retail price	Margin per pint
$70	$0.51	$2.55	$2.04
$80	$0.58	$2.92	$2.34
$90	$0.66	$3.28	$2.63
$100	$0.73	$3.65	$2.92
$110	$0.80	$4.01	$3.21
$120	$0.88	$4.38	$3.50
$130	$0.95	$4.74	$3.80
$140	$1.02	$5.11	$4.09
$150	$1.09	$5.47	$4.38
$160	$1.17	$5.84	$4.67
$170	$1.24	$6.20	$4.96
$180	$1.31	$6.57	$5.26
$190	$1.39	$6.93	$5.55
$200	$1.46	$7.30	$5.84

On a per unit basis, the taproom retail model has the best economic return, but you are limited in output. Wholesale distribution offers a path to mass distribution and the potential to grow into a regional or even a national brewery. Each brewery has a unique definition of success, and the right sales strategy will lie somewhere in this continuum of options.

WORDS OF WISDOM

You operate in Central America. How is craft beer accepted in that part of the world?

I love operating in less developed craft beer markets. The runway is a little bumpier but it's also much longer than it is in North America or some other places. I think having a personable customer-facing team is especially important to explain "why craft?" But, if you do a decent job, you can really open people's eyes and get them excited to try something new.

How is your pricing different than pricing of traditional Central American beers?

Well, compared to the generic continental lagers, we're more expensive. That said, we're retailing pints at our pub for $4, which is cheaper than any brewpub pint I've heard of in the US. It's all relative. Cost of doing business (and cost of living) is lower down there so pricing must be lower also.

What percentage of your audience in Nicaragua is expats versus native Nicaraguans?

I would say expat and tourists versus Nicaraguans is 65% to 35%.

In what channels do you sell in Nicaragua, and how are they different than the US? For example, in the US common channels might be bars/restaurants, grocery, convenience stores.

We're almost exclusively retail in Central America but changing that soon through the development of our Costa Rican production facility. Our distribution and sales channels plan for Costa Rica is pretty well balanced and similar to our strategy in the US.

The US has a three-tier system that requires sales through a distributor. Does anything like that exist in Nicaragua?

Nope! We'll be using our own sales reps creating new points of distribution and filling orders in Costa Rica and hiring a third-party delivery service. The main challenge that does exist, however, is that pay-to-play is basically legal. The macro beer company in Costa Rica offers discounted pricing to their highest volume accounts across their beer imports and liquor that they distribute in exchange for exclusivity commitments from retailers. In other words, these retailers aren't allowed to buy any sort of alcohol from any other supplier or distributor. This type of "blocking" is pretty common in Latin America across many different industries.

Matt Greenberg
San Juan del Sur Cerveceria, Nicaragua

8

OPERATING BUDGETS

Budgets are the most often ignored, but possibly most critical, component of financial management. A **budget** expresses the goals and objectives of an organization in numbers. They are helpful to keep financial performance on track, to hold key team members accountable, and can be a fantastic tool to develop employee engagement.

The budgeting process is not entirely an accounting task. The accounting department is typically charged with expressing the budget in financial terms, but the responsibility to write the budget is a shared effort among various departments. Each department should deliver a reasonable goal that supports the long-term vision of the company. The budgeting process is a rewarding experience for all involved because it provides an opportunity to review the business performance of the past at a micro level and encourages learning from prior periods. It also requires a company to clearly define lines of authority and responsibility.

The budgeting process requires a series of revisions and can take several months. In addition to being a practice of discipline and organization, drawing up a budget is an opportunity to build a stronger team. Budgets have a greater chance of acceptance if all levels of management have provided input into the budgeting process. Ideally, managers at each level will have provided input and agreed to the coming period's stated targets. This reinforces a team commitment to departmental and company goals. Budgets also provide a basis for evaluation. As an employee moves up to a higher level of managerial responsibility, a greater number of costs will fall under that employee's control. Therefore, when used for evaluation, budgets should only include the accounts that are under that manager's control.

A sample budget calendar is in appendix D.

TYPES OF BUDGET

A budget is a plan, and it may be expressed in dollars (financial budgets) or units (operating budgets). Operating budgets may be non-financial in nature. For example, defining a sales budget allows you to create your production plan; the production plan will inform your raw materials and direct labor budget, which are examples of operating budgets. Operating budgets should be completed before the financial budget is complete. Most small breweries will not have multiple departments with their own budgets. Even if only a few people are writing the budget for the entire company, I recommend approaching the project in the same sequence as a larger organization.

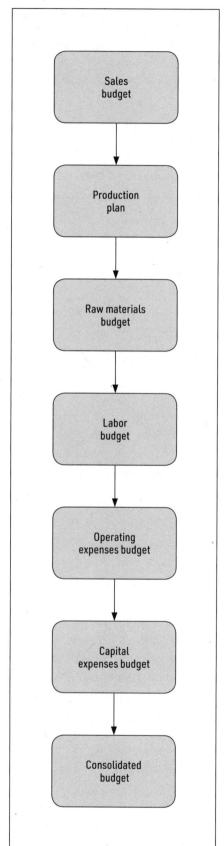

Figure 8.1. Preparation of departmental budgets for an organization should follow the correct sequence.

The proper sequence for the preparation of budgets is sales budget, production plan, raw materials budget, labor budget, operating expenses budget, capital expenses budget, and consolidated budget (fig. 8.1). Ideally, each budget will be displayed on a monthly frequency to provide more detail.

WORDS OF WISDOM

Do you use departmental budgets? Do you use them to hold accountable department heads?

We prepare departmental budgets in order to prepare a company-wide annual budget but, primarily, it is just the sales and marketing department who are held accountable for their budgets. We only recently starting preparing company-wide budgets but have been using budgets in sales and marketing for years. We haven't yet found an effective way to budget for production costs—other than labor—such that we can hold the department heads accountable.

Heather McCollum
CFO, Firestone Walker

Sales Budget

Writing the sales budget can be a huge undertaking, depending on the size of your organization and the level of detail that you use. At the most in-depth level, projections are created by month by SKU by distributor. This is informed by internal choices and conversations with distributors, and should include agreed-upon plans for a brewery's performance in the market. Factors that should be considered include pricing changes, product offerings, changes to retail channels, packaging changes, trends in velocity (how many units are sold at one point of distribution), and promotions (post-offs or incentive programs). Writing a good sales budget can require a herculean effort, but the payoff is that the goal of the budget period is clearly defined. The more detailed the sales budget is, the greater chance of writing an accurate budget for the other departments.

Every sales department also has expenses that should be forecasted. The departmental budget should include marketing expenses as well. Relevant marketing expenses include labor, travel expenses, promotional

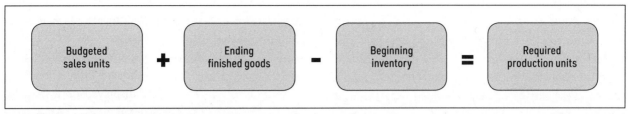

Figure 8.2. Determining the total required production units.

beer (valued at the *cost* of the beer, not the retail value), promotional items (giveaways), distributor and/or sales incentives, cents per case marketing expenses, auto expenses, dues and subscriptions, sponsorships, and advertising campaigns.

When putting together your sales budget, remember to consider the following:

- Over-budget for promotional beer. You will get many requests and it is low cost and a great way to get your name in the public eye; for example, for taproom promotional beer we use wooden nickels and give them out as promo items.
- Point of sale (POS) items (e.g., posters, tap handles, signs) may require development and some production. Many distributors print these items themselves, but art needs to be created by the brewery.
- Permanent POS (e.g., metal signs, neons, mirrors) will also require development and production. Expect that the cost will be split between the brewery and the distributor.
- Incentives for third party distribution
- Industry events like CBC and GABF® can be costly because of the travel and food expenses associated with these events.
- Local guild membership and meetings

Larry Chase
Standing Stone Brewery

Production Plan

Once the top-line sales goals are set, you plan the production plan that is needed to meet those goals. The total required production units equals the budgeted sales units plus desired ending finished goods inventory minus beginning inventory (fig. 8.2). Small sub-level goals are nested within the larger production plan: raw materials, packaging materials, brewery labor, overhead, and excise tax. The production planning process is an opportunity to review the materials contracts and consider if adjustments should be made, or if there are cost savings to be had by shopping for another vendor.

WORDS OF WISDOM

When it comes to budgeting for sales, carefully look at each different brand's finished production time. Too often shortcuts are taken here in an effort to push through more sales. Similarly, packaging costs and lead time are important factors that get overlooked. The production cycle for each brand will be different and should be considered in the production planning and sales forecast.

Larry Chase
Standing Stone Brewery

The production planning process also forces the production team to consider if the facility has the capacity to meet the projected sales demand. Considerations should include available capacity, efficiency of current equipment, gains to be made if new equipment is purchased, and resale value of existing equipment. This analysis will result in a capital expenses budget.

Administrative Budget

The administrative budget should include estimates for all operating expenses that do not fall to other department heads as a controllable cost. This includes administrative labor, rent, insurance, interest, supplies, and more.

Once all departmental budgets by month have been written the accounting staff should compile them. In fact, the accounting staff should be communicating with department heads along the way to assist in performing calculations and finding data.

It's my belief that each department head should be responsible for budgeting the items that are under his or her control, but there are significant expenses that are not under a department leader's control that must be included in a departmental budget; examples include rent and employee benefits. The accounting department should work with department leaders to ensure that these line items are reflected appropriately in the budgets after an overarching budget of the expense is received from the administrative department. This fine-tuning generally takes place in the latter part of the process.

The consolidated budget should be reviewed and agreed to by all department heads and executive team members. Usually there are one or two revisions before the process is considered final. The result is a static budget, showing planned results for one budgeted activity level.

WORDS OF WISDOM

What do you know now that you wish you knew when you were starting your operation?

I recently saw a line from Joe Gebbia (founder of Airbnb) that resonates: "Starting your own venture is like jumping off a cliff and assembling your parachute on the way down." The quotation speaks to the fact that I knew very little! So it's hard to pinpoint one thing that I wish I knew. For our brewpub operation though, I wish we had built the brewery with more room to grow and means to expand our production. For our eventual USA import operation I wish I knew how long the ramp-up would be for new points of distribution (PODs) through our self-distribution model in certain states. I'm not sure I would have done anything differently but at least my projections and expectations could have been a bit more accurate.

How frequently do you review financial reports and what reports are most helpful?

I review our KPIs weekly. For our USA business this is mostly just sales and AR because our expenses are quite regular. For our brewpub I look at our P&L [income statement] bi-weekly and sales/expense projections weekly. This includes profit margins on three categories: food, beer, and cocktails. Our expenses are a little more variable in the retail business so it's important to stay on top of them.

Do you use departmental budgets? Do you use them to hold department heads accountable?

I pretty much control all budgeting and spending myself with the exception of food.

Matt Greenberg
San Juan del Sur Cerveceria, Nicaragua

Other Budgeting Approaches

The process described above is very regimented and may not suit smaller breweries. If your company does not have specific department leaders or departmental budgets, then the head of the accounting department will be the most likely person on staff to help guide budget writing. For many breweries, one person, often the founder, is responsible for everything, budgets included!

Flexible Budget

If you want to introduce a more sophisticated budget process, create a flexible budget. The flexible budget refines the expected financial outcome that corresponds to the *actual* level of output. A flexible budget projects budget data for various levels of activity. For example, a static budget may show the expected outcome for sales of 1,000 barrels in one month. Assume that only 800 barrels were actually sold (perhaps there was a retail chain that did not take on your beer, but you had planned to include those sales). The flexible budget will show budgeted numbers based on the actual output of 800 barrels. Flexible budgets may be helpful for start-ups due to the volatility of the business. Employing a flexible budget takes more work than a static budget, but the benefits are great.

Rolling Forecast

Another way to take budgeting to the next level is to implement a rolling forecast. A rolling forecast starts with a static budget by month. At the end of each period, the performance of the last month informs the proposed forecast a year into the future. For example, at the end of January 20X1, that month's actual data, in conjunction with the existing budget for the remainder of 20X1, is used to help create a budget for January

20X2. This practice results in continuous budgeting, which can be a useful tool for forward planning. Work with your wholesalers and get their input each month. Promotions, features, and incentives all play a factor in the forecast. This is also a great way of keeping a constant touchpoint with distributors.

The rolling forecast allows managers to make continuous improvements and anticipate problems. At the end of the first full year, the company will have shifted its budget process so that the annual process is replaced by a smaller monthly process. It is advisable that the company continue to review the entire budget annually for items like capital expenses, insurance renewals, and the like.

CONCLUSION

A budget does not provide assurance that the company will achieve its objectives, rather it is a map so that you can see if the company is veering off course. Budgets are reviewed throughout the year to measure performance across smaller time periods, usually a month. It is recommended that each month a brewery reviews the budget versus actual report along with the balance sheet, income statement, and statement of cash flows. If you have more than one department (e.g., production, taproom, multiple locations) it is recommended that the budget versus actual report be segmented so that each department is shown separately. This monthly review will help you stay focused and it can expose areas that need attention. You may realize that you are spending much more than intended on certain line items. On the other hand, it may expose areas of great efficiency. Imagine that you review the numbers and realize that the sales expense as a percentage of revenue is 5% lower than what you have budgeted. You could then take that amount that hasn't been spent and host a special event, or increase advertising to support sales in the pub, or hire an additional body to lessen the workload for overburdened staff.

The budgeting process is part of the ongoing maintenance of a company. It is not a one-time affair. It's a constant process of planning, analyzing, and revising. Healthy companies embrace this as part of their company culture. Structured planning can make all the difference to the growth of your business. It will enable you to concentrate resources on improving profits, reducing costs, and increasing returns.

In a world of noise, reviewing actual performance against budgeted amounts, and setting an accurate forecast, provides sound financial information on which to base decisions. It improves the focus of your actions and allows business owners to make decisions with greater confidence.

WORDS OF WISDOM

At Stone Brewing, the topline number always came from me. It was not a number I thought we had to break our backs to stretch to, and thus rarely hit, but rather a number that I believed we could realize if all our people did all the things we expected of them. We (the executive team) realized that our customers were the ones who decided how much beer we were going to sell, not us. Our job was to make their choices easier by way of effectively and efficiently being in front of their eyes in the stores and at the front of their minds when searching. Everything we did was to support that assumption. Because of this style of forecasting, we never overshot our capabilities. We were always very, very close to realizing our projections, which made investing a more confident endeavor. Many breweries set their dollar goals as what is needed to achieve (a) certain CEO goals, (b) certain investor returns, or (c) some other non-reality-based measure. Then, they tell their sales team to "Make it happen!" While I believe this is a ridiculous way to plan for expenses, capital expenditures, etc. it is more common than you might imagine. Plus, it kills morale and sets everyone up for failure, not success.

I would lock myself away in my office, or at home, and put up last year's monthly depletions from each distributor. I had loaded them into a spreadsheet that shows each package's depletions from that distributor each month. From that, it was easy to see as my eyes move left to right what happened with each package. I could see seasonality and growth inclines. I would then set up my forecast to be a continuation of that page such that months 13–24 follow the same seasonality and curves. I would then make adjustments for things like new packages, planned outages, pricing changes, distributor changes, and retail changes. Once dialed in, I'd convert those "expected depletions" into how and when they would get shipped to each distributor. Many distributors would take beer every other month. Special release beers with long shelf lives might get shipped a month ahead of the release date. Since my revenue came from my shipments, these shipping volumes were the most accurate depiction of how much was shipped and when it was shipped to each distributor. Each distributor had different pricing and shipping costs so those were applied at that point. From then on, I was working with volume numbers and dollars for each package, both of which would eventually be tallied at the bottom of the spreadsheet. Barrelage would come from the totals of the package numbers.

I'd go through each and every distributor. Near the end of my term at Stone, we had well over 100 distributors, so it was a huge task. By the end of the week, or thereabouts, I'd have it all done and I would come up with a dollar growth number and a volume growth number (not always the same but always close). I'd ask myself if these made sense. It was my final gut check. If it all felt good, I'd send the budget along. I'm proud to say that over the many years I did the projections this way, I was within 5% of dollars and volume; most years, I was within 3%. I remember Steve Wagner telling me how crazy it was that I'd spend an entire week on this project and that we should just find prediction software. I disagreed with that solution because, at the time, I had talked to a couple of firms who had this stuff and they claimed it could be 20–25% from accurate. With sales over $100 million, a $20 million variance is massive and would never pass muster. I kept doing it my way until my last day.

I will note that in the last couple of years I enlisted my regional sales managers to forecast sales for their distributors, and I'd take it from there. Even after significant training, I was never able to fully rely on their numbers. Even though they each had the same information about what was coming, they each were far too optimistic. I ran dueling projections for two years. Mine were much more accurate. I attribute that to experience, an even hand, and a realistic approach to the business. Someone in an organization needs to have that position for final approval of forecasting and budgeting. It could be an optimistic accountant or a level-headed sales guy. Neither are easy to come by!

I found that if the final budget is completed by November 1, things run a lot more smoothly beginning in January. In fact, you can get a head start on putting programs together. In practice, though, I have found it really difficult to get it done by then. Often, final budgets come together around Dec 31

at 11 p.m. Distributor annual business plan meetings and fall sales objectives keep everyone busy until November, which is what makes the November deadline so difficult. I do, however, prefer to complete our distributor annual business plans before final budgets. There is often new information that is learned and plans that are made from these meetings that will impact how you want your following year to go. I try to schedule those planning meetings in October so that we can meet our November deadline for budgets.

I find that the budgeting process can feel too "corporate" for many small breweries. I would get asked regularly how to make it feel more organic. I would always suggest having discussions over a beer or two about what people see happening in the next year. These "meetings" feel more like hang sessions. As long as things stay on topic, it is a lot more fun and the answers tend to be more real. Budgeting is really important, and forecasting was the most difficult part. It involves experience, and knowledge of what is going down in the future within the organization and in the business environment. It also requires a fair amount of intuition, an understanding of the strengths and weaknesses of your sales staff and your distributors, and your ability to keep cash during the upcoming year. It is very "holistic."

Arlan Arnsten
Former Sr. Vice-President of Sales
Stone Brewing Co.

WORDS OF WISDOM

What do you know now that you wish you knew when starting your operation?
As related to financing and getting the funds we learned a couple of things. For one, it takes years of planning. My husband and I started the brewery and it took two-and-a-half to three years to write a solid business plan that we could present to investors. We were working full-time jobs, so at the time it was hard to focus, get the plan down on paper, and get the financial projections correct. Once the business plan was written it took another year to fully fund the operation as well as find a building, sign a lease, and purchase equipment. Everything fell into place in June 2016. We were fully funded through private loans and investment. Through that process we had a big learning curve to learn how to do that legally and correctly.

Family and friends were our biggest supporters. Even if they said no to investing in the brewery initially, they may have known someone else interested in investing. For example, my father's boss is one of our investors, as well as some of my former coworkers. It never hurts to ask people who they know who may be interested. Investors can also be a great resource for helping build the business. One of our major investors has an MBA and serves on our board of directors. We get the benefit of his experience.

How frequently do you review financial reports and what reports are most helpful?

We have two people who oversee the finances of the brewery: me (I have a background in analytics) and my father (who has a bookkeeping background). I review cash flow management and my father gets the expenses in the right place and produces accrual-based reports. I focus on financial projections and daily cash flow projections. We look at a P&L [income statement] once a week.

We also rely heavily on our scheduling system, Homebase, which shows managers' profitability by the hour and integrates with our POS system, Clover.

Do you use departmental budgets? Do you use them to hold accountable department heads?

Our team is currently 13 people and only four of them are in management. We have just one budget that is pretty basic, so we do not hold department heads accountable to their budget. We have three brewers (head, lead, and assistant) and the department's financial performance is not currently reflected in personnel reviews, but I'd like to implement that in the future.

If you financed your operation by selling equity to other investors, what minefields would you warn against? Why do you prefer raising money through equity as opposed to a bank?

In our experience, bankers weren't interested in lending to us without at least two years of sales. If you can finance privately, do it. Trying to work out a deal with bankers as a start-up can waste a lot of time. We found that it really comes down to what the founders own personally. Unless you have a home to collateralize, it's hard to get funding. You can try to go the SBA route, but we found that very

challenging. In my mind, the only way that we were able to fund this was through private funding.

We have found a lot of value in creating a board of directors. These are the people who help us make decisions, and we are stronger because we can leverage their knowledge and skills. Our investors are friends and family who are in it for the long term, and they are more forgiving of challenging financial results. They are patient and, as long as we can distribute enough cash to cover any tax liability caused by the company, they are OK with a longer timeline for their returns.

People are going to invest in you because they like you as a person or they like beer. Most of the investors are not in it for the money, they are in it because they want to support the owners, or because they are stoked about owning part of a brewery. Be cautious when approaching any angel investors. If their experience is in a different industry, like technology, their expectations may be much different than what is realistic for the brewery.

Also, be aware of regulatory requirements. When applying for a TTB license, we had to provide the background checks for everyone involved.

What two or three KPIs do you find most useful when monitoring the success of your business?

We also keep track of short-term debt versus long-term debt, and the relationship of short-term debt to cash. I also watch net income.

Nicole Smith
South Lake Brewery, Tahoe, CA

9

SOURCES OF CAPITAL

The natural course of a business is a series of expansion and contraction cycles. Contraction occurs when there is a constraint in the operating cycle that holds a company back from maximizing its resources to the fullest. In order to grow, a company must take steps to unblock constraints.

Expansion in the context of a brewery can take several forms:

- moving into a new pack type;
- opening a new location;
- adding to an existing facility to increase capacity;
- increasing the points of distribution of products, either through self-distribution or third-party distribution.

> **Pack type** is an industry term meaning how your product is packaged. It could be in kegs, cans, or bottles. Common pack types include:
>
> 12×22 = twelve 22 fl. oz. bottles
> 4×6×12 = four six-packs of 12 fl. oz. cans or bottles
> 6×4×16 = six four-packs of 16 fl. oz. cans or bottles
> Half-barrel keg
> Quarter-barrel keg
> Sixth-barrel keg (sixtel)

The meaning of the term "expansion" can vary within a small brewery context, and it almost always requires additional capital. Starting a brewery is a capital-intensive endeavor, and many breweries follow the same path as Happy Hour Brewing Company did in the chapter 1 narrative: gather enough money to get the doors open and then figure it out from there. Few companies have all phases figured out in the beginning. The vast majority of small breweries will go through some type of expansion in their life cycle. There are two general categories of capital to access for the expansion: debt and equity.

> Debt is money that is owed, equity is ownership interest.

DEBT VERSUS EQUITY

If you borrow money (debt), then the money borrowed (principal) is paid back to the lender with interest. Conceptually, the lender is willing to part with cash knowing it eventually will be paid back, and the lender will make money by charging interest to the debtor. The original amount loaned is called the principal. Usually, short-term loans will have a lower interest rate than long-term loans, because the longer that cash is out of the lender's hands, the greater the risk that it will *not* be paid back. To compensate the lender for the increased risk of forfeiting the principal, a larger amount of interest is owed. A lender generally does not have the right to direct the affairs of the business, so the current owner(s) stays in control of the company. Note that lenders may obtain some rights to assets via contract. For example, they could be in **first position** for repayment, meaning that they will get paid back before other creditors.

It is possible that the loan agreement may require the debtor to provide financial reports and/or tax returns on a periodic basis, in addition to other financial requirements known as **loan covenants**. In some cases, particularly with larger institutional lenders, the debtor may have to provide audited financial statements to the lender. These requirements can be costly. For example, an audit may cost $5,000–$10,000 or more. Most banks will require individuals who own 20% or more of the company to personally guarantee loans, which is a promise to personally repay loans if the company cannot fulfill the payments. These rules may be relaxed as a company grows and becomes an established entity with positive cash flow, but almost all commercial lenders will require a guarantee on loans in the first few years of a brewery's life. Furthermore, with certain types of loans, a lender may have the right to "call" the loan, meaning that the money must be paid back on demand.

Despite these conditions that can apply, loans can still be beneficial for the owner in the long term. One of the primary benefits is that, when the loan becomes due, the debtor pays back the loan but retains 100% ownership of the company.

Equity, on the other hand, is when founders or investors put money into a business with no intention of being paid back in the near term, but instead are investing in a long-term future payoff. They are buying an ownership stake in the company. The company pays no interest on the invested funds, and no loan payments are due. If a business owner is unable or unwilling to self-fund an expansion, the company may issue ownership units to other investors in exchange for cash.

Although equity funding saves the company from paying interest, these deals can be costly in other ways. Most investors expect financial reports from the company on at least a quarterly basis. Also, there may be an explicit or implicit expectation from investors that they be paid distributions on a regular basis. It is generally expected that over the long term the cost of equity (the expected return on equity) is higher than the cost of debt (the interest rate you'd pay a bank on a loan).

Additionally, investors may have a right to vote on matters that affect how the company makes certain decisions. Even if they do not have the contractual right to make decisions, investors may sometimes behave as if they have a right to weigh in on the direction of the company. The "costs" of others' contributions, therefore, whether financial or otherwise, can result in the current owner/founder owning and controlling less of the business. That said, investors can be a source of more than just financial capital. They can also offer great wisdom, experience, and connections from which your company may benefit.

There is no strategic advantage to either debt or equity that can be applied universally to businesses. The funding sources depend on the goals and values of each organization (table 9.1). If faced with a need to raise

TABLE 9.1 ANALYSIS OF DEBT VERSUS EQUITY

DEBT		EQUITY	
Pro	**Con**	**Pro**	**Con**
No dilution of ownership	Less cash available for business operations	No interest expense; no debt on the books	Dilution of ownership
Interest expense is a deduction and can reduce the tax you pay	Interest expense is a deduction and can reduce your net income	More cash available on an ongoing basis to reinvest in the company	Less freedom to make decisions for the company without investor input
		Potential skills or connections from investor group that can be leveraged	The process of finding the right investors can be long and costly

capital, consider your end goal before deciding which path to pursue. Are you building a company that you hope to sell in ten years? Are you building a company to leave to your children? Are you creating a lifestyle that suits you for the long term?

You may also want to consider a debt/equity hybrid model. In this model, a business both borrows money from and sells equity to the same party. For example, a company may offer $10,000 of equity in the company, but only if the investor also loans $10,000. Therefore, an investor will have to put up $20,000 to participate in the round of financing; half is a loan that will be repaid and half is an equity investment. This novel approach to financing can be a win-win for both the lender and debtor.

See appendix E for a sample term sheet that can be used for a hybrid offering.

WORDS OF WISDOM

If you financed your operation by selling equity to other investors, what minefields would you warn against? Why do you prefer raising money through equity as opposed to a bank?

I could not get a bank loan to start the business so I had to go the investor route. It was a real balancing act raising the money. I was able to maintain 51% of the company and sold the other 49% to investors. I have seven other entities other than myself. It took up until lease signing to get all the money in. We financed with each investor, say, putting in $100,000. We took 50% as an equity investment and the other was a loan to be paid back in seven years.

Minefields—I have not had any. My investment group has been very supportive. I believe you need to get all the information on the table for the investors. You need to get a very good attorney to get the Operating Agreement right. Also, you will need to pay a securities attorney to make sure your disclaimers are done correctly so you are protected. It was quite a process.

John Harris
Ecliptic Brewing

Table 9.2 is a short list of various sources of capital to consider as options for financing your brewery.

TABLE 9.2 OPTIONS FOR SOURCING CAPITAL TO FINANCE A BREWERY

Source of capital	Examples
Self-funding	You pay out of your own pocket
Friends and family	Investments, loans, or gifts from people who are close to the founder
Other investors	Investments or loans from other individuals
Institutional financing	From a bank or other third party
Alternative lenders	Examples at time of writing include American Express Merchant Finance, Square, QuickBooks, and Kabbage
State/municipal development funds	Loans with favorable terms for small businesses, or grants from municipal agencies
Government grant programs	Programs designed to fuel economic development for women-owned businesses, minority-owned businesses, certain geographical areas, or other factors
Angel investors	Smaller amounts from individuals or small groups
Venture capital	Institutions or larger groups of investors
Crowdfunding	Online platforms such as Kickstarter or GoFundMe
Trade credit	Credit terms with vendors or credit cards
Equipment leasing	Leasing or lease-to-own instead of buying
Bottle and mug clubs	Individuals who donate to a brewery's start-up fund in exchange for discounted beer in the future

WORDS OF WISDOM

There are a few areas that we see somewhat consistently where small brewery start-ups trip up. The first, and most common, is probably a lack of understanding of just how much money they will need as a runway as they get the brewery off the ground. We all love the story of the small brewery that was founded by die-hard beer lovers who bootstrapped their way to success, but the reality is that a lot of these breweries unnecessarily struggle early on because they simply lack the capital or capital equipment to be able to take advantage of the opportunities that being small and agile affords you. For example, a lot of smaller brewers utilize mobile canning/bottling in order to get their beer out in the market. This is a great way to establish a presence and test your market without significant investment in packaging equipment. However, relying on mobile packaging means that you are going to have to accept much slimmer margins and you'll be at the mercy of the schedule of the mobile canner (as well as any potential quality control issues they may deal with). Simply financing a canning or bottling line will more than likely cost you less per month than hiring that work out (and will give you a nice write-off).

Another major financial stumbling block for young or start-up breweries is a lack of understanding of credit and how it will impact their ability to borrow. We see applicants that put their heart and soul into developing a great business plan and a wonderful brand, only to get derailed because of either unrealistic expectations in terms of the kind of funding that is available to startup breweries, or because the partners never took the time to honestly discuss their personal credit with one another. Nothing hurts worse than having your dream squashed because your partner isn't paying his mortgage and can't qualify for financing.

Rick Wehner
Brewery Finance

EXPERT ADVICE

In the United States, many breweries take advantage of loans from the Small Business Administration (SBA). The SBA is a federal agency that exists to further the economic development of small businesses, because such businesses are the backbone of the US economy. The SBA offers loans and educational resources to small businesses. The agency's primary function is to enable small businesses operating in the US to get loans:[1]

> The SBA works with lenders to provide loans to small businesses. The agency doesn't lend money directly to small business owners. Instead, it sets guidelines for loans made by its partnering lenders, community development organizations, and micro-lending institutions. The SBA reduces risk for lenders and makes it easier for them to access capital, which makes it easier for small businesses to get loans. . . .

> Lenders and loan programs have unique eligibility requirements. In general, eligibility is based on what a business does to receive its income, the character of its ownership, and where the business operates. Normally, businesses must meet size standards, be able to repay, and have a sound business purpose. Even those with bad credit may qualify for startup funding. ("Loans," SBA.gov)

Loans guaranteed by the SBA range from tens of thousands of dollars to millions of dollars and can be used for most business purposes, including long-term fixed assets and operating capital. Some loan programs set restrictions on how you can use the funds.

WORDS OF WISDOM

If you financed your operation by selling equity to other investors, what minefields would you warn against? Why do you prefer raising money through equity as opposed to a bank?

Cash flow is obviously very important for small businesses, so not being handcuffed to loan service allows us to reinvest profits when they are generated.

In terms of minefields of having a number of smaller, minority partners, they make you less agile to make structural changes when needed. We are in the process of legally restructuring our company to account for the addition of new lines of business and companies in new countries. It becomes a lot of communication, explanation, and "cat-herding" to facilitate a basic legal change that will be in everyone's best interest.

Matt Greenberg
San Juan del Sur Cerveceria, Nicaragua

An important consideration for the lender is its ability to recoup loaned funds in a worst-case scenario. If cash is loaned to a party that defaults, then the lender may only be able to sell the hard assets (e.g., fixed assets) of the company to recoup the cash that was loaned. When a loan is secured with the value of assets, this is called collateral. Not all fixed assets have the same value as collateral. To **collateralize** an asset means that it is

---

[1] "Loans," SBA.gov, accessed April 27, 2019, https://www.sba.gov/funding-programs/loans.

pledged to a lender; the lender has a right to the asset if the debtor defaults (is unable to pay) on the loan.

Brewery equipment can be moved from one location to another, it is often made of stainless steel (which has inherent value), and there is a market demand for used equipment. In a worst-case scenario, if a brewery defaults on a loan, then the bank has a reasonable chance of recouping its investment by reselling the brewery equipment. Compare this to leasehold improvements, which are upgrades made to the real property; examples include installing floor drains or pouring concrete pads for tanks. Leasehold improvements are often specific to the particular building and become part of the building, thus, they cannot be moved to another location. There is little chance that leasehold improvements would have any resale value, especially if you are a tenant rather than a building owner. For these reasons, leasehold improvements have little chance of being resold to another party. In the eyes of a banker, brewing equipment is a more attractive asset to collateralize.

EXPERT ADVICE

After assessing the availability of sufficient cash flow to service a proposed loan (the primary source of repayment) a bank lender will then consider the potential salability and value of its collateral as a secondary source of repayment. The comments below are tailored toward new and used brewery equipment along with the other major long-term asset category of a brewery, leasehold improvements.

The collateral related variables contemplated by the banker will generally be the following:

1. *Does the collateral "hold its value" over time?* The answer tends to be a combination of supply and demand for the collateral coupled with functional viability of the collateral. For example, well-maintained conditioning tanks generally command good resale value at this time due, in part, to the overall growth in the industry, which in turn drives strong demand. Secondly, tanks can be useful for many years, even decades, without much need for expensive maintenance and costly replacement parts.

2. *In the event of a liquidation of the business, can the lender have access to the collateral for removal and resale? Should the equipment be sold piecemeal or as a total, in place, system?* While a total production system sale may simplify a liquidation, major brewing components are readily sold as stand-alone items without material degradation of value. Some equipment can be part of the building, so separating and selling as discrete items may not bring incremental value back to the lender. Leasehold improvements, such as drain systems, floor coating, utility upgrades, a back bar, bathroom improvements, etc., while costly, are not the type of collateral that are readily transferrable. Arguably, such assets are integral with the real property and are, therefore, much less attractive to an equipment lender as collateral, unless a buyer intends to occupy the property currently housing the current defaulting borrower.

3. *Is the collateral broadly marketable?* A highly customized item of equipment generally has a much smaller pool of potential buyers than general-purpose equipment.

4. *What are the various ways a lender protects its collateral security?* Concurrent with a promissory note/security agreement or equipment lease, the lender files a UCC-1 financing statement as a public record. Much like a deed of trust/mortgage secured by a residence or commercial building, the UCC-1 states to the world that the lender has a security interest in either specific assets or a "blanket" security interest in all business assets. Those UCC-1 filings on specific items of equipment will include a description of the equipment financed and should list the serial number(s). In many states, a Landlord Consent Agreement document is required by lenders so that, in the event of a liquidation of the business assets, the lender has the legal right to access the premises and remove the collateral for resale purposes. Finally, the borrower is required to carry sufficient business insurance coverage, with the lender named as loss payee.

5. *How is the equipment valued?* The lender looks to the (new) cost of the item being financed, less any shipping, tax, or installation related expense, as the primary value of new equipment. A bank or lessor will lend up to 100% of the cost of the new equipment, depending on the strength of the borrower. Many banks insist on a 10%–20% down payment by the borrower as a condition of the loan. For used equipment financings, most bank lenders rely on

the account officers to prepare written support on small equipment financings, say, up to $250,000 or perhaps even $500,000. For larger transactions, a "desktop" valuation might be performed. Lenders / funding sources will lend 80% to 100% of the "orderly liquidation value" of the appraised equipment. On-site appraisals by a certified professional are undertaken on larger transactions involving used equipment, usually in excess of $1 million. Tenant improvements financing, often avoided, might be financed 80% to 100% if either other collateral is available or the borrower is very strong. Often, particularly with early stage breweries, SBA financing is used to support loan requests where large amounts of loan proceeds are earmarked for tenant improvements.

6. Lenders place less collateral weight on brewery inventory due to regulatory barriers to reselling beer coupled with branded packaging items that have a limited marketability. Perishability of the product is also a limitation for brewery inventory value.

7. Accounts receivable, often due from distributors, represent a potential source of repayment to a lender who is liquidating a brewery, but often by the time a lender can intercede, the AR has been paid and the proceeds spent.

8. Brand value is a difficult asset to quantify, especially in the smaller craft beer market. Nevertheless, major industrial brewers buy and sell brands with regularity based on long established histories of broad sales generation experience.

In conclusion, many banks/funding sources will look at the overall risk of payment default by the borrower to determine the amount of leasehold improvement exposure they are comfortable with. The less perceived risk that is present, the more likely that the lender will be more aggressive in supporting weaker collateral.

Patrick McCarthy
Banker

_____

When applying for a loan, one of the biggest factors that determines approval is an applicant's creditworthiness. There are five primary considerations of creditworthiness, often called the Five Cs of Credit.

Character—a lender's opinion of an applicant's sense of responsibility and reliability. While this judgment is the most subjective of the five, it can be verified by references and professional credentials. Behavior, reputation, and lending history are important elements of character.

Capacity—one's ability to make loan payments. This is a more objective measurement because lenders use an applicant's financial projections to measure debt service coverage ratios. Debt service coverage is the earnings before interest and tax divided by required principal and interest payments of a period. A common required debt service coverage ratio is 1.25. That is, net income must exceed debt service payments by 25%.

$$\text{debt service coverage ratio} = \left(\frac{\text{EBIT}}{\text{principal} + \text{interest payments}} \right)$$

For example, if earnings before interest and taxes for Year 1 is $100,000, and required loan payments (interest and principal included) for Year 1 is $70,000, the debt service coverage ratio is 1.43.

Capital—the amount of money invested in a business by the owner(s). A lender is more likely to approve an applicant who has invested personal funds into a project, than an applicant who relies primarily on loaned money.

Conditions—industry climate. The economic conditions of an applicant's industry and region will impact the lender's decision to extend credit. Much of this is outside the control of the applicant, so be sure to plan for challenges in the business environment and be prepared to discuss how your company is prepared to address them.

Collateral—what will the lender get if the applicant defaults on the loan? This is a worst-case scenario consideration, but certainly affects a lender's decision. If an applicant can collateralize an asset that the bank can easily sell and recover loan principal from, then there is a stronger likelihood that the loan will be approved. It is also an excellent reason to form a corporate structure that can protect your personal assets.

WHO SHOULD INVEST

Friends and family may be the most obvious option when you need to raise money for your company. They may be the most sympathetic to your cause and easiest to get involved. More often than not, these individuals will see your passion and believe in your dream. Of course, this can be fraught with its own set of frustrations. You should consider how borrowing from those close to you may impact your relationships. Outside of friends and family, consider other individuals who are interested in investing in small businesses, breweries in particular.

When a private company offers investment opportunities to others, the investors must be "accredited or sophisticated," which is language from the Securities and Exchange Commission Regulation D. Regulation D allows an organization to issue a private offering to raise debt or equity without officially registering the offering to "go public." This exemption reduces the amount of paperwork required, lessening the time and money it takes to actually raise capital.[2] To be accredited, an individual must have $1 million net worth, excluding the value of a primary residence. In this context, sophisticated means that the potential investor has superior business and financial knowledge. Sophisticated individuals have the business acumen to understand that no investment is without risk.

A reputable attorney can help you ask appropriate questions of investors to ensure that you are complying with all regulations. Legal advice may be expensive, but it is worth it. Regardless of how casual a conversation about an investment may seem, you can get into hot water fast if you are not aware of all the risks associated with your offering. Poorly written operating agreements and equity offerings can rear their ugly heads years after people enter into an agreement. It is well worth your time to find a legal expert who is experienced in the alcohol industry and/or securities offerings.

FOUR MUST-HAVE DOCUMENTS WHEN WORKING WITH INVESTORS

Offering investment in your brewery falls under securities regulations, and you should carefully follow those rules. Consult your attorney or read more at https://www.sec.gov/smallbusiness. Some of the common regulations are:

- Avoid advertising and general solicitation
- Don't mention the investment in media
- No social media references to the investment are allowed
- Avoid presenting to large groups about terms
- No mass mailings pertaining to the investment are allowed
- Records of solicitations must be kept on hand
- You must approach only knowledgeable investors

Consider developing an investor packet. Investors should receive a clear, concise introduction to the concept of the brewery, basic pro forma financials, basic financial metrics, and the financial commitment of investors. If you choose to include a business plan, make it concise and put your business vision into plain English. You may also want to include a **term sheet** that outlines the nuts and bolts of the deal and lays out in clear detail what the investor can expect. It should include the dollar amount per unit of investment, and clearly define the rights of each investor.

I highly recommend having all legal documents prepared by an attorney. Providing these formal documents is important because it allows all parties to have a written, common understanding of your agreement.

Term Sheet

A term sheet usually has separate sections for the transaction summary, parties involved, closing date, operating agreement terms, capitalization, distributions, general voting rights, governance, rights of the investor, and any other conditions.

> Appendix E has a sample term sheet that is applicable to a debt/equity hybrid offering.

Pro Forma Financials

Many breweries in start-up phase will seek to raise money from investors. Most investors will want to

---

[2] "Differences Between Accredited Investors & Sophisticated Investors," Accredited Investor Leads, accessed April 26, 2019, https://www.accreditedinvestorleads.com/accredited-vs-sophisticated/.

see a representation of your financial expectations for the business. Pro forma financials communicate a best guess for performance over a period of time. Pro formas should include a balance sheet and an income statement. A statement of cash flows is optional. I recommend preparing annual pro forma balance sheets for the first three years of operations; monthly pro forma income statement for the first year of operations, and quarterly income statements for Years 2 and 3 of operations. By expressing the financial expectations in dollars, even though purely hypothetical, potential investors can see what is expected for payback period, timeline for estimated distributions, and return on investment.

The pro forma process starts by establishing a list of start-up costs. Estimate how much will be needed for major one-time items like build-out, brewhouse, and professional fees. Then consider how much you will need to run the business before you start to sell beer. The total of start-up expenses plus an extra cushion of cash, minus what founders are personally contributing or borrowing from others, will dictate how much money you need to raise.

Amount to be raised from investors =
Start up costs + working capital – owners investment – loans

Then compile a budget (see chapter 8), beginning with the month in which you expect to start sales. Set assumptions for revenue, COGS, and operating expenses, and build the financial statements around those assumptions.

Finally, put a timeline to these assumptions. Consider when you will need to pay the start-up expenses and when you will receive cash inflows. This timeline serves a basic cash flow statement that highlights periods of low cash. The resulting pro forma financials should be included in summary form in the materials presented to investors.

Pro forma financials can be used for any planned transaction such as an acquisition, merger, change in capital structure, or a new capital investment. The models express the anticipated result of the transaction and indicate the projected status of a company in the future based on current financial statements. (See the exercise at the end of this chapter.)

Operating Agreement

You will also need an operating agreement, which is a legal document that defines how the company will make decisions and enumerates the agreed-upon rules of the ownership group. The operating agreement governs how the organization is structured and stipulates the rights of investors.

Subscription Agreement

Another necessary document is the subscription (or admission) agreement. This document officially admits investors into the entity as an owner.

HOW TO MANAGE INVESTOR EXPECTATIONS

Once you have accepted an investor's financial commitment, it is important to manage expectations of when and how the investors will get their money back. Frequent and clear investor communication can put brewery owners in a proactive position by addressing the topic of distributions and sharing with investors the status of the business.

Best practices for working with investors include annual meetings and quarterly updates.

Annual Investor Meetings

The investor meeting is an opportunity for the company management to connect with investors, share updates about the business and discuss plans for future growth.

- Ideally all investors can attend in person. The agenda usually consists of a business update by the management.
- Review the state of the business, in particular the financials for the year, plans for the future, and challenges from the prior year.
- Frequently a brewery's CPA and/or attorney is in attendance to answer any questions.
- The investor meeting is a critical touchpoint that solidifies the relationship with investors and keeps them engaged.

Quarterly Updates

Quarterly investor updates are an important part of investor communications because they keep investors engaged and abreast of company developments. The quarterly updates provide the same content as the annual meeting, but condensed.

Investor Distributions

Be proactive about addressing the topic of investor distributions. Even if you are not discussing profit distributions, you may need to address distributions for taxes.

It is natural for investors to want to receive distributions. This is, of course, one major reason why most investors put money into businesses. Often there are competing interests between investors and managers when it comes to determining if the time is right for a distribution. It is inevitable that business owner/operators want to reinvest profits into the expansion of the brewery or pay down debt, but they also feel pressure to keep investors happy and at bay. The best option is to define parameters that outline when money will be distributed and how the distribution will be calculated. These standards can appear in your operating agreement. If your operating agreement is already written, then memorialize the process at your next board or investor meeting.

Be prepared to offer a tax distribution that is separate from a distribution of profits. Technically, a tax distribution is the same as a distribution of profits, but it may be treated differently in the operating agreement and may be seen differently by investors. Tax distributions are intended to cover any tax liability that may be incurred by owners in a **flow-through entity**. For example, if a company is established as a flow-through entity and has $100,000 of profits in one year, investors will end up with taxable income from the entity. However, it is quite likely that the company may use any available cash to either pay down debt, reinvest in the company, or keep on hand for upcoming expenses. In that case, no money will remain for distribution to the partners, yet the partners are left with tax to pay because of the investment. Companies usually will issue a tax distribution to cover the amount of that tax liability, to relieve investors of the added tax burden. There is no authoritative guidance for how to calculate a tax distribution, but a common method is to calculate the tax on the flow-through income assuming that each partner is taxed at the highest bracket. Following this method of calculating tax ensures that no one will have to pay out of pocket for tax on the investment; the company bears that burden. Remember that tax distributions are not an expense for the company. They reduce each partner's capital account, just as any other distribution would. But make sure to include this in your cash flow forecasts!

WORDS OF WISDOM

What do you know now that you wish you knew when starting your operation?

I would have moved quickly into cans, because sometimes you lose your opportunity if you don't get to market swiftly. I would have spent more time on innovation.

Also, it's important to have a good quality control program in place. That gives a distributor a sense that you are taking the product seriously, and it's important to protect yourself from recalls. By focusing on quality, shelf life increases and the beer tastes better.

How frequently do you review financial reports and what reports are most helpful?

I only look over financial reports sporadically. The production manager pores over the P&L [income statement] on a weekly basis. Our production manager also works with the sales team on forecasts.

Do you use departmental budgets? Do you use them to hold accountable department heads?

Yes and yes. That process is relatively new for the company. We are getting more into budgets and sticking with them on a per period basis. It helps us foresee costs and plan for capex [capital expenses]. It has been a big step for us. Our departmental budgets include production and brewpubs (GMs responsible for each location's front-of-house budget and the executive chef is responsible for the back-of-house budget).

We sell beer to ourselves at a wholesale price. It is important to do that so that the brewpubs have visibility into the true performance of each location.

If you financed your operation with bank financing, what aspects of your banking partners do you most appreciate? Why do you prefer raising money through a bank as opposed to selling equity?

I'd say it's most important to get a good relationship and don't be afraid to interview several bankers. We consider if our banking relationship is meeting our needs on an annual basis, or as changes in terms come up.

What two or three KPIs do you find most useful when monitoring the success of your business?

Labor is watched quite closely. Beer is a seasonal business and often is affected by weather. The production manager watches to make sure we're not hitting overtime. The other metric we review is cost per barrel. It's important to us to avoid cost overruns. We're continuously looking at ways to be more efficient with beer. Our production manager reviews that every 4 weeks and he can identify when unusual costs come up. We also have pricing tiers that align with the cost, which ensures every beer is priced to make money. Some breweries like to do line pricing, but, in my opinion, you are leaving money on the table because you are not showcasing your premium product. We usually only put specialty beers on draft in our taproom to avoid packaging costs and label approval costs.

Overall, I encourage brewers to look at peer-reviewed sources. For example, use ProBrewer.com, MBAA [Master Brewers Association of Americas], state brewers guilds, and the Brewers Association. Lean on the available industry knowledge. Many communities have SCORE (Service Corps of Retired Executives) counselors available, or small business development centers [SBDCs]. Small brewers often cannot afford to have a CFO, so lean on the resources available to you.

Aaron Brodniak
Minister of Beer Quality,
Diamond Knot Brewery, Seattle, WA

HOW TO PREPARE PRO FORMA FINANCIAL REPORTS

To begin preparing pro forma financials you need to have a set of assumptions. If you have prepared a business plan you probably have already considered your assumptions. They should include:

- Anticipated sales
- Anticipated changes to cost of goods
  - With higher production can you acquire raw materials at a lower unit price?
  - Can recipes be adjusted to produce the same beer with different ingredients?
  - Will you be producing a style that requires more expensive ingredients?
- Change in employee headcount
  - How will new equipment affect headcount? If you purchase an automated brewhouse, can you reduce headcount because the new equipment is more efficient?
- Expected raises
  - Discretionary raises, or mandatory raises due to an increase in minimum wage
- Adjustments for rent
- Capital equipment to be purchased
  - How will you pay for it? If a loan is required, what are the terms of the loan?
  - Example: In the fourth quarter of next year you know you are signing with a new distributor. To do that you will need to buy a new tank. You know you will pay half in March when you order and the remainder in May when you install. When forecasting, put half the balance in March as a Prepaid Asset and the full balance in May.

Once your assumptions are set, you can begin to compile pro forma financials.

Now you try it! Using the given assumptions, calculate the pro forma balance sheet and income statement for 20X1.

ASSUMPTIONS:

1. The company plans to increase sales by an additional 2 percent in 20X1 due to minor price increases. In addition, the brewery plans to sign with a distributor in a new state. The marketing costs of the launch are anticipated to be $40,000 and to add an additional $300,000 in sales during 20X1. Assume that the margin on the sales to the new distributor is the same as existing sales.

2. The company plans to invest an additional $600,000 in additional tanks and a canning line in 20X1. The equipment will be depreciated over 7 years. (Note: assume the plant and equipment come online the first day of 20X1).

3. Payroll and benefits for new employees are estimated at $30,000 for 20X1.

4. The equipment that existed as of 12/31/X0 will continue to depreciate in 20X1. The depreciation on that equipment will be the same for 20X1 as it was in 20X0.

5. The company plans to finance the new equipment by taking on $400,000 in long-term debt. The terms of the transaction include a 5% interest-only loan with full principal due in 10 years. Interest payments are due on December 31 for each of the next ten years. Existing interest payments will stay the same.

6. The two partners plan to contribute $50,000 each to bridge the amount of cash needed for the new equipment. The contribution is expected to occur on July 1, 20X1.

7. Inventory decreases by 10% from 12/31/X0 to 12/31/X1.

8. In this example, assume Accounts Receivable, Accounts Payable, Credit Card, and Note Payable balances stay the same.

9. If no change is listed above, assume that income statement accounts will be the same as last year. If no change is listed for a balance sheet account, assume the balance is unchanged from the prior year.

EXERCISE XYX PRO FORMA BALANCE SHEET

	12/31/20X0	12/31/20X1
ASSETS		
Current Assets		
Cash and Equivalents	73,211	
Accounts Receivable	65,227	
Inventory	54,090	
Other Current Assets		
Total Current Assets	**192,528**	
Long Term Investments		
Property, Plant and Equipment, Gross	961,749	
Less: Accumulated Depreciation	(252,723)	
Total Non-Current Assets	**709,026**	
Total Assets	**901,554**	
LIABILITIES AND PARTNER CAPITAL		
Current Liabilities		
Accounts Payable	62,285	
Credit Cards	73,099	
Total Current Liabilities	**135,384**	
Non-Current Liabilities		
Note Payable	61,585	
Bank Loan	445,887	
Total Non-Current Liabilities	**507,472**	
Total Liabilities	**642,856**	
Partner Capital		
Partner A Capital	138,267	
Partner B Capital	57,290	
Retained Earnings	63,141	
Total Partner Capital	**258,698**	
Total Liabilities/Partner Capital	**901,554**	

XYZ PRO FORMA INCOME STATEMENT

	12/31/20X0	12/31/20X1
Total Revenue	653,560	
Cost of Goods Sold, Total	257,088	
Gross Profit	**396,472**	
Operating Expenses		
Payroll and Benefits	68,769	
Guaranteed Payments	70,000	
Rent	48,000	
Sales and Marketing	18,420	
Insurance	36,291	
Depreciation/Amortization	73,629	
Other Expenses	17,446	
Interest Expense	776	
Net Income	**63,141**	

ANSWER KEY XYX PRO FORMA BALANCE SHEET

	12/31/20X0	12/31/20X1
ASSETS		
Current Assets		
Cash and Equivalents	73,211	215,309
Accounts Receivable	65,227	65,227
Inventory	54,090	48,681
Other Current Assets		
Total Current Assets	192,528	329,217
Long Term Investments		
Property, Plant and Equipment, Gross	961,749	1,561,749
Less: Accumulated Depreciation	(252,723)	(412,066)
Total Non-Current Assets	709,026	1,149,683
Total Assets	901,554	1,478,900
LIABILITIES AND PARTNER CAPITAL		
Current Liabilities		
Accounts Payable	62,285	62,285
Credit Cards	73,099	73,099
Total Current Liabilities	135,384	135,384
Non-Current Liabilities		
Note Payable	61,585	61,585
Bank Loan	445,887	845,887
Total Non-Current Liabilities	507,472	907,472
Total Liabilities	642,856	1,042,856
Partner Capital		
Partner A Capital	138,267	188,267
Partner B Capital	57,290	107,290
Retained Earnings	63,141	140,487
Total Partner Capital	258,698	436,044
Total Liabilities/Partner Capital	901,554	1,478,900

XYZ PRO FORMA INCOME STATEMENT

	12/31/20X0	12/31/20X1
Total Revenue	653,560	966,631
Cost of Goods Sold, Total	257,088	380,239
Gross Profit	396,472	586,392
Operating Expenses		
Payroll and Benefits	68,769	98,769
Guaranteed Payments	70,000	70,000
Rent	48,000	48,000
Sales and Marketing	18,420	58,420
Insurance	36,291	36,291
Depreciation/Amortization	73,629	159,343
Other Expenses	17,446	17,446
Interest Expense	776	20,776
Net Income	63,141	77,346

215,309 The balance sheet must balance, and all other accounts have defined changes. Cash is adjusted to balance the balance sheet.

65,227 No change

48,681 See assumption 7. Prior year balance * 90%. $54,090 * .9 = $48,681

1,561,749 See assumption 2. Prior year balance + $600,000. $961,749 + $600,000 = $1,561,749

(412,066) Accumulated depreciation = Prior year accumulated depreciation + Current year depreciation expense. $252,723 + $159,343 = $412,066

62,285 No change

73,099 No change

61,585 No change

845,887 See assumption 5. Bank loan will increase by $400,000. Prior year bank loan balance = $445,887. $445,887 + $400,000 = $845,887

188,267 See assumption 6. Prior year partner capital balance + $50,000. $138,267 + $50,000 = $188,267

107,290 See assumption 6. Prior year partner capital balance + $50,000. $57,290 + $50,000 = $107,290

140,487 Prior year balance + current year net income = $63,141 + $77,346 = $140,487

966,631 See assumption 1. Prior year sales * 1.02 + $300,000 = ($653,560*1.02) + $300,000 = $966,631

380,239 Prior year COGS/Prior year revenue * Current year revenue = ($257,088/$653,560) * $966,631 = $380,239

98,769 See assumption 3. Prior year payroll and benefits + $30,000 = $68,769 + $30,000 = $98,769

70,000 No change

48,000 No change

58,420 See assumption 1. Prior year sales and marketing = $40,000. $18,420 + $40,000 = $58,420

36,291 No change

159,343 See assumptions 2 and 4. Depreciation on assets placed in service before year 20X1 will depreciate at the same rate ($73,629). Add 1/7 of the cost of new equipment placed in service on 1/1/20X1. $73,629 + ($600,000/7) = $159,343

17,446 No change

20,776 See assumption 5. Same interest expense as 20X0 + ($400,000*.05). $776 + $20,000 = $20,776

10

BUSINESS LIFE CYCLE

When brewery owners first open their doors, it's unlikely that they are thinking about how long their brewery will be around. Many blindly assume that it will keep going forever, or, if they're honest, don't even consider what the life cycle of the company might be. No matter how much a business feels like an expression of you, the owner, it eventually takes on a life of its own. There is a cycle that is followed (fig. 10.1).

Your business needs are different in each phase of its life cycle. Of course, businesses in the start-up phase will require more hands-on attention and organizational processes may be barely existent. By the adolescence phase, however, a company is forced to develop processes in order to scale; in this phase budgets become increasingly more important.

The course of a life cycle takes you through the nascence of start-up, the headstrong sprinting of early stage, the introduction of discipline in adolescence, the comfort of coming into your own in maturity, and, finally, the winding down of operations at exit. Understanding each phase and recognizing its business indicators can make you more adept at managing your company through these growth periods.

For breweries in particular, the business life cycle is marked by certain indicators relevant to either revenue, production, or number of full-time equivalent employees, depending on your business model (table 10.1). Note that comments in table 10.1 around sales and production management indicate what to expect as businesses reach the top end of the phase.

Note that the "Exit" column is blank in table 10.1. The reason for this is twofold: first, an exit is a point in time, rather than a phase; second, exits can come at any time, based on the needs of the company or the opportunities that are presented. Although anything is

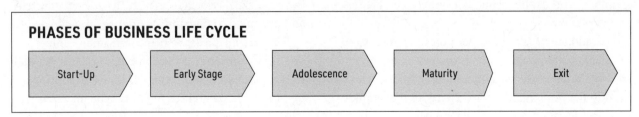

PHASES OF BUSINESS LIFE CYCLE

Start-Up > Early Stage > Adolescence > Maturity > Exit >

Figure 10.1. Phases of business life cycle.

TABLE 10.1 COMMON INDICATORS FOR EACH PHASE OF A BREWERY'S LIFE CYCLE

	Start-up	Early stage	Adolescence	Maturity	Exit
Revenue	$0–$300K	$300K–$4 million	$4–$12 million	$12–$30+ million	?
Production	Less than 1K bbl.	1K–15K bbl.	15K–40K bbl.	40K– ~100K bbl.	?
Production Full-Time Equivalent Employees	2 per 1K bbl. of production	+1 per 5K bbl. of production	+1 per 7K bbl. of production	+1 per 10K bbl. of production	
Sales Mix	≥80% draft	Up to 50% draft, 50% packaged	30%–50% draft, 50%–70% packaged	≥70% packaged	?
Production Management	Clipboards, spreadsheets	Spreadsheets to inventory management software	Production planning, inventory management software	Enterprise resource planning software	

possible, for the purposes of this text, we will assume that exit happens after the maturity phase.

I will offer the caveat that every brewery's path is different. In this book, I have assumed that a brewery is following the course of significant growth. As the industry continues to evolve, I believe that you'll see the traditional growth model wane, with more breweries leveling off and reaching maturity at an earlier age. That may mean that a company tops out at a lower dollar amount of revenue.

One of the beautiful things about the brewing industry is that there is enough variance in business models that all operations don't fit into one bucket. Your business model may differ, and for good reason. As long as you are reaching your own definition of success, you are winning. Also, note that table 10.1 is in reference to a production brewery, not a brewpub or brewery/restaurant combo.

In those glorious days of the early stage, managers have to be hands-on with all aspects of the business. As you scale, though, you will have to let go of the operations of some of the departments. And as the team grows, and other people fill leadership positions, clarity and communication become paramount. How can you ensure that the end product will meet your standards for quality without crystal clear process and expectations?

Operationally, scaling will likely mean graduating to production planning and/or inventory management software in the early-stage-to-adolescent phase. You'll need to develop organizational charts so that employees are clear about the chain of command.

Designing your operations team is outside the scope of this book, but I will offer the following accounting organizational charts ("org charts") for each particular phase.

START-UP

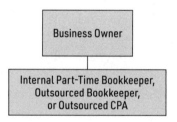

During the start-up phase it is important for the owner to stay close to the numbers so that he or she can understand where and how money is spent. The owner will generate and send invoices, call clients about collections if needed, process payroll, and pay bills. A bookkeeper should be hired to handle transaction entry for payables, record payroll, prepare month-end adjustments, prepare bank reconciliations, and prepare financial reports for the owner. The owner and bookkeeper should do a line-by-line review of the financial reports each month. A CPA should review the financial performance with the owner quarterly and prepare the company's tax return annually.

The start-up phase also includes many important one-time decisions for the company. Perhaps the decision of paramount importance is choice of entity. Note that there are differences in entity type for tax versus legal. The short list is:

Tax	Legal
Sole proprietor	Limited liability company
Single member limited liability company	General partnership
Partnership	Limited partnership
S corporation	Corporation
C corporation	

The article "Choice of Entity: Significant Tax and Other Considerations", provided by law firm Davis Wright Tremaine and included in appendix F, is a fantastic summary of each entity type.

WORDS OF WISDOM

What do you know now that you wish you knew when you were starting your operation?

I wish I would have had a crystal ball to see what our growth projectile would have been like, especially in the last 10 years. If I would have fully grasped the level of growth, I would have ramped up staffing much earlier, especially in key administrative/executive type positions. We didn't have an IT position nor an HR position until six years ago.

Heather McCollum
CFO, Firestone Walker

EARLY STAGE

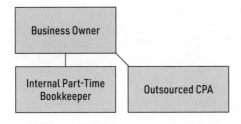

As a company graduates to early stage (producing up to 15,000 bbl.), the number of transactions will increase, and things will start happening much faster. There is less wiggle room, forcing more attention to detail and a hawk-eyed view of cash flow. At this stage it will be more economical for a brewery to hire a part-time in-house bookkeeper. When hiring into the company, the hourly rate should be lower than an external bookkeeper and, given the number of hours needed, it will be more economical overall than outsourcing. An accounting manager should be hired to review the books on a monthly basis and should review the financials with the brewery owner. This is important because early stage is perhaps the most precarious stage of a company's development. You need the constant attention of a part-time bookkeeper, but you also need access to a higher-level skill set on a regular basis. Your business needs will start to become more complex, and cash flow will become ever more critical. You can find an outsourced accounting manager by looking for a fractional CFO, or your CPA firm may offer this service. Many firms have expanded their offerings to include client advisory services.

Small microbreweries generally spend the first couple of years of operation in start-up phase. Their primary focus is on producing beer to satisfy taproom demand. Reporting requirements for excise tax are less rigorous than those for larger breweries. Often, these entities are working with a handful of team members for their internal recordkeeping. Some COGS processes may be skipped or adjusted to meet staff levels. Even though it may seem tedious at times, microbreweries are best served by following best practices when possible. Better data allows owners to make better business decisions during the early stage.

ADOLESCENCE

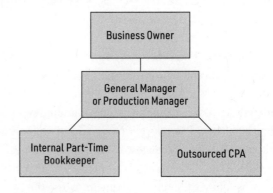

During adolescence (usually producing 15,000–40,000 bbl.) the company focuses on expanding sales and finding profitability. It grows to a level where the business owner needs to step away from being involved in every department. You can expect at this level that your intimate knowledge of each vendor, terms, and check that is written will go away. It's important to develop a team underneath you whom you trust, and who has access to the tools and resources needed to adequately complete its job. At this point, a brewery has usually been in business for a few years, and its sales and production strategies must accommodate higher demand.

The adolescence phase is typically when a brewery begins to distribute beer. As the sales strategy shifts, the brewery should budget for additional equipment needs. Before entering the distribution channel, brewers should have a solid costing system and understand the true cost of selling their beer through a distributor. Remember that profitability is not the same in each region. It may make sense to sell to your neighboring state, but not a state across the country. Remember to include labor and overhead in your analysis of beer cost.

Ideally, the management will have a good grasp of the brewery's cost structure and will still focus on cash balances and cash flow. In the adolescence phase you are likely ready to hire a full-time bookkeeper. The level of activity is probably not so great that you need an in-house accounting manager or controller; most breweries in adolescence can get by with their outsourced manager. Finally, you still need the outsourced CPA for annual tax returns, and I'd recommend continuing to keep that quarterly meeting schedule you've had since start-up. If you have chosen to work with a CPA who specializes in the industry, she will have insights into macro trends and benchmarking data and can offer a valuable and unique perspective.

Breweries in adolescence may consider implementing a perpetual inventory software package or upgrading accounting systems to one with more capabilities. Generally speaking, before switching or adding systems, a brewery should conduct a study of internal needs and options to make the most cost-effective and needs-based decision. An enterprise resource planning (ERP) system would require all departments to use the same system, so brewery and brewpub operators should ensure all departments agree to the chosen system.

Before deciding on systems and software, a brewery can work with a trusted advisor, such as their CPA, who can provide guidance regarding all considerations and options. An advisor who has seen multiple system selection processes and implementations can help brewery and brewpub operators avoid common mistakes. Software vendors may understate potential difficulties in implementing their product, while an independent advisor can provide valuable advice and support.

WORDS OF WISDOM

If you financed your operation with bank financing, what aspects of your banking partners do you most appreciate? Why do you prefer raising money through a bank as opposed to selling equity?

Until recently, we used bank financing to grow our operation. I greatly appreciate a banking partner that understands our industry; and I need a banking partner that can move quickly. Meaning once we have established a relationship with a bank, I appreciate when they can approve a loan in a matter of days, not weeks.

If you financed your operation by selling equity to other investors, what minefields would you warn against? Why do you prefer raising money through equity as opposed to a bank?

In 2015 we sold an equity interest in our company to Duvel Moortgat. They have been an incredible industry partner. They have let us continue to run our operation as we best see fit; of course, there is oversight from them, but they are a true partner in our enterprise.

Heather McCollum
CFO, Firestone Walker

MATURITY

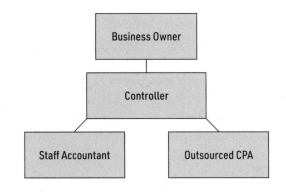

At maturity (producing 40,000+ bbl.) the brewery is focused on maximizing profitability. It will have a full internal staff, including a CFO (if needed), controller, and multiple staff accountant or clerk positions. Its day-to-day finance needs will be addressed internally, and an external CPA will be used for the tax return, tax planning, audit (if needed), and business valuation services.

In the maturity phase the annual revenue growth rate slows. The ability to increase topline is limited and most gains in profitability come from finding efficiencies in the operation. This may come in the form of upgrading equipment, efficient team management, a focus on SKU profitability analysis, or taking view of the operations with an engineer's mind.

The accounting department usually has a solid costing system in place and is regularly reviewing it to catch operational changes or changes that need to be made in the costing. The accounting department usually manages cash balances and cash flow. Breweries usually implement budgeting by department at this level of production. If it hasn't already, a brewery of this size should consider implementing GAAP-compliant accounting for internal accounting purposes. At this part of the life cycle GAAP-compliant financials may be required by investors or lenders. The accounting department should be working with production to determine capital expenditures that could improve brewing efficiency. Accounting should also be monitoring profitability on a monthly basis. If brewery or brewpub operators note significant profitability fluctuations, the accounting department should work with production to identify the cause.

Because a brewery's costing systems are more complex by the maturity phase, accounting should provide regular product cost reporting to management and the sales department to enable informed pricing decisions. Ideally, the brewery would develop a five-year financial model to estimate what future revenue growth will be required from a capital expenditure and labor cost structure standpoint. The financial model should include modeling out product costs.

A larger regional brewery (producing 50,000+ bbl.) should have an accounting department with a strong voice in the company's leadership. At this size, a brewery should have a strong CFO and strong controller, as well as a sizeable accounting department to support them. Generally speaking, a brewery of this size has GAAP-compliant financials and is most likely audited by a third party.

The production department of a large regional brewery should be calculating return on investment (ROI) for all capital expenditure requests. The brewery should have a rolling five-year financial model to estimate what future revenue growth will require from a capital expenditure and labor cost structure standpoint. The financial model is most effective when it models out product costs.

WORDS OF WISDOM

What do you know now that you wish you knew then?
The problem is that if I knew then what I know now, I would have never started the business. We were just so naive. We had so little understanding of the industry that looking at it now, it was totally irresponsible to dive in thinking we did.

We missed huge periods of growth because we didn't realize those periods existed. Our lack of a cogent plan is largely why we missed them.

How really important a professional sales team was. We were so focused and enamored with the production process but the key to success lay in a strong and successful sales plan.

Adam Firestone
Firestone Walker

EXIT

Your business's life cycle wouldn't be complete without an exit. At the very basic level, there are only two ways to exit: transfer ownership to another party, or simply close the doors. In regard to transfer of ownership, there are myriad ways to achieve that: sell to another party, create an employee stock ownership plan (ESOP) that places ownership in the hands of its employees, or sell to key employees or family members.

WORDS OF WISDOM

SUCCESSION PLANNING

Can you provide a quick definition of succession planning; what type of advisor will help you with this?

- Succession planning is about assuring a company's success through ownership and management changes, both the unexpected changes (e.g., death, disability, or other events that force unintended change) as well as predictable changes (e.g., retirement, a business plan to build/grow/sell, etc.)
- Business succession/transition consultants, investment bankers, attorneys, accountants are the typical advisors. Franchise businesses are often helped by the franchisor.

How far in advance of ownership transfer should succession planning start?

- In all cases the answer is "as early as possible" but it depends on the transition type. A family transition takes years-to-decades to grow the next generation's capabilities, and the best/most effective gifting transfers can take a decade or more to complete. Planning a business sale to an investor or competitor should be a minimum of a year or more in advance.

What are the general steps in the process of ownership transfer?

1. Define objectives.
2. Test the business' ability to accomplish the desired transition and remain competitive.
3. Test the owners' personal financial goals against the value they are likely to get from the business transition to see if it's motivating.
4. Adjust the objectives based on the business and owners' likely outcomes (could be any adjustment, from changing timing to changing to a completely different transition).
5. Make any business and management changes necessary to increase likelihood of success.
6. Start the succession when appropriate.
7. If the succession isn't immediate (most are not), make sure contingency plans are in place and are consistent with the desired outcome.

What should a business owner look for in a succession plan advisor?

- Experience and expertise, a defined process, agnostic/not conflicted on the outcome

Describe some of the advantages to both buyer and seller of having a well-structured plan.

- It actually happens, and with less hysteria and friction getting there. Most failed transitions are a result of poor planning or no planning at all. Whether the desired framework is an internal sale, family transition, or external sale, a comprehensive strategy is what ensures success. The reality is that every business transitions. The primary question is would the owner(s) prefer to dictate how that happens or let unknowns determine the outcome (e.g., death, disability, change in industry, competition, or other events that force unintended change).

Patrick Corcorran
Principal, Rainier Group

Through an Employee Stock Ownership Plan (ESOP), a company establishes a stock ownership trust and contributes stock to the trust each year. Employees have accounts within the ESOP trust and they earn the stock that is allocated to them over a certain vesting period. The structure of an ESOP motivates employees to work toward profitability and productivity since their labors are contributing directly to their own investment.

According to Rocky Fiore at Prairie Capital,[1] here are five reasons you may want to consider an ESOP:

- Provides full or partial liquidity to shareholder(s)
- Realize a tax efficient transfer of ownership
- Maintain brewery independence
- Reward employees with an opportunity to participate in equity ownership
- Build an exciting and rewarding employee ownership culture

---

[1] Rocky Fiore, "Is an ESOP right for your craft brewery? Consult this checklist from Prairie Capital Advisors," Craft Brewing Business, January 2, 2018, https://www.craftbrewingbusiness.com/featured/esop-right-craft-brewery-consult-checklist-prairie-capital-advisors/. Used by permission.

ESOPs work best in breweries with the following characteristics:

- Dedicated management team
- Good operating model and market position
- Stable or growing margins and cash flows
- Strong balance sheet
- Excellent financial management and controls

CONCLUSION

There is a quote from Heraclitus, a Greek philosopher: "Change is the only constant in life." Business owners, take that to heart! Be flexible and operate today like the brewery you want to be in three years. Don't wait until you are exhausted and out of options before thinking about how you will exit a company. Moving from one phase to another takes time and intention, so understand where you are headed on the roadmap of life, but be adaptable as to the route you take.

APPENDIX A

WHAT TO INCLUDE IN YOUR BUSINESS PLAN

While the specifics of your plan will be unique to your vision, most business plans do follow the same general outline. The headings below are an example of what to include in any business plan.

Executive Summary

The executive summary is the elevator pitch for your company. In a few short paragraphs you describe the product offerings, the need or problem you are solving, and differentiators for your product that make you unique.

Company Description

The company description provides information about the company's legal structure, founders, and managers. This is also the section to provide basic information, such as where you are located and when the company was formed. To give historical perspective, provide background on the relevant experience of the founders and measures of success to date. For a brewery business plan, this might include any beer awards or recognition that you have earned, experience within the industry, or relevant business, management or leadership achievements. Briefly describe the stages of future growth (e.g., will the brewery grow through distribution or by opening multiple taprooms) and provide basic forecasted financial information.

Products and Services

The products and services section describes your line of offerings; for example, standard or traditional styles, sours, barrel-aged, or experimental beers. Give character to your various offerings and describe how each style plays an important role in your portfolio of beers. Here are some examples of how each group could be validated:

"Market demand requires that we brew an IPA."

"Our brewers are acclaimed for their barrel-aged beers and blending techniques."

"Experimental beers will give us a fresh face in the market."

This is a natural area of the business plan to discuss strengths or differentiators as it relates to the beers you will offer. Don't limit yourself to describing the liquid—it could be an innovation in packaging, or a unique experience. It's becoming more common to see destination breweries, where customers can spend time to either take a tour, participate in some way, or host special events. Some breweries have even built lodgings to create a full experience for their guests.

Market Analysis

Do a basic SWOT analysis—strengths, weaknesses, opportunities, and threats. Give the reader information about the competitive landscape and show how you are positioning yourself relative to others in the space. To the best of your ability, discuss market forces and how you see yourself evolving.

Strategy and Implementation

In the previous sections you've described your vision and the landscape in which you work. The strategy and implementation section describes how you will achieve this vision. For example, assume that your vision is to open three taprooms over a seven-year period and achieve EBITDA of 15% on average over that period. Your strategies may include a requirement that potential locations meet a set of pre-determined guidelines. That strategy would be implemented by defining those guidelines: gathering economic data on a potential location, interviewing the landlord, conducting a SWOT analysis on the specific location, and creating pro forma financial reports. This section of the business plan provides the structure for how your vision will be realized.

Organization and Management

While the strategy and implementation section is the playbook for the actions to be taken, the organization and management section is the team roster who will execute the plan. Create a short-term and long-term organizational chart to help readers visualize how the personnel will look in the future and how roles and responsibilities will be assigned.

Financial Plan and Projections

The financial plan and projections section should include pro forma financial statements for the first three years of the company. Include information about the planned timeline for distributions, if possible. Discuss how you will handle tax liabilities for investors that may arise from the company's operations. Will you make tax distributions? How will those be calculated? How will you determine when to make a regular distribution to investors, and at what frequency?

Conclusion

The concluding section briefly summarizes key points from the business plan and reinforces the vision of the company.

APPENDIX B

SAMPLE CHART OF ACCOUNTS

TABLE B.1 SAMPLE BREWERY CHART OF ACCOUNTS WITH RESTAURANT OPERATIONS

Number	Account	Type
1000	Cash on Hand	Bank
1020	Checking	Bank
1040	Undeposited Funds	Other Current Asset
1100	Accounts Receivable	Accounts Receivable
1200	Credit Cards Receivable	Other Current Asset
1500	Inventory	Other Current Asset
1510	Inventory:Finished Goods	Other Current Asset
1512	Inventory:Finished Goods:Cases Packaged	Other Current Asset
1514	Inventory:Finished Goods:Kegs	Other Current Asset
1516	Inventory:Finished Goods:Serving Tanks	Other Current Asset
1520	Inventory:Growlers and Glassware	Other Current Asset
1522	Inventory:Hat Inventory	Other Current Asset
1524	Inventory:Shirts	Other Current Asset
1530	Inventory:Raw Materials	Other Current Asset
1540	Inventory:Packaging Materials	Other Current Asset
1550	Inventory:Taproom Inventory	Other Current Asset
1552	Inventory:Taproom Inventory:Food	Other Current Asset
1554	Inventory:Taproom Inventory:Guest Tap	Other Current Asset
1556	Inventory:Taproom Inventory:In-House Kegs	Other Current Asset
1560	Inventory:Work in Process	Other Current Asset
1562	Inventory:Work in Process:Barrel-Aging	Other Current Asset
1600	Prepaid Expenses	Other Current Asset

Number	Account	Type
1700	Brewery Equipment and Machinery	Fixed Asset
1702	Brewery Equipment and Machinery:Barrel Racks	Fixed Asset
1704	Brewery Equipment and Machinery:Barrels	Fixed Asset
1710	Computer	Fixed Asset
1720	Equipment	Fixed Asset
1730	Leasehold Improvements	Fixed Asset
1740	Start-up costs	Fixed Asset
1750	Taproom Equipment	Fixed Asset
1752	Taproom Equipment:Computers	Fixed Asset
1754	Taproom Equipment:Equipment	Fixed Asset
1756	Taproom Equipment:Furniture and Fixtures	Fixed Asset
1760	Trademark	Fixed Asset
1780	Vehicles	Fixed Asset
1798	Accumulated Depreciation	Fixed Asset
1799	Accumulated Amortization	Fixed Asset
1800	Assets Not Yet In Service	Other Asset
1900	Security Deposit	Other Asset
2000	Accounts Payable	Accounts Payable
2010	Credit Card	Credit Card
2100	Accrued Federal Excise Tax	Other Current Liability
2110	Accrued Interest Payable	Other Current Liability
2120	Equipment Lease	Other Current Liability
2130	Gift Card Liability	Other Current Liability
2140	Keg Deposits Received	Other Current Liability
2200	Line of Credit	Other Current Liability
2300	Notes Payable	Other Current Liability
2400	Payroll Liability	Other Current Liability
2410	Tips Payable	Other Current Liability
2500	Sales Tax Payable	Other Current Liability
2600	Bank Loan	Long Term Liability
3000	Members Equity	Equity
4000	Draft Sales	Income
4100	Packaged Sales	Income
4200	Dock Sales:Kegs	Income
4300	Food	Income
4400	Liquor	Income
4500	Merchandise Sales	Income
4510	Merchandise Sales:Growlers	Income
4520	Merchandise Sales:Hats	Income
4530	Merchandise Sales:Shirts	Income
4600	Miscellaneous	Income
4700	N/A Beverage	Income

Number	Account	Type
4800	Wine	Income
4999	Discounts Given	Income
5000	Cost of Goods Sold	Cost of Goods Sold
5010	Cost of Goods Sold:Beer - Kegged	Cost of Goods Sold
5020	Cost of Goods Sold:Beer - Packaged	Cost of Goods Sold
5030	Cost of Goods Sold:Beer Loss	Cost of Goods Sold
5040	Cost of Goods Sold:Inventory Adjustment	Cost of Goods Sold
5100	Excise Tax	Cost of Goods Sold
5200	Groceries	Cost of Goods Sold
5300	Keg Expense	Cost of Goods Sold
5310	Keg Expense:Barrel Expense	Cost of Goods Sold
5400	Liquor Sold	Cost of Goods Sold
5500	Merchandise	Cost of Goods Sold
5510	Merchandise:Growlers	Cost of Goods Sold
5520	Merchandise:Hats	Cost of Goods Sold
5530	Merchandise:Shirts	Cost of Goods Sold
5600	Online Sales Revenue Share	Cost of Goods Sold
5700	N/A Beverage Sold	Cost of Goods Sold
5800	Wine Sold	Cost of Goods Sold
5900	Payroll COGS	Cost of Goods Sold
5910	Payroll COGS:Back House Labor	Cost of Goods Sold
5920	Payroll COGS:Front House Labor	Cost of Goods Sold
5940	Shipping & Delivery	Cost of Goods Sold
5960	Depreciation Expense:COGS Depreciation	Cost of Goods Sold
6000	Amortization	Expense
6010	Bank Service Charges	Expense
6020	Business Licenses	Expense
6030	Cash Under/Over	Expense
6040	Charitable Contributions	Expense
6050	Telephone/Cable/Internet	Expense
6060	Computer and Internet Expenses	Expense
6070	Depreciation Expense	Expense
6080	Dues and Subscriptions	Expense
6090	Equipment Rental	Expense
6100	Fines and Penalties	Expense
6110	Gift Cards	Expense
6120	Gifts	Expense
6130	Guaranteed Payment	Expense
6140	Hiring Expenses	Expense
6150	Insurance Expense	Expense
6160	Insurance Expense:Dental Insurance	Expense
6162	Insurance Expense:General Liability Insurance	Expense

Number	Account	Type
6164	Insurance Expense:Health Insurance	Expense
6166	Insurance Expense:Worker's Compensation	Expense
6170	Interest Expense	Expense
6180	Janitorial Expense	Expense
6182	Janitorial Expense:Laundry	Expense
6190	Lab Supplies	Expense
6200	Landscaping	Expense
6210	License & Permits	Expense
6220	Marketing and Advertising	Expense
6230	Merchant Fees	Expense
6240	Office Supplies	Expense
6250	Payroll	Expense
6252	Payroll:Bonuses	Expense
6254	Payroll:Commissions	Expense
6256	Payroll:Manager Salaries	Expense
6258	Payroll:Payroll Service Fee	Expense
6260	Payroll:Payroll Taxes	Expense
6270	Payroll:Temporary Staff	Expense
6280	Postage and Delivery	Expense
6290	Professional Fees	Expense
6292	Professional Fees:Accounting	Expense
6294	Professional Fees:Consulting	Expense
6296	Professional Fees:Legal Fees	Expense
6298	Professional Fees:Marketing	Expense
6300	Rent Expense	Expense
6302	Rent Expense:Hops Storage Fee	Expense
6310	Repairs and Maintenance	Expense
6320	Sales Expense	Expense
6322	Sales Expense:Automobile Expense	Expense
6324	Sales Expense:Cell Phone	Expense
6326	Sales Expense:Meals	Expense
6328	Sales Expense:Parking	Expense
6330	Sales Expense:Samples	Expense
6332	Sales Expense:Travel	Expense
6340	Small Equipment	Expense
6350	Smallwares	Expense
6360	Supplies	Expense
6362	Supplies:Brewery Supplies	Expense
6364	Supplies:Pub Supplies	Expense
6370	Taxes	Expense
6372	Taxes:Local	Expense
6374	Taxes:State	Expense

Number	Account	Type
6376	Taxes:Property Taxes	Expense
6380	Uniforms	Expense
6390	Utilities	Expense
6392	Utilities:Garbage Service	Expense
6394	Utilities:Natural Gas	Expense
6396	Utilities:Power	Expense
6398	Utilities:Security	Expense
6400	Utilities:Water	Expense
7000	Gain/Loss on Sale of Equipment	Other Income
7100	Interest Income	Other Income
8000	Theft Loss	Other Expense

TABLE B.2 SAMPLE BREWERY CHART OF ACCOUNTS

Account	Type	Description	Accnt. #
10000 · Checking Account #1	Bank	Checking account	10000
11000 · Accounts Receivable	Accounts Receivable	Amounts owed to the company for goods or services, but not yet paid.	11000
12000 · Undeposited Funds	Other Current Asset	Funds received, but not yet deposited to a bank account.	12000
12100 · Inventory	Other Current Asset	Parent account for inventory items.	12100
12100 · Inventory:12101 · Raw Materials	Other Current Asset	Parent account for raw materials.	12101
12100 · Inventory:12101 · Raw Materials:12103 · Malt	Other Current Asset	Cost of malt owned by the company (stored on-site or off-site).	12103
12100 · Inventory:12101 · Raw Materials:12104 · Hops	Other Current Asset	Cost of hops owned by the company (stored on-site or off-site).	12104
12100 · Inventory:12101 · Raw Materials:12105 · Chemicals	Other Current Asset	Cost of chemicals used in the production of finished goods.	12105
12100 · Inventory:12101 · Raw Materials:12106 · Packaging Materials	Other Current Asset	Cost of bottles, cans, trays, labels, etc.	12106
12100 · Inventory:12101 · Raw Materials:12108 · Adjuncts	Other Current Asset	Cost of additives used in the production of finished goods.	12108
12100 · Inventory:12130 · Merch Inventory	Other Current Asset	Cost of merchandise owned by the company to be sold.	12130
12100 · Inventory:12150 · Work in Process	Other Current Asset	Parent account for beer that is at a stage of process between raw ingredients and finished goods.	12150
12100 · Inventory:12150 · Work in Process:12151 · Bright Beer	Other Current Asset	Cost of beer that is at the bright beer stage of the production process.	12151
12100 · Inventory:12150 · Work in Process:12152 · Dry Hopped Beer	Other Current Asset	Cost of beer that is at the dry hopped stage of the production process.	12152
12100 · Inventory:12150 · Work in Process:12153 · Green Beer	Other Current Asset	Cost of beer that is at the green beer stage of the production process.	12153
12100 · Inventory:12200 · Finished Goods	Other Current Asset	Parent account for finished goods.	12200
12100 · Inventory:12200 · Finished Goods:12201 · Packaged Inventory	Other Current Asset	Cost of finished beer that has been packaged in bottles or cans.	12201

Account	Type	Description	Accnt. #
12100 · Inventory:12200 · Finished Goods:12202 · Draft Inventory	Other Current Asset	Cost of finished beer that is bulk or kegged.	12202
12102 · Inventory Asset	Other Current Asset	Cost of inventory purchased for resale.	12102
19000 · Prepaid Expenses	Other Current Asset	Cost of expenses for future accounting periods that is paid in advance.	19000
15000 · Brewery Machinery & Equipment	Fixed Asset	Cost to acquire and prepare brewing equipment for use by the company. Includes tanks, brewhouse, etc.	15000
15000 · Brewery Machinery & Equipment:15001 · Office Equipment	Fixed Asset	Cost to acquire and prepare office supplies for use by the company.	15001
15200 · Leasehold Improvements	Fixed Asset	Cost of improving a leased building. The improvement will revert to the lessor at the end of the lease. Can include services such as engineering fees or architect fees.	15200
15300 · Taproom Equipment	Fixed Asset	Cost to acquire and prepare taproom equipment for use by the company. Includes crowler machines, etc.	15300
17000 · Accumulated Depreciation	Fixed Asset	Amounts of fixed assets' cost that have been allocated to Depreciation Expense since the company has owned the fixed asset.	17000
18000 · Organizational Costs	Other Asset	Initial cost incurred to create a company. Includes legal and promotional fees, licensing costs, etc.	18000
18050 · Trademark Costs	Other Asset	Costs incurred to file and protect company trademarks.	18050
20000 · Accounts Payable	Accounts Payable	Amounts owed by the company for goods or services, but not yet been paid.	20000
20100 · Credit Card #1	Credit Card	Amounts owed by the company for credit card debt.	20100
22000 · Keg Deposits	Other Current Liability	Amounts held by the company as security deposits on keg shells.	22000
25100 · Federal Excise Tax	Other Current Liability	Amounts of federal excise tax owed by the company, but not yet paid.	25100
25200 · State Excise Tax	Other Current Liability	Amounts of state excise tax owed by the company, but not yet paid.	25200
25500 · Sales Tax Payable	Other Current Liability	Amounts of sales tax owed by the company, but not yet paid.	25500
25550 · Payroll Tax Payable	Other Current Liability	Amounts of payroll tax owed by the company, but not yet paid.	25550
21000 · Bank Loan #1	Long-Term Liability	Amounts of principal due a year or more in the future to a financial institution.	21000
30100 · Partner Contributions	Equity	Amounts contributed to a company by an owner. There is no expectation of being paid back.	30100
32000 · Retained Earnings	Equity	Earnings of the corporation that have accumulated from prior periods.	32000
40000 · Brewery Sales	Income	Parent account for the sale of product outside of the company's retail location.	40000

Account	Type	Description	Accnt. #
40000 · Brewery Sales:40100 · Packaged Sales	Income	Amounts earned from selling packaged beer.	40100
40000 · Brewery Sales:40200 · Draft Sales	Income	Amounts earned from selling draft beer.	40200
40000 · Brewery Sales:40300 · Brewery Discounts	Income	Amounts discounted on beer sales. Examples include promotional discounts.	40300
40000 · Brewery Sales:40400 · Brewery Refunds-Allowances	Income	Discounts given for unsaleable product.	40400
45000 · Taproom Sales	Income	Parent account for the sale of product at the company's retail location.	45000
45000 · Taproom Sales:45100 · Taproom Packaged Sales	Income	Amounts earned from selling packaged beer.	45100
45000 · Taproom Sales:45200 · Taproom Draft Sales	Income	Amounts earned from selling draft beer.	45200
45000 · Taproom Sales:45300 · Taproom Discounts	Income	Amounts discounted on beer sales. Examples include mug club discounts, employee discounts, etc.	45300
47000 · Merchandise	Income	Parent account for the sale of merchandise.	47000
47000 · Merchandise:47001 · Glassware	Income	Amounts earned from selling glassware.	47001
47000 · Merchandise:47002 · T-Shirts	Income	Amounts earned from selling t-shirts.	47002
47000 · Merchandise:47003 · Hats	Income	Amounts earned from selling hats.	47003
47000 · Merchandise:47100 · Merch Discounts	Income	Discounts given on merchandise. Examples include promotional discounts, employee discounts.	47100
47000 · Merchandise:47200 · Shipping, Delivery Income	Income	Amounts earned on shipping or delivery of product sold.	47200
50000 · Cost Of Goods Sold	Cost of Goods Sold	Parent account for cost of goods sold.	50000
50002 · Brewery COGS	Cost of Goods Sold	Parent account for brewery cost of goods sold.	50002
50002 · Brewery COGS:50004 · Packaged COGS	Cost of Goods Sold	Cost of ingredients used in the production of packaged beer sold in the accounting period.	50004
50002 · Brewery COGS:50006 · Draft COGS	Cost of Goods Sold	Cost of ingredients used in the production of draft beer sold in the accounting period.	50006
50002 · Brewery COGS:50500 · Brewery Direct Labor	Cost of Goods Sold	Parent account for brewery labor COGS.	50500
50002 · Brewery COGS:50500 · Brewery Direct Labor:50505 · Brewery Payroll	Cost of Goods Sold	Cost of payroll directly associated with the production of beer sold in the accounting period.	50505
50002 · Brewery COGS:50500 · Brewery Direct Labor:50510 · Brewery Benefits	Cost of Goods Sold	Cost of benefits for employees directly associated with the production of beer sold in the accounting period.	50510
50002 · Brewery COGS:50500 · Brewery Direct Labor:50515 · Brewery Payroll Taxes	Cost of Goods Sold	Cost of payroll taxes related to employees directly associated with the production of beer sold in the accounting period.	50515
50002 · Brewery COGS:50500 · Brewery Direct Labor:50520 · Subcontractors - COS	Cost of Goods Sold	Cost of fees for subcontracted services directly related to the production of beer sold in the accounting period.	50520

Account	Type	Description	Accnt. #
50002 · Brewery COGS:50600 · Chemicals	Cost of Goods Sold	Cost of chemicals used in the production of beer sold in the accounting period.	50600
50002 · Brewery COGS:50700 · Brewery Supplies & Materials	Cost of Goods Sold	Cost of small supplies and materials used in the production of beer sold in the accounting period.	50700
50002 · Brewery COGS:50800 · Manufacturing Loss	Cost of Goods Sold	Cost of beer lost in the production process during the accounting period.	50800
50002 · Brewery COGS:50900 · Spoilage	Cost of Goods Sold	Cost of beer that spoiled or went out of date, thus becoming unsaleable, during the accounting period.	50900
50002 · Brewery COGS:51000 - Warehouse Loss	Cost of Goods Sold	Cost of beer lost in the cellaring process during the accounting period. Examples include a case being dropped, a forklift piercing a pallet, etc.	51000
55000 · Taproom COGS	Cost of Goods Sold	Parent account for taproom cost of goods sold.	55000
55000 · Taproom COGS:55050 · Packaged COGS	Cost of Goods Sold	Cost of packaged beer sold in the taproom during the accounting period.	55050
55000 · Taproom COGS:55070 · Draft COGS	Cost of Goods Sold	Cost of draft beer sold in the taproom during the accounting period.	55070
55000 · Taproom COGS:55100 · Taproom Direct Labor	Cost of Goods Sold	Parent account for taproom labor COGS.	55100
55000 · Taproom COGS:55100 · Taproom Direct Labor:55110 · Taproom Payroll	Cost of Goods Sold	Cost of payroll directly associated with the sale of beer in the taproom during the accounting period.	55110
55000 · Taproom COGS:55100 · Taproom Direct Labor:55120 · Taproom Payroll Taxes	Cost of Goods Sold	Cost of payroll taxes related to employees directly associated with the sale of beer in the taproom during the accounting period.	55120
55000 · Taproom COGS:55100 · Taproom Direct Labor:55130 · Taproom Benefits	Cost of Goods Sold	Cost of benefits of employees directly associated with the sale of beer in the taproom during the accounting period.	55130
55000 · Taproom COGS:55200 · Taproom Glassware	Cost of Goods Sold	Cost of glassware used to serve beer in the taproom.	55200
55000 · Taproom COGS:55300 · Music	Cost of Goods Sold	Cost of music in the taproom. Includes live performers as well as music subscription services.	55300
55000 · Taproom COGS:55400 · Nonalcoholic	Cost of Goods Sold	Cost of nonalcoholic beverages served in the taproom.	55400
56000 · Merch COGS	Cost of Goods Sold	Parent account for merchandise cost of goods sold.	56000
56000 · Merch COGS:50610 · Glassware	Cost of Goods Sold	Cost of glassware sold.	50610
56000 · Merch COGS:50620 · Hats	Cost of Goods Sold	Cost of hats sold.	50620
56000 · Merch COGS:50630 · T-Shirts	Cost of Goods Sold	Cost of t-shirts sold.	50630
56000 · Merch COGS:50660 · Merch Freight & Delivery	Cost of Goods Sold	Cost of freight and delivery of merchandise sold in the accounting period.	50660
60200 - Bad Debts	Expense	Amounts due to the company that cannot be recovered.	60200
60400 · Bank Charges	Expense	Amounts charged for banking services.	60400
61000 · Administrative	Expense	Parent account for administrative expense.	61000

Account	Type	Description	Accnt. #
61000 · Administrative:61100 · Administrative Labor	Expense	Parent account for admin labor expense.	61100
61000 · Administrative:61100 · Administrative Labor:61110 · Administrative Payroll	Expense	Cost of payroll of admin department employees.	61110
61000 · Administrative:61100 · Administrative Labor:61120 · Administrative Payroll Taxes	Expense	Cost of payroll taxes of admin department employees.	61120
61000 · Administrative:61100 · Administrative Labor:61130 · Administrative Benefits	Expense	Cost of benefits of admin department employees.	61130
62400 · Depreciation Expense	Expense	A reduction in value of an asset in the accounting period due to normal use.	62400
62500 · Dues & Subscriptions	Expense	Amounts paid for membership or subscriptions.	62500
63300 · Insurance	Expense	Parent account for insurance expense.	63300
63300 · Insurance:63301 · Workman's Comp Insurance	Expense	Premiums paid for workers comp insurance.	63301
63300 · Insurance:63302 · Disability	Expense	Premiums paid for disability insurance.	63302
63300 · Insurance:63303 · Liability	Expense	Premiums paid for liability insurance.	63303
63400 · Interest Expense	Expense	Amounts paid for borrowing money.	63400
64300 · Meals	Expense	Amounts paid for business-purpose meals.	64300
64400 · Entertainment	Expense	Amounts paid for business-purpose entertainment (e.g., sports event tickets, etc.)	64400
64900 · Office Expenses	Expense	Amounts paid for office expenses.	64900
65000 · Sales	Expense	Parent account for sales expense.	65000
65000 · Sales:65100 · Sales Labor	Expense	Parent account for sales labor expense.	65100
65000 · Sales:65100 · Sales Labor:65110 · Sales Payroll	Expense	Cost of payroll of sales department employees.	65110
65000 · Sales:65100 · Sales Labor:65120 · Sales Payroll Taxes	Expense	Cost of payroll taxes of sales department employees.	65120
65000 · Sales:65100 · Sales Labor:65130 · Sales Benefits	Expense	Cost of benefits of sales department employees.	65130
65000 · Sales:65300 · Commissions and Fees	Expense	Amounts paid to a salesperson in exchange for services in facilitating a sales transaction.	65300
65000 · Sales:65400 · Sales Auto Expense	Expense	Amounts paid for gas, parking, mileage for sales employees	65400
66000 · Advertising	Expense	Parent account for advertising expense.	66000
66000 · Advertising:66001 · Design	Expense	Amounts paid for design services.	66001
66000 · Advertising:66002 · Promotional	Expense	Amounts paid for promotional services.	66002
66700 · Legal & Professional Fees	Expense	Amounts paid for legal, accounting, or other professional consulting services.	66700
67100 · Rent or Lease	Expense	Parent account for rent or lease expense.	67100
67100 · Rent or Lease:67101 · Building	Expense	Amounts paid for rent of a location.	67101
67100 · Rent or Lease:67102 · Equipment	Expense	Amounts paid for rent of equipment.	67102
67200 · Repair & Maintenance	Expense	Amounts paid for repairs and maintenance of facilities or equipment.	67200

Account	Type	Description	Accnt. #
68400 · Travel	Expense	Amounts paid for business travel.	68400
68400 · Travel:68401 · Travel Meals	Expense	Amounts paid for meals of employees who are traveling on business.	68401
68600 · Utilities	Expense	Parent account for utilities expense.	68600
68600 · Utilities:68601 · Telephone	Expense	Amounts paid for telephone utility.	68601
68600 · Utilities:68602 · Gas & Electric	Expense	Amounts paid for gas and electric utility.	68602
68600 · Utilities:68603 · Internet	Expense	Amounts paid for internet utility.	68603
68600 · Utilities:68604 · Water & Sewer	Expense	Amounts paid for water and sewer utility.	68604
68600 · Utilities:68605 · Trash Removal	Expense	Amounts paid for trash service.	68605
70100 · Other Ordinary Income	Other Income	Other income amounts.	70100
70200 · Interest Earned	Other Income	Amounts earned by lending money to others.	70200
80500 · Other Expense	Other Expense	Other expense amounts.	80500
90100 · Purchase Orders	Non-Posting	Purchase orders specifying items ordered from vendors	90100

APPENDIX C

SAMPLE FULL BUDGET SPREADSHEET

See Second Retail Location, Sales Budget for Second Taproom, Second Retail Breakeven, Raise Pint Prices, and Unadjusted Income Statement tables on the following pages.

TABLE C.1 SECOND RETAIL LOCATION

	Projected Y2 Month 1	Projected Y2 Month 2	Projected Y2 Month 3	Projected Y2 Month 4	Projected Y2 Month 5	Projected Y2 Month 6
Ordinary Income/Expense						
Income - Taproom 1						
Draft Sales	47,650.30	43,419.23	49,905.97	40,718.82	46,175.74	48,113.73
Packaged Beer	7,926.23	7,222.43	8,301.45	6,773.24	7,680.95	8,003.32
Merchandise Sales	678.00	771.00	786.00	465.00	717.00	918.00
Income - Taproom 2						
Draft Sales	39,650.76	36,130.00	45,680.53	37,271.23	42,266.13	44,819.50
Packaged Beer	7,347.44	6,695.03	8,464.78	6,906.51	7,832.08	8,305.23
Merchandise Sales	698.00	781.00	796.00	465.00	737.00	938.00
Total Income	103,950.74	95,018.69	113,934.73	92,599.80	105,408.90	111,097.79
Cost of Goods Sold						
Beer - Guest	1,650.82	895.78	555.88	1,203.32	1,205.36	1,416.78
Beer - House	17,460.21	15,909.85	19,117.30	15,598.01	17,688.37	18,586.65
Mobile Packaging	9,638.45	11,424.48	9,321.35	10,570.55	11,079.15	11,574.72
Excise Tax	436.51	397.75	477.93	389.95	442.21	464.67
CO_2	1,532.04	1,715.28	1,689.30	1,584.70	1,763.18	1,165.34
Merchandise	236.00	267.00	272.00	165.00	249.00	316.00
Payroll COGS	7,133.81	7,133.81	7,133.81	7,133.81	7,133.81	7,847.19
Total COGS	38,087.83	37,743.94	38,567.57	36,645.34	39,561.08	41,371.33
Gross Profit	65,862.91	57,274.75	75,367.16	55,954.46	65,847.82	69,726.45
Expense						
Guaranteed Payment	4,000.00	4,000.00	4,000.00	4,250.00	4,250.00	4,250.00
Insurance Expense	1,866.95	1,866.95	1,866.95	1,866.95	1,866.95	1,866.95
Interest Expense	2,500.00	2,500.00	2,500.00	2,500.00	2,500.00	2,500.00
Marketing and Advertising	3,000.00	3,000.00	3,000.00	3,000.00	3,000.00	3,000.00
Office Supplies	741.14	531.00	327.22	1,097.72	423.86	328.40
Payroll	7,910.00	7,910.00	7,910.00	8,305.50	8,305.50	8,701.00
Professional Fees	500.00	2,000.00	3,500.00	500.00	2,000.00	0.00
Rent Expense	12,500.00	12,500.00	12,500.00	12,500.00	12,500.00	12,500.00
Repairs and Maintenance	116.74	216.00	1,314.00	1,841.20	893.68	216.00
Taxes						
Local	0.00	0.00	200.00	0.00	0.00	0.00
State	0.00	0.00	150.00	0.00	0.00	0.00
Property Taxes	0.00	0.00	0.00	0.00	0.00	0.00
Total Taxes	0.00	0.00	350.00	0.00	0.00	0.00
Utilities	11,364.27	10,634.04	9,062.83	9,266.89	9,762.98	11,183.27
Other Expenses	4,491.31	2,489.41	3,425.97	2,880.28	6,158.77	1,883.98
Total Expense	51,589.18	50,022.87	52,605.33	50,323.54	54,296.97	49,207.04
Net Ordinary Income	14,273.73	7,251.88	22,761.83	5,630.93	11,550.85	20,519.41
Net Income	**14,273.73**	**7,251.88**	**22,761.83**	**5,630.93**	**11,550.85**	**20,519.41**

TABLE C.1 SECOND RETAIL LOCATION (CONT.)

Projected Y2 Month 7	Projected Y2 Month 8	Projected Y2 Month 9	Projected Y2 Month 10	Projected Y2 Month 11	Projected Y2 Month 12	Projected Y2 TOTAL
49,847.63	44,800.00	39,600.00	48,400.00	37,400.00	33,000.00	529,031.43
8,291.74	7,452.11	6,587.13	8,050.94	6,221.18	5,489.28	88,000.00
832.50	580.00	580.00	620.00	660.00	660.00	8,267.50
47,590.25	41,800.00	37,620.00	45,980.00	35,530.00	31,350.00	485,688.39
8,818.66	7,745.71	6,971.14	8,520.28	6,583.85	5,809.28	90,000.00
842.50	590.00	580.00	640.00	660.00	680.00	8,407.50
116,223.28	102,967.82	91,938.27	112,211.22	87,055.03	76,988.56	1,209,394.82
758.92	700.00	700.00	700.00	700.00	700.00	11,186.86
19,487.58	17,320.00	15,444.00	18,876.00	14,586.00	12,870.00	202,943.96
10,321.71	9,179.64	11,219.56	8,669.66	7,649.70	7,649.70	118,298.67
487.19	433.00	386.10	471.90	364.65	321.75	5,073.60
2,469.70	1,700.00	1,700.00	1,700.00	1,700.00	1,700.00	20,419.54
287.50	203.33	203.33	216.67	230.00	230.00	2,875.83
7,847.19	8,203.88	8,203.88	8,203.88	8,203.88	8,203.88	92,382.79
41,659.78	37,739.85	37,856.87	38,838.10	33,434.23	31,675.33	453,181.25
74,563.50	65,227.97	54,081.40	73,373.11	53,620.81	45,313.23	756,213.57
4,500.00	4,500.00	4,500.00	4,750.00	4,750.00	4,750.00	52,500.00
1,866.95	1,866.95	1,866.95	1,866.95	1,866.95	1,866.95	22,403.40
2,500.00	2,500.00	2,500.00	2,500.00	2,500.00	2,500.00	30,000.00
3,000.00	3,000.00	3,000.00	3,000.00	3,000.00	3,000.00	36,000.00
551.04	570.00	570.00	570.00	570.00	570.00	6,850.38
8,701.00	9,096.50	9,096.50	9,096.50	9,096.50	9,096.50	103,225.50
500.00	2,000.00	0.00	500.00	2,000.00	0.00	13,500.00
12,500.00	12,500.00	12,500.00	12,500.00	12,800.00	12,800.00	150,600.00
1,216.00	830.00	830.00	830.00	830.00	830.00	9,963.62
0.00	0.00	0.00	0.00	0.00	0.00	200.00
0.00	0.00	0.00	0.00	0.00	0.00	150.00
0.00	0.00	0.00	7,500.00	0.00	0.00	7,500.00
0.00	0.00	0.00	7,500.00	0.00	0.00	7,850.00
11,012.28	10,439.40	10,439.40	10,439.40	10,439.40	10,439.40	124,483.57
4,893.11	3,424.94	3,983.52	5,183.62	5,842.22	6,863.12	51,520.24
54,145.96	53,301.99	51,584.83	61,541.75	55,871.45	54,640.68	639,131.58
20,417.54	11,925.98	2,496.57	11,831.36	(2,250.64)	(9,327.45)	117,081.99
20,417.54	**11,925.98**	**2,496.57**	**11,831.36**	**(2,250.64)**	**(9,327.45)**	**117,081.99**

TABLE C.2 SALES BUDGET FOR SECOND TAPROOM

	Month 1	Month 2	Month 3	Month 4
Year One revenue from Taproom 1	$40,090.76	$36,626.00	$42,023.75	$34,176.94
Less: revenue earned outside of Taproom 2's operating hours	$4,000.00	$4,500.00	$4,540.00	$4,440.00
Additional revenue if we had charged $6 per pint from the beginning	$3,153.71	$2,838.73	$1,357.55	$1,016.39
Draft revenue subtotal	$39,244.47	$34,964.73	$38,841.30	$30,753.33
Average ticket	$14.50	$15.20	$16.25	$18.45
Number of customer turns	2707	2300	2390	1667
Difference in average ticket from sampler tray group vs big beer drinkers	$7.00	$7.00	$7.00	$7.00
Increase in number of sampler tray drinkers	30%	30%	30%	30%
Incremental revenue from shifting customers to sampler trays*	$5,683.68	$4,830.65	$5,019.49	$3,500.38
Draft revenue subtotal	$44,928.15	$39,795.38	$43,860.80	$34,253.71
Adjustment in sales for established brand	$898.56	$795.91	$877.22	$(229.50)
Draft revenue total	$45,826.71	$40,591.29	$44,738.01	$34,024.21
Packaged beer revenue	$4,400.80	$3,898.03	$4,296.25	$3,267.39
Total revenue	$50,227.51	$44,489.32	$49,034.26	$37,291.60

* Number of customer turns × Difference in average ticket from sampler tray group vs big beer drinkers × Increase in number of sampler tray drinkers

TABLE C.2 SALES BUDGET FOR SECOND TAPROOM (CONT.)

Month 5	Month 6	Month 7	Projected Month 8	Projected Month 9	Projected Month 10	Projected Month 11	Projected Month 12	Projected TOTAL
$40,195.75	$44,214.00	$47,471.25	$46,720.00	$42,540.00	$48,265.00	$40,750.00	$36,970.00	$500,043.45
$4,640.00	$4,260.00	$6,000.00	$4,500.00	$4,500.00	$4,500.00	$4,500.00	$4,500.00	$54,880.00
$1,278.08	$1,452.78	$1,594.40	$1,561.74	$1,380.00	$1,628.91	$1,302.17	$1,137.83	$19,702.29
$36,833.83	$41,406.78	$43,065.65	$43,781.74	$39,420.00	$45,393.91	$37,552.17	$33,607.83	$464,865.74
$22.00	$19.35	$17.88	–	–	–	–	–	–
1674	2140	2409	2479	2232	2570	2126	1903	26597
$7.00	$7.00	$7.00	$7.00	$7.00	$7.00	$7.00	$7.00	–
30%	30%	30%	30%	30%	30%	30%	30%	–
$3,515.96	$4,493.76	$5,058.05	$5,205.79	$4,687.16	$5,397.48	$4,465.07	$3,996.08	$55,853.55
$40,349.78	$45,900.54	$48,123.70	$48,987.53	$44,107.16	$50,791.39	$42,017.25	$37,603.90	$520,719.29
$(270.34)	$(307.53)	$(322.43)	$(328.22)	$(295.52)	$(340.30)	$(281.52)	$(251.95)	$(55.62)
$40,079.44	$45,593.01	$47,801.27	$48,659.31	$43,811.65	$50,451.09	$41,735.73	$37,351.96	$520,663.67
$3,848.88	$4,378.36	$4,590.42	$4,672.82	$4,207.29	$4,844.88	$4,007.94	$3,586.96	$50,000.00
$43,928.32	$49,971.36	$52,391.69	$53,332.13	$48,018.93	$55,295.97	$45,743.67	$40,938.91	$570,663.67

TABLE C.3 SECOND RETAIL BREAKEVEN

Capital expenses	
Leasehold Improvements	$160,000
Computers	$3,000
Architect Fees	$5,000
Furniture and fixtures	$30,000
Total capital expenses	$198,000
Kegs	$5,000
Rent - prior to opening	$6,000
Payroll - prior to opening	$4,000
Utilities - prior to opening	$6,000
Smallwares	$4,000
Legal fees	$3,000
Total start-up costs	**$226,000**
Monthly net income from second location	
Estimated revenue	$47,000
Cost of beer	($8,000)
Mobile Canning	($3,000)
Additional excise tax	($100)
Taproom labor, payroll tax, benefits	($4,500)
Rent	($6,500)
Utilities	($4,000)
Other expenses	($8,000)
Estimated net income	**$12,900**
Number of months to break even	**18**

TABLE C.4 RAISE PINT PRICES

	Month 1	Month 2	Month 3	Month 4	Month 5	Month 6
Ordinary Income/Expense						
Income						
Draft Sales	39,650.76	36,130.00	41,527.75	33,882.94	38,423.75	40,745.00
Packaged Beer					1,318.00	2,897.00
Merchandise Sales	440.00	496.00	496.00	294.00	454.00	572.00
Total Income	40,090.76	36,626.00	42,023.75	34,176.94	40,195.75	44,214.00
Cost of Goods Sold						
Beer - Guest	825.41	447.89	277.94	601.66	602.68	708.39
Beer - House	7,930.15	7,226.00	8,305.55	6,776.59	7,684.75	8,149.00
Mobile Packaging					3,802.00	
Excise Tax	198.25	180.65	207.64	169.41	192.12	203.73
CO_2	766.02	857.64	844.65	792.35	881.59	582.67
Merchandise	151.33	169.00	167.33	102.00	154.00	190.67
Payroll COGS	168.62	1,882.51	1,990.20	3,902.15	3,985.00	4,203.35
Total COGS	10,039.79	10,763.69	11,793.31	12,344.16	17,302.14	14,037.80
Gross Profit	30,050.97	25,862.31	30,230.44	21,832.78	22,893.61	30,176.20
Expense						
Guaranteed Payment	0.00	0.00	0.00	2,500.00	2,500.00	3,000.00
Insurance Expense	1,122.09	1,122.09	1,122.09	1,122.09	1,122.09	1,122.09
Interest Expense	0.00	0.00	0.00	0.00	0.00	0.00
Marketing and Advertising	1,144.00	1,732.09	485.25	361.50	185.25	3,178.00
Office Supplies	370.57	265.50	163.61	548.86	211.93	164.20
Payroll	0.00	1,866.76	2,013.66	1,984.28	2,175.25	2,782.06
Professional Fees	3,205.00	1,000.00	3,347.00	800.00	705.00	0.00
Rent Expense	6,235.00	6,235.00	6,235.00	6,235.00	6,235.00	6,235.00
Repairs and Maintenance	58.37	108.00	657.00	920.60	446.84	108.00
Taxes						
Local	0.00	0.00	200.00	0.00	0.00	0.00
State	0.00	0.00	150.00	0.00	0.00	0.00
Property Taxes	0.00	0.00	0.00	0.00	0.00	0.00
Total Taxes	0.00	0.00	350.00	0.00	0.00	0.00
Utilities	7,391.98	6,827.34	5,777.89	5,971.70	6,258.64	7,210.46
Other Expenses	2,673.52	2,607.21	2,308.32	2,407.86	4,059.58	2,047.60
Total Expense	22,200.53	21,763.99	22,459.82	22,851.89	23,899.58	25,847.41
Net Ordinary Income	7,850.44	4,098.32	7,770.61	(1,019.12)	(1,005.97)	4,328.79
Net Income	**7,850.44**	**4,098.32**	**7,770.61**	**(1,019.12)**	**(1,005.97)**	**4,328.79**

TABLE C.4 RAISE PINT PRICES (CONT.)

Month 7	Projected Month 8	Projected Month 9	Projected Month 10	Projected Month 11	Projected Month 12	Projected TOTAL
42,590.25	41,800.00	37,620.00	42,845.00	35,530.00	31,350.00	462,095.45
4,366.00	4,500.00	4,500.00	5,000.00	4,800.00	5,200.00	32,581.00
515.00	420.00	420.00	420.00	420.00	420.00	5,367.00
47,471.25	46,720.00	42,540.00	48,265.00	40,750.00	36,970.00	500,043.45
379.46	350.00	350.00	350.00	350.00	350.00	5,593.43
8,518.05	8,000.00	7,200.00	8,800.00	6,800.00	6,000.00	91,390.09
	3,512.00			3,800.00		11,114.00
212.95	200.00	180.00	220.00	170.00	150.00	2,284.75
1,234.85	850.00	850.00	850.00	850.00	850.00	10,209.77
171.67	143.33	143.33	143.33	143.33	143.33	1,822.67
3,876.56	4,000.00	4,000.00	4,000.00	4,000.00	4,000.00	40,008.39
14,393.54	17,055.33	12,723.33	14,363.33	16,113.33	11,493.33	162,423.10
33,077.71	29,664.67	29,816.67	33,901.67	24,636.67	25,476.67	337,620.35
3,000.00	3,500.00	3,500.00	3,500.00	3,500.00	3,500.00	28,500.00
1,122.09	1,122.09	1,122.09	1,122.09	1,122.09	1,122.09	13,465.08
1,249.00	1,250.00	1,250.00	1,250.00	1,250.00	1,250.00	7,499.00
2,008.69	0.00	2,000.00	2,000.00	3,000.00	0.00	16,094.78
275.52	285.00	285.00	285.00	285.00	285.00	3,425.19
3,008.06	3,842.00	3,842.00	3,842.00	3,842.00	4,520.00	33,718.07
0.00	400.00	1,200.00	300.00	1,200.00	300.00	12,457.00
6,235.00	6,235.00	6,235.00	6,235.00	6,400.00	6,400.00	75,150.00
608.00	415.00	415.00	415.00	415.00	415.00	4,981.81
0.00	0.00	0.00	0.00	0.00	0.00	200.00
0.00	0.00	0.00	0.00	0.00	0.00	150.00
0.00	0.00	0.00	5,000.00	0.00	0.00	5,000.00
0.00	0.00	0.00	5,000.00	0.00	0.00	5,350.00
7,136.23	6,744.70	6,744.70	6,744.70	6,744.70	6,744.70	80,297.74
4,462.12	2,830.22	2,985.01	4,063.19	4,259.61	4,410.56	39,114.81
29,104.71	26,624.01	29,578.80	34,756.98	32,018.40	28,947.35	320,053.48
3,973.00	3,040.66	237.87	(855.31)	(7,381.73)	(3,470.68)	17,566.87
3,973.00	**3,040.66**	**237.87**	**(855.31)**	**(7,381.73)**	**(3,470.68)**	**17,566.87**

TABLE C.5 UNADJUSTED INCOME STATEMENT

	Month 1	Month 2	Month 3	Month 4	Month 5	Month 6
Ordinary Income/Expense						
Income						
Draft Sales	39,650.76	36,130.00	41,527.75	33,882.94	38,423.75	40,745.00
Packaged Beer					1,318.00	2,897.00
Merchandise Sales	440.00	496.00	496.00	294.00	454.00	572.00
Total Income	40,090.76	36,626.00	42,023.75	34,176.94	40,195.75	44,214.00
Cost of Goods Sold						
Beer - Guest	825.41	447.89	277.94	601.66	602.68	708.39
Beer - House	7,930.15	7,226.00	8,305.55	6,776.59	7,684.75	8,149.00
Mobile Packaging					3,802.00	
Excise Tax	198.25	180.65	207.64	169.41	192.12	203.73
CO_2	766.02	857.64	844.65	792.35	881.59	582.67
Merchandise	151.33	169.00	167.33	102.00	154.00	190.67
Payroll COGS	168.62	1,882.51	1,990.20	3,902.15	3,985.00	4,203.35
Total COGS	10,039.79	10,763.69	11,793.31	12,344.16	17,302.14	14,037.80
Gross Profit	30,050.97	25,862.31	30,230.44	21,832.78	22,893.61	30,176.20
Expense						
Guaranteed Payment	0.00	0.00	0.00	2,500.00	2,500.00	3,000.00
Insurance Expense	1,122.09	1,122.09	1,122.09	1,122.09	1,122.09	1,122.09
Interest Expense	0.00	0.00	0.00	0.00	0.00	0.00
Marketing and Advertising	1,144.00	1,732.09	485.25	361.50	185.25	3,178.00
Office Supplies	370.57	265.50	163.61	548.86	211.93	164.20
Payroll	0.00	1,866.76	2,013.66	1,984.28	2,175.25	2,782.06
Professional Fees	3,205.00	1,000.00	3,347.00	800.00	705.00	0.00
Rent Expense	6,235.00	6,235.00	6,235.00	6,235.00	6,235.00	6,235.00
Repairs and Maintenance	58.37	108.00	657.00	920.60	446.84	108.00
Taxes						
Local	0.00	0.00	200.00	0.00	0.00	0.00
State	0.00	0.00	150.00	0.00	0.00	0.00
Property Taxes	0.00	0.00	0.00	0.00	0.00	0.00
Total Taxes	0.00	0.00	350.00	0.00	0.00	0.00
Utilities	7,391.98	6,827.34	5,777.89	5,971.70	6,258.64	7,210.46
Other Expenses	2,673.52	2,607.21	2,308.32	2,407.86	4,059.58	2,047.60
Total Expense	22,200.53	21,763.99	22,459.82	22,851.89	23,899.58	25,847.41
Net Ordinary Income	7,850.44	4,098.32	7,770.61	(1,019.12)	(1,005.97)	4,328.79
Net Income	**7,850.44**	**4,098.32**	**7,770.61**	**(1,019.12)**	**(1,005.97)**	**4,328.79**

TABLE C.5 UNADJUSTED INCOME STATEMENT (CONT.)

	Projected	Projected	Projected	Projected	Projected	Projected
Month 7	Month 8	Month 9	Month 10	Month 11	Month 12	TOTAL
42,590.25	40,000.00	36,000.00	44,000.00	34,000.00	30,000.00	456,950.45
4,366.00	4,500.00	4,500.00	5,000.00	4,800.00	5,200.00	32,581.00
515.00	420.00	420.00	420.00	420.00	420.00	5,367.00
47,471.25	44,920.00	40,920.00	49,420.00	39,220.00	35,620.00	494,898.45
379.46	350.00	350.00	350.00	350.00	350.00	5,593.43
8,518.05	8,000.00	7,200.00	8,800.00	6,800.00	6,000.00	91,390.09
	3,512.00			3,800.00		11,114.00
212.95	200.00	180.00	220.00	170.00	150.00	2,284.75
1,234.85	850.00	850.00	850.00	850.00	850.00	10,209.77
171.67	143.33	143.33	143.33	143.33	143.33	1,822.67
3,876.56	4,000.00	4,000.00	4,000.00	4,000.00	4,000.00	40,008.39
14,393.54	17,055.33	12,723.33	14,363.33	16,113.33	11,493.33	162,423.10
33,077.71	27,864.67	28,196.67	35,056.67	23,106.67	24,126.67	332,475.35
3,000.00	3,500.00	3,500.00	3,500.00	3,500.00	3,500.00	28,500.00
1,122.09	1,122.09	1,122.09	1,122.09	1,122.09	1,122.09	13,465.08
1,249.00	1,250.00	1,250.00	1,250.00	1,250.00	1,250.00	7,499.00
2,008.69	0.00	2,000.00	2,000.00	3,000.00	0.00	16,094.78
275.52	285.00	285.00	285.00	285.00	285.00	3,425.19
3,008.06	3,842.00	3,842.00	3,842.00	3,842.00	4,520.00	33,718.07
0.00	400.00	1,200.00	300.00	1,200.00	300.00	12,457.00
6,235.00	6,235.00	6,235.00	6,235.00	6,400.00	6,400.00	75,150.00
608.00	415.00	415.00	415.00	415.00	415.00	4,981.81
0.00	0.00	0.00	0.00	0.00	0.00	200.00
0.00	0.00	0.00	0.00	0.00	0.00	150.00
0.00	0.00	0.00	5,000.00	0.00	0.00	5,000.00
0.00	0.00	0.00	5,000.00	0.00	0.00	5,350.00
7,136.23	6,744.70	6,744.70	6,744.70	6,744.70	6,744.70	80,297.74
4,462.12	2,785.22	2,944.51	4,092.06	4,221.36	4,376.81	38,986.18
29,104.71	26,579.01	29,538.30	34,785.85	31,980.15	28,913.60	319,924.85
3,973.00	1,285.66	(1,341.63)	270.82	(8,873.48)	(4,786.93)	12,550.50
3,973.00	**1,285.66**	**(1,341.63)**	**270.82**	**(8,873.48)**	**(4,786.93)**	**12,550.50**

APPENDIX D

TEN-WEEK BUDGET CALENDAR

Date	Responsible Party	Activity
Week 1	CFO CEO Director of Restaurants/Taproom Director of Brewery Sales Director of Marketing	CFO to deliver budget worksheets to department heads.
Week 2	Director of Restaurants/Taproom Director of Brewery Sales Director of Marketing	Initial budgets submitted to CFO.
Week 3	CFO	Initial budgets are consolidated and delivered to leadership team.
Week 4	CFO CEO Department heads	Budget work session with leadership team.
Week 5	CFO	Distribute updated budgets with notes from work session.
Week 6	Director of Restaurants/Taproom Director of Brewery Sales Director of Marketing	Second round of budgets due from department heads.
Week 8	CFO	Consolidate second round of budget and deliver to leadership team.
Week 9	CFO CEO Director of Restaurants/Taproom Director of Brewery Sales Director of Marketing	Final leadership team work session.
End of Week 10	CEO	Sign off on final budget.
End of November/ Early December	CFO	Final consolidated and departmental budgets issued.

APPENDIX E

SAMPLE TERM SHEET FOR XYZ BREWING COMPANY, LLC

The following does not constitute a legally binding agreement, nor is it an offering of securities. It is intended to explain the possible investment options in XYZ Brewing Company, LLC. This undertaking is by its nature risky, and potential investors are encouraged to closely examine the potential risks of investment.

XYZ Brewing Company, LLC is a manager-managed LLC, with Individual A and Individual B serving as the managers. This document sets forth the manner in which membership in the LLC will be offered, but in and of itself is *not* an offer of membership.

XYZ Brewing Company, LLC will be initially capitalized with $650,000 in start-up funds from the founders, a loan, and membership units. Founders Individual A and Individual B have contributed a combined $50,000 of initial capital and will retain 60% of the LLC's membership units. The remaining 40% of the membership units will be offered to prospective investors in order to raise $300,000 in capital from the sale of equity and $300,000 in funds from private debt. Ownership interests will be offered in the form of membership units, with each unit priced at $7,500 and equal to a 1% ownership interest at the conclusion of the first round of funding. In order to purchase an interest in the company, an initial minimum investment of $20,000 will be made, which will include purchase of 1.33 units for $10,000 and a loan of $10,000 to the LLC. The loan will be documented in a promissory note issued by the LLC, to be paid in annual payments over an 8-year period at 7.5% interest, with no payments the first year, interest-only payments in years 2 and 3, and interest and principal payments in years 4 through 8. Thus, if an investor would like to invest $50,000 in XYZ Brewing Company, the investor would purchase 3.33 units for $25,000 (3.33% of the company at the conclusion of initial funding), and a promissory note for $25,000 to be paid over 8 years at 7.5% interest.

For each $25,000 investment, the projected return according to our business plan is shown in the table (be aware that all returns on membership interest are approximate, and pure speculation, particularly after year 3).

	Year 1	Year 2	Year 3	Year 4-8*	Year 9
1 Unit of Membership Income/(Loss)	($1,000)	$100	$1,800	$25,000	$6,000
Promissory Note of $25,000	$1,875	$2,016	$2,016	$6,360	$0.00
Total	$875	$2,116	$3,816	$31,360	$6,000

* Projections for year 4–8 returns on membership are cumulative totals.

Please note that ownership and transfer of the membership units will be subject to the terms of the company's operating agreement. Individual A and Individual B will have the first right to purchase membership interests in the event of any transfer. Investor participation is subject to qualification of the investor. Each potential investor will be asked to complete an accredited investor questionnaire and make representations as to the investor's sophistication.

Additional documentation will be provided to interested parties following execution of a nondisclosure agreement. Please feel free to ask either Individual A or Individual B any questions about investment in XYZ Brewing Company, LLC. We will be glad to talk about this prospectus, as well as our plans for the brewery. We want to make this brewery work for you as well as for us.

APPENDIX F

CHOICE OF ENTITY: SIGNIFICANT TAX AND OTHER CONSIDERATIONS

Courtesy of Davis Wright Tremaine

One of the first steps in setting up a brewery involves selecting the specific type of entity to form for purposes of running the business. Operating through an entity both professionalizes the business (versus operating individually under a DBA or as a sole proprietor) and, if done properly, helps protect the brewery's owners from liability for the business's operations.

There are numerous factors to consider when selecting the entity type. The following is a high-level summary of some of the more important federal income tax and non-tax considerations involved in choosing between the following types of entities for federal income tax purposes:

- a C corporation ("C Corp");
- an S corporation ("S Corp"); and
- a partnership, such as a multi-member limited liability company ("LLC") that has not checked the box to be taxed as a C Corp or an S Corp.

This summary focuses on multi-member LLCs that have not checked the box to be taxed as a C Corp or an S Corp.

Note that there are other entity types that can be taxed as partnerships (such as general partnerships and limited partnerships), but a detailed discussion of these entity types is outside the scope of this summary since it is becoming increasingly rare for breweries to select these types of entities.

In addition, a business that is wholly-owned by one person cannot be formed as a "partnership" (since this requires more than one owner). However, the business can be formed as an LLC that is disregarded for federal income tax purposes (or the LLC can check the box to be taxed as a C Corp or an S Corp, although this is less common). A discussion of LLCs that are disregarded for federal income tax purposes is also outside the scope of this summary.

Each of the above entity types has its advantages and disadvantages, and the following summary provides some helpful comparisons between the various options to assist in the entity selection process.

LLC VERSUS C CORP

LLC Advantages/C Corp Disadvantages

- **Single Level of Tax.** LLCs are pass-through entities, meaning their income is subject to only one level of tax at the member (i.e., the owner) level. Conversely, a C Corp's income is subject to tax at the entity level, and any dividend distributions of earnings to the C Corp's shareholders are also taxable to the shareholders. This means that in the C Corp context income is effectively taxed. Due to the pass-through nature of LLCs, this "double tax" is avoided.

- **Pass-Through of Losses.** Subject to certain limitations, losses, deductions, credits, and other tax benefits pass-through to an LLC's members and may offset the member's personal taxable income. Although the ability to utilize these pass-through benefits is subject to various restrictions—such as the passive activity loss limitation rules, at risk limitation rules, basis limitation rules, and other similar limitations—a C Corp's losses do not pass-through to its shareholders. Therefore, the LLC structure provides the opportunity for pass-through tax benefits in the form of deductions from a shareholder's personal taxable income, which are not available in the C Corp context, although these benefits are not guaranteed.

- **Tax-Free Property Contribution.** Under one of the broadest non-recognition provisions in the IRC (IRC Section 721), appreciated property can generally be contributed to LLCs tax-free. Conversely, tax-free capitalizations for C Corps must comply with the more restrictive provisions of the IRS (IRC Section 351) to achieve a similar tax-free result. For brewery owners who want to contribute appreciated brewing equipment to the business, it will be easier to avoid negative tax consequences and cumbersome IRS requirements if the entity is an LLC versus a C Corp.

- **Tax-Free Distributions of Appreciated Property.** An LLC can distribute appreciated property (e.g., real estate or stock) to its members without gain recognition to the LLC or its members, facilitating spin-off transactions. A C Corp's distribution of appreciated property to its shareholders is subject to tax at the corporate level and possibly tax at the shareholder level as well. Because of the ability to distribute appreciated property without gain recognition, breweries that own both the operating business and the underlying real property, or that have a multi-tier entity structure, should consider an LLC.

- **Basis Step-Up.** Members receive a basis step-up in LLC interests that they inherit from another partner. This means that the member who receives the interest adjusts its value to the current fair market value, not the historical cash basis originally paid. This is important because it can minimize the gain when the interest is sold. This benefit is not available for C Corps or S Corps.

- **Investor Interest.** Although certain types of investors prefer C Corp investments (as discussed further below), investors, including private equity groups active in the brewery space, are increasingly (and in many instances, exclusively) interested in investing in LLCs. In fact, prior to an acquisition or majority investment, many C Corp breweries are forced to undertake expensive restructurings in order to convert into LLCs. Because industry investors are increasingly interested in investing or acquiring LLCs, this entity structure is often preferable to C Corps for breweries looking toward investment or exit.

- **Operating Flexibility.** LLCs are notoriously flexible entity structures. With few exceptions, nearly all of the provisions governing LLCs can be customized, including the terms governing ownership, management, decision-making, and economics. For example, LLCs can have numerous classes of ownership, with various tiers of equity and economic preferences (e.g., preferred returns, complicated waterfall mechanics, and creative allocations of profits and losses). LLCs can also have either very formal or very flexible management structures, depending on the preferences of the entity and its owners. Conversely, C Corps are creatures of statute, and it is more difficult (and in some instances, impossible) to stray from the statutory requirements related to ownership and governance. The flexibility of LLCs provides a customized structure while avoiding some of the rigidity that arises in the context of C Corps. Because of this flexibility, many breweries elect to operate as an LLC notwithstanding that C Corps are more common in certain other industries (e.g., technology).

C Corp Advantages/LLC Disadvantages

- **Early-Stage and Traditional VC Investment; IPOs.** Investors in early-stage companies, such as angel investors or venture capital investors, often prefer C Corp investments, particularly if the investors are most familiar with the tech space (where C Corps are the standard). One reason for this is that there are various standard form documents for C Corp investments that many early-stage investors like to use for efficiency and consistency reasons (conversely, the cost of the flexibility afforded by LLCs can be significant and is a deterrent for very early stage businesses and investors). In addition, many venture capital investors prefer to invest through convertible preferred stock, which is only available for C Corps (a similar structure can be achieved in the LLC context, but it can be prohibitively expensive to create this level of customization). In addition, if a company is looking toward an IPO, a C Corp entity structure is essentially a requirement. Depending on the type of investor and the type of investment, a C Corp may be the preferable structure.

- **Traditional Equity Compensation is Available.** C Corps can issue traditional stock options and "incentive stock options." It is more complex for LLCs to issue the LLC-equivalent of stock options. In addition, it is possible for LLCs to issue equity incentives in the form of "profits interests" so employees can share in the business's appreciation, but this creates some accounting and administrative complexity that many smaller companies find daunting. For a brewery for whom issuing traditional (and, therefore, commonly understood) stock options or incentive stock options is an important part of the ownership plan (e.g. to the head brewer or other key employees), a C Corp may be the better option.

- **No Pass-Through Taxation.** As discussed above, members of an LLC recognize pass-through income, and therefore each member receives a Form K-1 to report such LLC-level income on the member's personal tax returns. However, just because the members are *taxed* on the LLC's income does not mean the members actually received a distribution of cash. This can result in members having to pay taxes on income without the cash to do so, and also leads to additional complexity on the member's personal returns, which often requires a more proficient, and often more expensive, accountant. For many closely-held breweries, members cannot afford to personally pay these taxes. Although many LLCs mitigate this issue by making annual or quarterly tax distributions to members, this has to be specifically negotiated *and* the entity has to have cash available for distributions. Because C Corps do not have pass-through income, there is no analogous issue in the C Corp context.

- **Self-Employment Taxes; Fringe Benefits.** C Corp shareholders are not subject to self-employment taxes on the C Corp's income. Conversely, an LLC's members are generally subject to self-employment tax on their distributive share of ordinary trade and business income. One often-unexpected impact of this is that members who are also employees must treat their "salary" as a partnership distribution, as opposed to a traditional salary that is subject to withholding. In addition, C Corps often have tax-favorable fringe benefits, which are not available for LLC member-employees (since they are not "employees" for federal income tax purposes). These differences can lead to a significant tax surprise for employee-members who are caught unawares.

- **Retention of Earnings/Reinvestment of Capital.** As mentioned above, a C Corp's income does not pass-through as taxable income to its shareholders. This makes it easier to retain and accumulate capital in the business. Conversely, an LLC's pass-through taxation structure makes conservation of operating capital difficult; for example, LLCs typically have to distribute cash to help the members pay taxes on the pass-through income. If this tax distribution was not necessary (i.e., in the C Corp context), the capital could be utilized for other purposes, such as expansion or capital improvements. This feature makes C Corps the preferable option for many companies that expect significant ongoing capital needs for the business.

- **Qualified Small Business Stock Benefits.** C Corps can issue "qualified small business stock." LLCs cannot issue qualified small business stock, thus, LLC owners are ineligible for qualified small business stock benefits, such as the 50% gain exclusion for gain on the sale of qualified stock held for more than five (5) years (for an effective capital gains tax rate of 14%) and the ability to roll over gain on the sale of qualified stock into other qualified stock.

- **State Income Tax Return Filing Requirements.** Each member of the LLC may be required to a file a tax return in multiple states. This is not the case with C Corps because there is no pass-through taxation.

- **Complexity/Uncertainty.** The flexible nature of LLCs makes them more complex, and, often, more expensive. With the rigidity of C Corps also comes some efficiency and certainty. In addition, partnership tax is substantially more complex than C Corp tax, affecting both the company and its owners. A good accountant who is familiar with partnership tax rules and limitations is a necessity in the LLC context.

- **Tax Rates.** Individual tax rates can be higher than C Corp tax rates. Up until the recent change in tax law (Tax Cuts and Jobs Act that went into effect in December 2017), it most often made sense for a small business to not be a C Corp. The individual and corporate tax rates were similar and the income from a C Corp was subject to two levels of tax. (one tax hit at the corporate level, and a second tax assessed on dividends distributed to stockholders). Under the new law, the corporate tax rate is a flat 21%. The individual rates range from 10% to 37%. Under this tax structure some entities are choosing to have a C Corp structure even though there are still two levels of tax. I cannot stress enough that tax strategy is a complex matter and most business decisions should be made with the guidance of a CPA and attorney. A knowledgeable professional can consider all angles of tax planning to achieve the best result.

- **Withholding on Foreign Member's Distributive Shares.** An LLC has to withhold taxes on certain types of income allocated to foreign persons, regardless of whether distributions are made. In addition, due to the pass-through taxation for LLCs, foreign members of an LLC are required to file US federal taxes. Since this is not an ideal outcome for many foreign investors, the tax "shield" provided by a C Corp is often preferable.

S CORP VERSUS VS. LLC

LLC Advantages/S Corp Disadvantages

- **Flexibility of Ownership.** LLCs are not limited with respect to who can be an owner. For example, LLCs can typically have an unlimited number of members. Conversely, S Corps can only have up to 100 shareholders. In addition, S Corps cannot have any entity owners or certain types of trusts as owners, which is cumbersome and difficult to manage for owners who want to complete estate-planning transfers. Similarly, whereas S Corps cannot have any foreign owners (i.e., all shareholders must be US residents or citizens), foreign owners are permitted in the LLC context. However, as mentioned above, a foreign owner may not want to own an interest in an LLC since the member may become subject to US tax laws (including certain withholding requirements for the company) and have to file a US tax return. If an S Corp "busts" its election by having impermissible owners, the S Corp will be automatically converted into an entity taxed as a C Corp. For breweries with numerous owners, entity owners, aging owners, or foreign investors, or for whom compliance with detailed and complicated ownership requirements is not a core competency, the risks of electing to be taxed as an S Corp may simply not be worth taking. The flexibility of an LLC leaves more options for owners to create compensation plans for key employees, which is an important succession planning consideration. In addition, if a brewery plans to grow and take on investment, it may be challenging to do so as an S Corp because many investors prefer to invest through an entity.

- **More Certainty in Tax Status.** As mentioned above, S Corps must meet certain criteria to elect S Corp status, and then must file an election with the IRS. After this filing, the S Corp (and its owners) must then take care not to bust the election by violating one of the eligibility criteria. This can lead to administrative complexity, risk, and lack of certainty. Conversely, LLCs with multiple members are automatically (i.e., without an election) treated as pass-through entities, and it is very difficult to inadvertently bust this status unless the LLC becomes a single-member entity (which just means it becomes disregarded for tax purposes) or it affirmatively makes an election to be treated as an S Corp or a C Corp (which is difficult to do inadvertently).

- **Special Allocations of Tax Attributes.** An S Corp's tax attributes must be allocated to shareholders based on the number of shares they own, and only one class of stock is permitted. Conversely, an LLC can have multiple different classes of ownership, and has flexibility to allocate tax attributes in ways other than pro rata based on ownership.

- **Debt in Basis.** An LLC member's basis for purposes of deducting pass-through losses includes the member's share of the entity's indebtedness. This is not the case with S Corps. Most bank loans require anyone who owns more than 20% of the business to guarantee a loan. Debt that is personally guaranteed increases the amount of losses that can be taken on personal taxes. Think of this as your skin in the game for your brewery. It represents what you stand to lose if the brewery doesn't work out. The IRS doesn't allow a taxpayer to deduct more than what he or she stands to lose. By having debt basis, a brewery owner can use losses from the business to offset income from other sources. In an S Corp, the rules are different. A shareholder can only get debt basis for money that he or she directly lends to the company. In an LLC taxed as a partnership, simply being on the hook for debt will increase your basis; in an S Corp, a shareholder must directly lend money to the business.

- **Tax-Free Distributions of Appreciated Property.** As mentioned above, an LLC can distribute appreciated property to its members without gain recognition to the LLC or its members. Conversely, an S Corp's distribution of appreciated property to its shareholders results in the recognition of gain by the S Corp on the appreciation, which gain then passes through to the S Corp's shareholders. It is therefore less tax advantageous to complete a spin-off transaction in the S Corp context.

- **Profits Interests.** As mentioned above, it is possible to grant incentive equity (i.e., that is issued in exchange for services and not for cash) to service providers by issuing "profits interests" under Rev. Proc. 93-27 (*see also* Rev. Proc. 2001-43). Because S Corps can only have one class of equity, S Corps cannot give "cheap" equity to service providers without adverse tax consequences to the recipients (i.e., the recipients will be taxed on the value of the equity received).

- **Ease of Tax-Free Formation.** As mentioned above, appreciated property can be contributed tax-free to LLCs. Contributions of appreciated property to S Corps in exchange for stock must comply with more restrictive provisions of the IRC to be tax-free (i.e., IRC Section 351), although this is not usually a problem.

S Corp Advantages/LLC Disadvantages

- **Traditional Equity Compensation Available.** With certain constraints (i.e., that a single class of shares is required), S Corps can adopt traditional stock option plans and can grant "incentive stock options." It is very complex for LLCs to issue the equivalent of stock options (although they can more easily issue the equivalent of cheap stock through the issuance of "profits interests," as described above). Incentive stock options also are not available for LLCs. As a result, breweries that want to incentivize their employees with traditional stock options may prefer an S Corp structure.

- **Simplicity of Structure.** If the S Corp is formed as a corporation and subsequently elects to be taxed as an S Corp (vs. an LLC that subsequently elects to be taxed as an S Corp) the S Corp will have a simpler corporate structure. Because S Corps can only have one class of stock (common stock), the governing documents are simplified (vs. the expansive flexibility—and therefore complexity—that is available in the LLC context).

- **Self-Employment Taxes.** S Corp shareholders are not subject to self-employment taxes, and S Corp employee-shareholders are taxed as W-2 employees (vs. K-1 partners, as is the case for LLC employee-members). This allows for simpler accounting and tax filings for both the S Corp and its employee-shareholders than what is available in the LLC context. This can often be a huge advantage for owners. Under an LLC, members who participate in the operation of the business will pay self-employment tax on all ordinary income in addition to income tax. This is, roughly, an additional 15% tax. It represents the Social Security and Medicare tax (both the employee and employer portion since the individual is self-employed). Note that income attributed to an owner is based on ownership percentage, not what an owner *receives* through guaranteed payments or distributions. On the other hand, in an S Corp, a member who participates in the operation of the business will receive a W-2 and will only be responsible for half of the self-employment taxes (the business will pay the other half as payroll tax). The ordinary income of the business attributed to the member will be subject to income tax, but not self-employment tax. The self-employment tax is paid via withholdings from the member's paycheck and payroll taxes paid by the company. There are more details to consider, and a business owner should consult with a CPA to fully understand the requirements and tax implications.

- **Fringe Benefits.** Generally, all fringe benefits of LLCs are included in the income of the members, regardless of their percentage of ownership. Conversely, only shareholders holding 2% or more of the S Corp's shares need to include certain fringe benefits in income.

C CORP VERSUS S CORP

C Corp Advantages/S Corp Disadvantages

- **Traditional Investments Can Be Made; Multiple Classes of Stock.** Unlike S Corps, C Corps are not limited with respect to who can be a shareholder (i.e., shareholders can be foreign investors, entities, trusts, etc.). In addition, C Corps can issue many types of stock, including preferred stock, which is often used for early-stage and venture capital investment. Because S Corps cannot have entity owners (among other restrictions), and cannot issue preferred stock (or any other class of stock other than common stock), C Corps are preferable to S Corps for most investment options (with the possible exception of friends and family rounds).

- **No Pass-Through Taxation.** As with LLCs, shareholders of an S Corp recognize pass-through income on their personal tax returns (and may not always have the corresponding cash to pay these taxes). C Corps do not have this issue, since C Corps do not pass-through the entity's income to the shareholders.

- **Retention of Earnings/Reinvestment of Capital.** As mentioned above, it is easier to retain and accumulate capital in a business if the entity is a C Corp than if it is a pass-through entity such as an LLC or a C Corp. As with LLC, it can be difficult to conserve operating capital in an S Corp given the need for tax distributions to help shareholders pay their personal taxes. This makes C Corps preferable for companies with significant ongoing capital needs.

- **Eligibility for Qualified Small Business Stock Benefits.** Whereas C Corps can issue "qualified small business stock," this structure is not available to S Corps. As a result, some of the significant tax benefits arising from issuing qualified small business stock are not available to S Corp shareholders.
- **More Certainty in Tax Status.** A C Corp's tax status is more certain than an S Corp's, since a C Corp does not have to file an election to obtain its tax status. Conversely, S Corps must meet certain eligibility criteria, must elect S Corp status, and then not "bust" that status by violating one of the eligibility criteria. This leads to more certainty (and less administrative burdens) in the C Corp context.
- **No State Income Tax Complications for Investors.** Each shareholder in an S Corp may be required to file a tax return in multiple states where the S Corp does business. This is not the case for C Corps.

S Corp Advantages/C Corp Disadvantages

- **Single Level of Tax.** As with LLCs, S Corps are pass-through entities, meaning their income is subject to only one level of tax at the shareholder level. Conversely, a C Corp's income is subject to tax at the entity level, and shareholders are taxed on any dividend distributions made to them. Due to the pass-through nature of S Corps, this "double tax" is avoided.
- **Pass-Through of Losses.** Subject to certain limitations, losses, deductions, credits, and other tax benefits pass-through to an S Corp's shareholders and may offset the shareholder's personal taxable income. Conversely, a C Corp's losses do not pass-through to its shareholders. Therefore, an S Corp structure provides the opportunity for pass-through tax benefits in the form of deductions from a shareholder's personal taxable income, which are not available in the C Corp context, although these benefits are not guaranteed.

GLOSSARY

Adjusted basis

Adjusted basis is the historical cost of an asset plus the cost of improvements to the asset minus depreciation.

Accounts

An account is a method of classification. An account houses groups of transactions that are similar in nature. For example, Insurance Expense is an account that houses groups of accounting transactions that represent how much a company spends on insurance. All accounts of a company make up its chart of accounts.

Accounts receivable (AR)

Accounts receivable is the amount owed to a company resulting from the company providing goods and/or services on credit.

Accounts payable (AP)

Accounts payable is a current liability account in which a company records the amounts it owes to suppliers or vendors for goods or services that it received on credit.

Accrual accounting

The accrual basis method of accounting adheres to the matching principle. Revenues are recognized when earned, and expenses are recognized when incurred, regardless of when cash is received or disbursed.

Amortization

Amortization is an accounting method of allocating the cost of an intangible asset over time. Examples of costs that are amortized include loan fees, organizational costs, start-up costs, and intellectual property.

Assets

An asset is a resource with economic value that an entity owns that currently does, or is expected in the future to, provide an economic benefit. Assets are reported on a company's balance sheet and are bought or created to increase a firm's value.

Balance sheet

A balance sheet is a financial statement that summarizes a company's assets, liabilities, and shareholders' equity at a specific point in time. These three balance sheet segments give investors an idea as to what the company owns and owes, as well as the amount invested by shareholders.

Book-to-tax difference

The net income on a company's internal financial reports may differ from the net income on the company's tax return. This book-to-tax difference is the result of rules that are different for financial accounting than they are for tax accounting. These differences fall into two categories: temporary or permanent. An example of a temporary difference is depreciation. A company may choose to use a different depreciation method for tax (usually to accelerate deductions), but over time the available depreciation for an asset is the same for book as it is for tax. The temporary difference is simply a result of methodology used for tax. An example of a permanent difference is officers life insurance. Under US tax law, a deduction is not allowed for officers' life insurance premiums because the proceeds are not taxable. Therefore, a company may record an expense for their books, but the tax return will not reflect that deduction.

Breakeven

Breakeven is the amount of revenue that a company must generate in order to cover all costs. Every dollar after the breakeven point will result in a profit. Breakeven may also be expressed in units sold.

Budget

A budget is an estimation of revenue and expenses over a specified future period of time; it is compiled and re-evaluated on a periodic basis. Budgets can be made for a person, a family, a group of people, a business, a government, a country, a multinational organization, or just about anything else that makes and spends money. Among companies and organizations, a budget is an internal tool used by management and is often not required for reporting by external parties.

Capital expenses

See fixed assets.

Capitalize

To capitalize is to recognize the expense of an asset over a long period of time (generally more than one year), even though the cash is disbursed at one moment. For example, a car is purchased for $20,000 and recorded as an asset on the balance sheet. Each year a portion of the cost is recorded as depreciation expense, with a corresponding entry to accumulated depreciation.

Cash basis accounting

The cash basis method of accounting is widely used, but does not adhere to the matching principle. Under cash basis, revenues and expenses are recorded when cash is received or disbursed, not when revenues and expenses are earned or incurred.

Chart of accounts

A chart of accounts is a listing of each account a company owns, along with the account type and account balance, shown in the order the accounts appear in the company's financial statements. It includes both balance-sheet accounts and income-statement accounts. The chart of accounts shows assets, liabilities, equity, revenues, and expenses, all in one place and broken down into subcategories. Each chart is assigned a multi-digit number to identify the account type.

ISSN/ISBN

Collateralize

To collateralize an asset is to pledge the asset to a lender. The lender has a right to the asset if the borrower defaults on the loan.

Contra-accounts

Contra-accounts have a natural balance that is opposite the natural balance of other accounts with which it is grouped in the financial reports. An example is Accumulated Depreciation, which has a natural credit balance, and which is presented with the Fixed Asset accounts, which have a natural debit balance.

Contribution margin

Contribution margin is a product's price minus all associated variable costs, resulting in the incremental profit earned for each unit sold. The total contribution margin generated by an entity represents the total earnings available to pay for fixed expenses and to generate a profit.

Cost of goods sold

Cost of goods sold (COGS) are the direct costs attributable to the production of the goods sold by a company. This amount includes the cost of the materials used in creating the good along with the direct labor costs used to produce the good. It excludes indirect expenses such as distribution costs and sales force costs. COGS appears on the income statement and can be deducted from revenue to calculate a company's gross margin. Also referred to as "cost of sales," or COS.

Current assets

Current assets are balance sheet accounts that represent the value of all assets that can reasonably expect to be converted into cash within one year. Current assets include cash and cash equivalents, accounts receivable, inventory, marketable securities, prepaid expenses, and other liquid assets that can be readily converted to cash.

Current liabilities

Current liabilities are a company's debts or obligations that are due within one year, appearing on the company's balance sheet and include short term debt, accounts payable, accrued liabilities, and other debts. Essentially, these are bills that are due to creditors and suppliers within a short period of time. Normally, companies withdraw or cash current assets in order to pay their current liabilities.

Depreciation

Depreciation is an accounting method of allocating the cost of a tangible asset over its useful life. Businesses depreciate long-term assets for both tax and accounting purposes. For tax purposes, businesses can deduct the cost of the tangible assets they purchase as business expenses; however, businesses must depreciate these assets in accordance with IRS rules about how and when the deduction may be taken.

Earnings per unit

Earnings per unit, a measure of profitability, equals profit divided by the number of units outstanding in a company.

EBITDA

Earnings before interest, taxes, depreciation, and amortization.

Entity

An entity is an organization or business that has its own legal structure and distinct identity.

Equity

Equity represents the difference between assets and liabilities in a company. If all assets were to be liquidated, and all debts paid off, equity is what would remain.

First position

First position indicates that a lender has priority to be paid back in the case of a liquidation.

Fixed asset

A tangible good that has a useful life of more than one year. Fixed assets are also known as Property, Plant, and Equipment. Examples include brewing equipment, computers, vehicles, furniture, and fixtures.

Flow-through entity

A flow-through entity is a legal structure for businesses that passes all income through to the owners. Under US tax law, the entity does not pay income tax. All income is passed to the owners and business income is paid by the individual owners. Partnerships and S corporations are examples of flow-through structures.

Gross margin

Gross margin is a company's total sales revenue minus its cost of goods sold, divided by total sales revenue, expressed as a percentage. It represents the percent of total sales revenue that the company retains after incurring the direct costs associated with producing the goods and services it sells. The higher the percentage, the more the company retains on each dollar of sales, to service its other costs and debt obligations.

Horizontal analysis

A method of financial analysis in which a line item in a financial statement is compared across multiple time periods (e.g., months), or across multiple departments (e.g., brewery, tasting room).

Income statement

An income statement, also known as a profit and loss statement, is a financial statement that reports a company's financial performance over a specific accounting period. Financial performance is assessed by giving a summary of how the business incurs its revenues and expenses through both operating and non-operating activities. It also shows the net profit or loss incurred over a specific accounting period.

Indirect costs

Indirect costs are costs that are not directly associated with a single activity, event, or other cost object. Such costs are frequently aggregated into an overhead cost pool and allocated to various activities, based on an allocation method that has a perceived or actual linkage between the indirect cost and the activity.

Internal controls

Internal controls are processes defined by a company to ensure the accuracy, security, and integrity of financial reporting.

Inventory

Inventory is the raw materials, work-in-process products, and finished goods that are considered to be the portion of a business's assets that are ready or will be ready for sale. Inventory represents one of the most important assets of a business because the turnover of inventory represents one of the primary sources of revenue generation and subsequent earnings for the company's shareholders.

Key performance indicator (KPI)

A key performance indicator is a quantifiable measure used to evaluate the success of an organization or project. Key performance indicators are often used to determine how well targets are being reached.

Key ratio

A key ratio is a relationship between two accounting elements that illustrate the financial health of an organization. Key ratios are often used to compare the performance of companies in the same industry.

Ledger

An accounting record that represents a collection of transactions in the same account. Also referred to as a book or register.

Liability

A liability is a company's debts or obligations. This is a financial commitment that must be repaid in the future.

Loan covenants

A condition in a loan agreement that requires the borrower to meet certain conditions, or that restricts certain activities of the borrower.

Matching principle of accounting

The matching principle is a foundation of accrual basis accounting. It requires revenues to be recorded when they are earned and expenses when they are incurred, therefore matching economic activity to the proper period.

Non-cash expense

A non-cash expense appears on an income statement because accounting principles require them to be recorded as an economic outlay of resources, even though not being paid for with cash. Examples include depreciation and amortization.

Overhead

Overhead refers to all ongoing business expenses not including or related to direct labor, direct materials, or third-party expenses that are billed directly to customers. A company must pay overhead on an ongoing basis regardless of whether the company is doing a high or low volume of business. It is important not just for budgeting purposes but for determining how much a company must charge for its products or services to make a profit. For example, a service-based business that operates in a traditional white-collar office setting has overhead expenses such as rent, utilities, and insurance.

Payback period

The length of time required for an initial investment to be recovered by profits.

Price to retailer (PTR)

The price to retailer is the amount charged by a distributor (or by a brewery if self-distributing) to a retailer. The retailer, in turn, marks up the price to arrive at the shelf price.

Profit and loss statement

See income statement.

Ratio analysis

Ratio analysis is the use of ratios to determine a company's financial performance. A ratio is a relationship between two financial measures. It is generally expressed as two numbers separated by a colon, such as 1.25:1.

Reconciliation

A quality control process used in accounting in which the source document that supports an account balance is compared to what is presented on the financial statement to confirm that it is correct.

Return on capital employed

Return on capital employed is a ratio that measures how efficiently a company turns an investment into profit.

Selling, general, and administrative expenses (SG&A)

Selling, general and administrative expenses (SG&A) are reported on the income statement as the sum of all direct and indirect selling expenses and all general and administrative expenses of a company. There are many factors that go into manufacturing a product, such as a warranty, and therefore SG&A expenses are deducted to generate a net income. SG&A expenses are also monitored to ensure proper cash flow is being managed.

SKU

See stock keeping unit.

Standard costing

Standard costing is the practice of substituting an expected cost for an actual cost in the accounting records, and then periodically recording variances showing the difference between the expected and actual costs. Standard costing involves the creation of estimated (i.e., standard) costs for some or all activities within a company. The core reason for using standard costs is that there are a number of applications where it is too time-consuming to collect actual costs, so standard costs are used as a close approximation to actual costs.

Statement of cash flows

The statement of cash flows is one of the three statements in a complete set of financial reports. It shows the sources and uses of cash over a period of time.

Stock keeping unit

A stock keeping unit is a number assigned to a product to identify a unique item in a retail store. SKUs can also be used to identify unique items in a brewery's catalog of products.

Taproom

A retail establishment owned by a beverage manufacturer where the primary offering is self-made beverages. Food service in a taproom is usually limited, as opposed to a brewpub, which often has a full restaurant.

Term sheet

A term sheet is a summary of the basic terms and conditions of a business agreement. It is commonly provided to potential investors along with pro forma financial statements and a business plan summary.

Tracing

In accounting terms, to trace is to follow a financial document from it's original point of entry as a transaction all the way to the financial statements.

Vertical analysis

A method of financial analysis in which a line item in a financial statement is calculated as a percentage of a base amount. Common examples of base amounts include total revenue, total assets, or total equity.

Vouching

In accounting terms, to vouch is to follow a number on the financial statements back to the original source document or source transaction.

Working capital

Working capital is the funds available to a business for ongoing operations. It is calculated as follows: current assets – current liabilities.

INDEX